D1569805

Foreign
Teachers
in
China

LB
2285
.C55
P67
1990

Foreign Teachers

in

China

Old Problems for a New
Generation, 1979–1989

EDGAR A. PORTER

WITHDRAWN

GOSHEN COLLEGE LIBRARY
GOSHEN, INDIANA

Contributions to the Study of Education, Number 39

GREENWOOD PRESS
New York • Westport, Connecticut • London

Library of Congress Cataloging-in-Publication Data

Porter, Edgar A.
  Foreign teachers in China : old problems for a new generation,
1979-1989 / Edgar A. Porter.
    p. cm.—(Contributions to the study of education, ISSN
0196-707X ; no. 39)
  Includes bibliographical references.
  ISBN 0-313-27386-3 (lib. bdg. : alk. paper)
  1. Educational exchanges—United States. 2. Educational
exchanges—China. 3. Teachers, Foreign—China. 4. Education,
Higher—China. I. Title. II. Series.
LB2285.C55P67 1990
370.19'63'0951—dc20   89-78405

British Library Cataloguing in Publication Data is available.

Copyright © 1990 by Edgar A. Porter

All rights reserved. No portion of this book may be
reproduced, by any process or technique, without the
express written consent of the publisher.

Library of Congress Catalog Card Number: 89-78405
ISBN: 0-313-27386-3
ISSN: 0196-707X

First published in 1990

Greenwood Press, 88 Post Road West, Westport, CT   06881
An imprint of Greenwood Publishing Group, Inc.

Printed in the United States of America

The paper used in this book complies with the
Permanent Paper Standard issued by the National
Information Standards Organization (Z39.48-1984).

10 9 8 7 6 5 4 3 2 1

Copyright Acknowledgment

The author gratefully acknowledges permission to quote from the following:

Reprinted from Knight Biggerstaff: *The Earliest Modern Schools in China.* Copyright © 1961 by Cornell University. Used by permission of the publisher, Cornell University Press.

Every reasonable effort has been made to trace the owners of copyright materials in this book, but in some instances this has proven impossible. The publishers will be glad to receive information leading to more complete acknowledgments in subsequent printings of the book, and in the meantime extend their apologies for any omissions.

*This book is dedicated
to my wife, Ran Ying.*

Contents

Preface

"Why is it necessary to learn from the barbarians?"
Wo-jen's Objection to Western Learning, 1867 (quoted in Teng, 1961, p. 76)

When research for this book began in 1987, the goal was to gauge the relationship between Chinese educators and students and their foreign teachers in the post-1979 era.* It was in early 1979 that foreigners, especially Westerners, began to enter China in substantial numbers for the first time since the late 1940s when the Communist party took control of the country. The research would examine questions of the role, motivation, and future of this modern relationship, as seen through the eyes of Chinese and foreigners experiencing it firsthand. It was assumed that when the book was completed, the environment in China would still reflect the values of the post-1979 period. That proved a naive assumption, however, as the events surrounding the June 4, 1989, suppression of the pro-democracy movement have shown. With that single set of actions, China's relationship with the West entered a new era. Presented here is a grassroots summation of what we now see as a ten-year period that began in 1979 and ended on June 4, 1989. The post-1989 period is now being fashioned in the government and university offices in Beijing, Shanghai, Washington, D.C., New Haven, and countless other cities in China and the West. As usual, the future remains unclear.

Many of the central points raised throughout this book find reinforce-

---

*In China, foreign teachers are placed in one of two categories. They are invited as either foreign "experts" or "teachers." Experts hold the higher rank and receive more respect. This includes more comfortable living quarters and a higher salary than those classified as teachers. While most of the foreigners interviewed for this book are classified as experts, the more generic term, teacher, is used throughout with reference to those foreigners engaged in the teaching profession while in China.

ment from the events following June 4. When asked for a prediction of the future, several of those quoted below responded that the future of Chinese-Western relations always proves unpredictable. One Chinese responded with laughter, saying he had seen too much during his life in China ever to predict the future. One foreigner predicted that the relationship will be one of a continuously swinging door; open, then closed, then open again. Some on both sides have remained optimistic, arguing that the door cannot close again. They are wrong, for we now see the door closing, at least partially, to foreigners throughout China. No foreigner is hit harder by the closing door than the visiting teacher. This is evident through decisions on the part of both Chinese and foreigners following June 4.

In the late summer of 1989, the Chinese government announced that it would withdraw, for at least one year, its invitation to Fulbright professors to teach in Chinese institutions of higher learning.* It also withdrew its invitation to the first group of Peace Corps volunteers who were to enter China in 1989 as English teachers. Other visiting professors received notices from their Chinese sponsors withdrawing their invitations to China, at least for a period of time. The cancellation of these programs, especially the Fulbright program, provides major evidence that the door is indeed closing again. In a press release dated August 16, 1989, the U.S. Information Agency announced:

The Chinese government has informed the U.S. embassy in Beijing that it does not wish to participate in the Fulbright program this year. In recent years, the China Fulbright program has been one of the largest in the world, with 24 American professors teaching on Chinese campuses and a like number of Chinese graduate students and scholars studying at U.S. universities.

The Chinese government informed the U.S. that no American Fulbright professors would be permitted to teach in China, and no Chinese graduate students or research scholars would be allowed to travel in the U.S. The Chinese side also rejected our proposal for a reduced two-way exchange. . . .

We deeply regret the Chinese decision to suspend an educational exchange program that has been of mutual benefit.

Other nations and groups have also decided to cancel programs taking foreign teachers into China. The Yale-China Association, in its Summer, 1989, newsletter, stated:

In late June, the Trustees of Yale-China considered the consequences of the violent military suppression of China's nascent democracy movement for the Association's China-based programs. After considerable discussion the Trustees voted to suspend the English Languages Teaching (Bachelor) Program based at three schools in China for the 1989–1990 academic year.

---

*The Chinese government agreed in March, 1990 to resume the Fulbright program on a limited scale for the academic year 1990–1991.

To explain the suspension, Yale-China cited its inability to assure the safety of its young teachers in such an unstable atmosphere and a concern about the further possible deterioration of Sino-American relations. The quality of the teachers' experience in China would be:

much less rewarding than in previous years. Contact with Chinese people other than under strictly professional circumstances would be discouraged, school officials would be obliged to hew to the official line (however they may feel about that line as individuals), and our teachers would be expected to give at least tacit support to this lie, irrespective of their own views or the views of their students. Moreover, we do not believe that we are capable of adequately preparing newly appointed instructors for the situation they will confront in China in the fall. It is a situation which none of us have experienced and one which, indeed, we would have difficulty predicting with any great confidence. Finally, we also believe that a decision to continue our teaching programs this fall can be misrepresented by the Beijing authorities, who are parading foreign businessmen and other visitors before television cameras to lend plausibility to the line "business as usual."

Some programs sponsored by nongovernmental concerns, however, continue to provide foreign teachers in China. Johns Hopkins University has maintained its commitment to send professors to teach Chinese students at its center in Nanjing. The faculty at Yellow River University, established by American overseas Chinese in conjunction with Henan Province officials, retained its usual number of professors on the staff of the school. The same has proved true of the Christian-based English Language Institute, which sends hundreds of teachers to China each year; the recent problems have not affected its program at all, as it increased the numbers of its teachers entering China for the 1989–1990 academic year.

There have been watershed periods in China's history that foretold changes in its relationship with the West. Examples abound: Prince Kung's creation in 1861 of the Tong Wen Guan to teach English; the Boxer Rebellion of 1900 when foreigners were singled out for banishment, even death; and the Nationalist movement of the 1920s and 1930s that forced foreign teachers from schools that they had begun, as Chinese administrators and teachers took charge of these programs. Modern history shows the revolution culminating in the October 1, 1949, establishment of the People's Republic of China as one such turning point. In the years following this victory, China expelled or pressured out most foreigners, including those engaged in teaching. The year 1979 saw a re-opening to foreigners, especially to teachers from the West.

Now we have entered another period marked clearly by a date and an event. The actions of the Chinese government on June 4, 1989, foretold the expulsion of foreign teachers again, as seen through the actions surrounding the Fulbright and Peace Corps programs. It placed foreigners who were allowed to stay in China on notice that they would be watched more carefully than before, and any activities perceived as interference in China's internal affairs would be dealt with strictly. The decision to withdraw its teachers by Yale-China—the American program with the longest history and richest experience in China—points even more clearly to the fact that we have now entered a new period in Chinese-Western relations.

Such events have taken place before. They prove unique only in their particulars, not in any new ways of thinking on the part of Chinese or foreigners. Foreigners are suspect, in their motives and their actions, as they have been for centuries. Comments by Chinese officials after June 4 referred to corrupting influences on China by Western educators and others. This is no different from a century ago, when Wo-Jen said of the education offered by Westerners in China, "If these subjects are going to be taught by Westerners as regular studies, the damage will be great." Similarly, the Yale decision to abandon their English teaching program was based in large measure on the perception that American teachers would not have a meaningful experience while in China; in other words, the Yale teachers would not get what they desired out of the experience. Most of the Chinese officials care little about the Yale teachers' experiences. Their concern has focused on the meaningful English instruction they must now do without. The motives of each side clearly emerge here, and they do not match. They have not matched for centuries.

That the post-1979 era would end in 1989 proves to me, and should prove to others dealing with China, that to predict the future of China with any sense of authority, especially its relationship with the West, is a foolhardy exercise. We now await the twists and turns of the post-1989 period. Whatever happens, we should be mindful of the concern voiced by Wo-Jen, for in China today he has modern compatriots from the same school of thought. They are referred to in the pages that follow, and they cannot be discounted. They still speak for much of China.

Acknowledgments

Writing about China, especially when relating the words and ideas of Chinese confidants, friends, and colleagues, carries with it a heightened sense of responsibility. This is especially true since the June, 1989 crackdown on the democracy movement in China. Because all of the interviews included here took place before the crackdown and during a time of relative freedom of expression in China, the opinions expressed by those Chinese interviewed prove straightforward and refreshingly honest. It is, of course, now my responsibility to protect those scores of Chinese who spent time with me to explain their views of foreign educators in China. Therefore, no names used here are true identities. Whereas interviews did take place at the schools mentioned, titles are sometimes changed and locations of those interviewed are at times altered. Having expressed this concern, I want at this time to thank all those Chinese who participated in the interviews. Without them there would be no book.

Along the way there were others whose support proved invaluable to me. Foremost among these are the foreign teachers who shared perceptions of their role in China. As with their Chinese counterparts, their insights proved invaluable in the completion of this work.

While finishing graduate study at George Peabody College of Vanderbilt University I received the gentle encouragement of Dr. Thomas Stovall and Dr. Jack Miller. They guided me as I fumbled through the early stages of this project and instilled discipline that held me to the fire when the times did not always encourage such determination. I also am appreciative of the international travel grant received from George Peabody College that enabled me to travel to China in 1987 to carry out the interviews that make up such an important part of this book.

During the early drafts of this book I called on two international experts on the role of foreigners in China, Jonathan Spence and Ruth Hayhoe. Both read parts of the manuscript and made suggestions that were incorporated into the work. Without their assistance this work would be much weaker, and probably would not have found itself in print. With their help, especially the detailed review given by Ruth Hayhoe, this book now makes a modest contribution to the study of Chinese education and the role foreigners play in that system. All weaknesses found in the book fall completely on my shoulders. Many of the strengths can be traced to the assistance of Ruth Hayhoe and Jonathan Spence.

To prepare the original manuscript for publication, several persons at the University of Hawaii proved invaluable. Linda Miyashiro and Jennifer Kam spent countless hours at the word processor, making my scribbling legible. Stephen Fleming and Du Xiaoya made several suggestions relating to the document section of the book. The offices of Mark Juergensmeyer, Dean of the School of Hawaiian, Asian and Pacific Studies, and Rudolph Schmerl, Director of Research Relations, awarded grants to assure that the final production of this book be presented in an appropriate format.

Finally, I want to acknowledge the assistance of Ran Ying, my companion and colleague. Her support over the years has made this book possible. This support manifested itself through her ideas, translations, proofreading, and typing. For the most part, however, it was shown through her quiet and constant encouragement. It is to her that this book is dedicated.

Foreign Teachers in China

Chapter 1

Introduction

Since the 1600s, foreigners have entered China in various official capacities. Not until the latter half of the nineteenth century, however, did foreign educators, mostly Western missionaries, enter China as teachers, advisors, and administrators. While political turmoil and change have dictated the numbers, activities, and nationalities of those participating, there has been no period since the 1860s when foreign educators were absent from Chinese institutions of higher learning. The presence of foreigners in China's classrooms during this period has brought with it a contradictory, yet unavoidable, state of mutual attraction and conflict between the Chinese and the foreigner. The attraction lies in China's desire to learn from the West and the desire of Westerners to live in China so they may change and/or experience it. The conflict between China and its Western educators surfaces easily and often, given the vastly different roots from which each culture springs. This conflict finds expression in an educational setting in the context of mission. Specifically, to what end and in what manner does a nation educate its people?

The Chinese understanding of the mission of education relates directly, even today, to thousands of years of Confucian teaching. Confucianism, which at its roots amounts to conformity to a moral code of living, stresses that education exists for the improvement of society through the transformation of people into better citizens. Education's purpose is to create an environment that promotes peace and harmony, and to provide moral training as a way to achieve this. In other words, education's role in Confucian thought is to bring about a more just society (Hawkins, 1981). In traditional China, this morally grounded education was tied directly to training scholars for state offices. In modern China, the mission of education is not as far removed from the past as might be suspected.

Soon after the victory of the Communist party in 1949, the world saw

China call on its youth to "serve the people." While modern China no longer educates its people to serve only as officials, the use of this slogan shows that China still instills in its youth the idea that education is tied to a national mission (Hawkins, 1981, p. 93). Since the late 1970s, China has continued in this vein, exhorting its young people to study diligently so that the country may attain the "four modernizations" in science and technology, industry, agriculture, and defense. Again, the goal of education relates to the improvement of the country itself.

Western expectations for education concentrate on different goals. Ignas (1981) states that American education, for example, stresses the following: "(1) that the schools produce citizens with the necessary skills, knowledge, and attitudes to function in the nation's social, political, and economic structures, and (2) that every child be given the opportunity to learn whatever is needed to carry out basic life tasks" (p. 2). The difference between the Chinese and American goals proves striking. Whereas China educates its people to build a stronger and more just society, America educates its youth to function, or survive, within society's structures. Americans have no stated or expected moral obligation to work cooperatively in making society better. The second goal refers again to the individual meeting his or her needs in society. People must learn "whatever is needed" to survive in the world. By implication, the individual in America finds himself or herself pitted against the strains encountered in society rather than participating in the flow of society's advancement.

The role of the individual stands out as the most striking difference between Chinese and American educational missions. In China, the individual inescapably participates as a member of the Chinese collective. Individualistic behavior is relegated to a secondary role, if that. This is shown through the negative attitude most Chinese take toward the word individualism. As several Chinese friends have pointed out to me, this word in Chinese carries the connotation of the English word selfish.

Commenting on the role of individualism in Chinese society, Hsu (1985) writes:

Despite their erudition, the Chinese have produced no writings extolling self-reliance or attacking conformity. Their great literature deals with the means to achieve peace by wise government and by the elimination of causes of crime, corruption, and civil disturbance. Their problem has always been how to make the individual live according to the accepted customs and rules of conduct, not how to enable him to rise above them. (p. 135)

In contrast, in the American view, the individual remains paramount. While an American education may lead a student to a path that helps improve society, it may just as easily lead to riches or fame not tied to national pride or progress. Foreigners who go to China to engage in educational activities and who have little or no knowledge of this difference will encounter much confusion, frustration, and misunderstanding.

Tied to the problem of differences in mission are differences in pedagogy. An experience I had while teaching in China in the late 1970s provides an example. I had been in China for only a few weeks when a Chinese colleague asked me to visit her class and evaluate her teaching. As class began, I was impressed with the teacher's skill in relating a story to her class in English. What a pleasant and active way to begin class, I thought. The story lasted 8 to 10 minutes. When she finished, she asked her attentive students to tell parts of the same story. Much to my surprise, they recited exactly her own words. After a few minutes of this, the teacher took the floor again and repeated the whole story, using exactly the same vocabulary and inflection in her voice. I sat stunned as I opened the class text and began to follow her, word for word, through that day's assignment. She had spent hours memorizing the text, as had her students. That is how they learn English in China. It is also how they learn history, geography, education, and most other subjects. This teaching method relates directly to the Confucian tenets extolling student discipline, rote learning, and a teacher-centered classroom (Louie, 1984).

The gap between my more spontaneous, student-active approach to teaching and her structured recitation method (which, I soon learned, she shared with every other Chinese instructor in our department) proved too wide to bridge in a single after-class discussion. In fact, we never bridged the gap.

The experience illuminated a basic difference between Western education, with its emphasis on the role of the individual's contribution, and Chinese education. In most Western classrooms, what each student thinks merits consideration. In fact, instructors solicit creative input from their students, including opinions, criticism, and debate. For example, American education teaches that the individual must have the freedom to express his or her views simply because it is a person's right to do so. To limit this creative style of learning may seem personally and philosophically offensive to persons educated in this fashion. The roots of these views have been traced to America's early history:

The self-sufficiency of pioneer Americans was rooted in individualism. . . . Their self-sufficiency was a channel into which their individualism could flow without restraint, and which was necessary if families were to survive in a hostile environment. And unfettered individualism became an ideal that they inculcated into their children and by which they judged the worth of all mankind. (Hsu, 1985, p. 128)

Because they have a different agenda for their students and their nation, Chinese instructors are less concerned with spontaneous classroom participation. Their students have a foreign language to learn, and recitation has proved successful in accomplishing this aim for generations. The mastery of a subject for the benefit of the nation stands as the most important goal. The individual's need to express himself or herself about a subject proves little importance.

Beyond the question of the individual versus the collective, equally serious differences surround perceptions of motivation. What motivates foreigners to enter China as educators, and what motivates the Chinese to invite them? At what point do these motivations converge, and at what point do they conflict? When large numbers of foreigners entered China in the later half of the nineteenth century and the first half of the twentieth century, they arrived with their own cultural and religious motivations that connected directly to a specific educational mission. They met a China that, while steeped in a centuries-old tradition, saw some of its people struggling to break China out of the confinement imposed by that tradition, so that the nation could take its place as a modern power. Those who welcomed the foreigners, though few in numbers, were eager to adapt Western technology and science to their age-old culture. However, they showed little interest in the culture and religion of these visitors. What the foreigners perceived as their mission and what the Chinese actually desired from them were at odds from the beginning of the relationship, and they continue to be at odds today.

The differing perceptions indicate that the Chinese have welcomed foreign technology and concrete, applicable knowledge, but resented attempts by Westerners to sell their cultural and religious offerings. Westerners, however, have a history of combining the two. During those early years, most Westerners thought that Western technology and knowledge sprang from a superior culture and morality; it was thus only natural that the Chinese should buy the complete package. The Chinese, on the other hand, have always held their culture to be superior. These perceptions, viewed in a historical light, are best analyzed by Spence (1980) when he states:

Every technique that Western advisors had brought had eventually been assimilated: heliocentric theories and calendrical science, sophisticated medical surgery, economic planning, engineering, interdisciplinary universities, long-distance communications, mechanized warfare, nuclear physics. The Westerners had presented their expertise as the wrapping round an ideological package, however, and had tried to force the Chinese to accept both together. It was this that the Chinese had refused to tolerate; even at their weakest, they sensed that acceptance of a foreign ideology on foreign terms must be a form of submission. . . . As we look back across the cycle from 1620 to 1960, we can observe the standpoint of superiority sprang from two elements: the possession of advanced technological skills and a sense of moral rightness. Convinced that their goals were good and that their advice was sorely needed, the Westerners adopted a proprietary air toward China; Chinese refusal to accept the validity of their goals, and Chinese rejection of their advice, were met with Western bewilderment or anger. (pp. 289–290)

As seen here, China's mission in education historically derives from the need to instill in the collective a sense of justice and dedication to building the country. That was the case over two thousand years ago, and it remains true today. Borrowing aspects of Western technology continues to be viewed as an aid to this mission, rather than a replacement for it. The mission guiding most Western educators in China, by contrast, has revolved around the development and intrinsic worth of the individual and his or her movement in the direction of Western morals and Christian religion.

Chapter 2

History of Foreigners in Chinese Education

INFLUENCE OF CONFUCIAN CULTURE

The history of education in China, like its mission, is tied to the Confucian principle that the primary goal in life is to build harmonious relationships. Disorder and unrest must be cast aside. Order, in which each person knows his or her place in society, takes precedence in everyone's life (Hookham, 1972). To act harmoniously, people must first understand virtuous behavior, which can be attained only through proper conduct. But how does one know what constitutes proper conduct? The answer, according to Confucian ideas, must be understood solely in the search for wisdom through study. For the strict Confucian scholar, this study revolves around the precepts of prior sages and the lessons gained from history. If one pursues a study of these sages, one can find a proper place in society, thus fitting harmoniously in that society. One of the most important and intriguing ideas behind this concept holds that both individuals and human society are perfectible. Every person, regardless of status at birth, can become a sage, and every society can potentially become harmonious and fulfilling for all (Hucker, 1975).

Hu (1984) states that moral fiber and leadership ability have proved the best criteria for good leaders. He states further that traditionally the more education one held in China, the higher the moral superiority (that is, the closer to perfection). Because of this equation, the function of education in traditional China became one of preparing and producing men as scholars and eventually government officials. In other words, in Confucian-dominated China, the major goal of education was not to transmit knowledge or learn certain skills. The goal was to internalize a set of ethical principles that govern human behavior in all facets of life, to act out those principles, and to be rewarded by becoming a scholar or government official.

For centuries, scholars made up the elite in China. Understanding their role in a harmonious society, commoners usually accepted their own inferior positions relative to the educated elite as long as stability, or harmony, reigned. It was accepted that the elite did no physical labor and shunned practical matters. Their role in life centered on reading the classics, thus bettering themselves in their own positions and qualifying them further as leaders (Hu, 1984). Commenting on this system and the means by which scholars attained their positions, Max Weber wrote, "For twelve centuries social rank in China has been determined more by qualification for office than by wealth. This qualification, in turn, has been determined by education, and especially by examination" (quoted by Hu, 1984, p. 7).

Whereas the philosophy of education stresses maintaining harmony in society through the leadership of those best educated, the classical Chinese examination system demonstrates how this philosophy actually works its way into daily Chinese life. The system of examinations, within the framework of classical Confucian China, survived for centuries. As Gu (1984) points out, for almost three thousand years of Chinese history, young and old men participated in the examinations to attain that special rank of scholar. The first level of examinations was given locally; then successful candidates were invited to the capital, where a select few would be chosen for one final written and oral examination. The students were required to know Chinese classical literature and politics, and to have an undeniable understanding of Confucian ideas. To strive for such heights, it was not uncommon for young men to sacrifice much of their youth in hopes of passing the examination. One early Chinese poem shows this concern well:

> Shadows of pairing sparrows cross his book
>   of poplar catkins, dropping overhead . . .
> The weary student from his window-nook
>   Looks up to find that spring has long since fled.
>   (quoted in Giles, 1923, p. 238)

For countless generations, young and old in China were molded through their education to conform to an ideology supporting the state's universal moral correctness. Fostered by the belief that China stood alone at the center of the civilized world and that all others gathered below its empire, the Chinese have also believed, quite naturally, that they were the moral superior of all other cultures. And, as has been seen, moral superiority has come from attention to education. Thus, for centuries the Chinese have held that their educational level stood much higher than that of the rest of the world (Hu, 1984). It comes as no surprise to learn that foreigners played no role in China's examination (i.e., education) system other than as isolated observers during these many centuries.

NINETEENTH CENTURY TO 1949

For more than twenty centuries, from the time of Confucius until the nineteenth century, China delivered education through private and individual teaching. Although there were attempts to set up schools to train government officials as early as the Western Zhou dynasty of three thousand years ago, it was not until the Qing dynasty (1644–1911) that schools of a formal nature were actually established. The Chinese set up two types of schools. The first constituted what Westerners would call a state institution, whose purpose was to polish those who had already passed the first level of the state examination. The second type offered itself to those who had finished some basic education and were preparing for the initial examination. Most of this preparatory work was done on a private basis in a family setting. The quality of this second tier of schools varied in students and instruction (Hu, 1984). As in earlier centuries, foreigners had no role in these schools, but attempts by foreigners to involve themselves in Chinese education were on the horizon.

In 1786, foreign Roman Catholic missionaries established religious schools for Chinese youth. While the Chinese government forced most of these to close, by the 1840s Protestant missionaries were pursuing the earlier Catholic example and setting up schools in Hong Kong and Ningbo. As Bastid (1987) points out, none of these schools was established at the request of the Chinese. They were begun as attempts to gain converts to Christianity and to a new world outlook. The Chinese, understanding this, rejected their legitimacy and their relevance, and continued closing them at their discretion (Covell, 1978).

Following the Opium War defeat in 1840, some Chinese authorities began to question the outright rejection of Western educational practices and to advocate change in the country's educational system—a change, they argued, that would include learning from the West. These early advocates of change, according to Biggerstaff (1961) were motivated solely by a desire to strengthen China against the West. All regarded China as morally superior to all Western nations. They acknowledged, however, China's weakness as a military power and knew it was incapable of withstanding the coming armies and influences of Western powers. They pressed for Chinese study of Western mathematics, science, and language.

In the 1840s, Qi Kang, the governor of Guangzhou, advocated the addition of mathematics to the civil service exam. Wei Yuan, a historian of the time, advocated a Western approach to the study of arms manufacturing and ship navigation. The central authorities accepted neither proposal. The goal of China, the authorities said, was to destroy Western arms and strengthen moral character, not to copy the inferior West. All else would fall into place, if that were achieved.

One educator, Feng Guifu, argued in 1860 that China should study Western subjects and learn the language of the Westerners who were then arriving in China in large numbers. Recognizing that contact with the West was unavoidable and that only missionary-trained Chinese spoke English, Feng feared that the truly educated in China (that is, those who had passed through the examination system) would have to depend on foreignized Chinese "of uncertain social status" to represent China in negotiations. China could not negotiate from strength while locked in this position, he said, so he advocated the establishment of schools in Shanghai and Guangzhou to teach the language and culture of the West. Students would study mathematics and foreign languages under foreign teachers, but the classics would remain in the curriculum under the direction of Chinese scholars (Biggerstaff, 1961). China must, he stated, adopt Western technology while maintaining traditional Confucian virtues (Covell, 1978). By the early 1860s, government authorities finally responded to the paradoxical view of Feng and others that the best way to strengthen China against the threat from the West was to gain knowledge from the West.

On January 18, 1861, three regents under the child emperor Tong Zhi proposed a radical restructuring of China's relationship with the West. Led by Prince Kung, a relative of the emperor, these regents proposed the establishment of a foreign office to deal with the new and growing problems surrounding Westerners in China. This proposal included the idea of opening a new school of foreign languages in Beijing that would teach English and French. The proposal to establish this school was approved and steps were taken to locate qualified teachers. Ten students were selected initially, with twenty more scheduled to follow the next year. The school was eventually called Tong Wen Guan, or the Interpreters' College, in Beijing.

In 1862, the regents reported to the emperor that no Chinese teachers of merit had been found to teach language courses. They therefore suggested the employment of foreigners to teach the Chinese students chosen for this new-style school. They had seen foreigners in China learn language from native Chinese. Why, they argued, should foreigners not teach their native language to Chinese? They wrote:

Since there are no Chinese possessing a thorough knowledge of foreign languages, Kwangtung and Kiangsu lacking any who should be sent to Peking, we could not avoid seeking suitable persons among foreigners. The English [secretary of legation] Thomas Wade informed us that his countryman J. S. Burdon, who understands Chinese, might temporarily fill the chair [of English]. We ordered him to visit this office for an interview. Although we do not know this man well, still he appears to be sincere and if employed only to teach students there would seem to be no grounds for him to make demands. Because the ten students earlier ordered selected entered the school on July 11, he is being tried out as their teacher. As clearly stated to Wade in advance, religious teaching will not be tolerated after the language lessons. (quoted in Biggerstaff, 1961, p. 99)

This proposal and its ultimate acceptance paved the way for foreigners to participate officially in China's educational system for the first time. In 1863, similar schools were authorized in Shanghai and Guangzhou. By 1865, Tong Wen Guan brought on board two additional instructors, a missionary from France to teach French and an American missionary, W. A. P. Martin, to teach English. Like their British colleague, they received strict assignments in their teaching role and were told they could not give instruction in their religion. By 1866, Robert Hart, an Irishman who headed China's customs office, was commissioned to find foreign teachers to hold posts in the area of the natural sciences (Biggerstaff, 1961).

The establishment of this school, even though directed by Chinese authorities, caused great alarm among many of the Chinese elite. In 1867, a spokesman for this group offered a document to the emperor, calling for the cessation of this new type of foreign-taught and Western-slanted education. It said:

I have heard that the way to establish a state is to respect propriety and righteousness rather than power and scheming. The basic design is in men's minds not in their skills. Now if we pursue one of the secondary arts [mathematics] and also accept foreigners as teachers, we run the risk that the two-faced foreigners may not necessarily transmit their skills; even if the teachers teach with sincerity and the students study with sincerity, the products will be no more than mathematicians. In all history no one has been heard of who, relying on mathematics, was able to lift decline or to strengthen weakness. With the size of China, there is no need to worry about a lack of talent. If it is necessary to teach astronomy and mathematics, a wide search will necessarily disclose persons versed in these arts. Why should it be foreigners? Why must we learn from foreigners? . . . If now it is recommended that the outstanding accomplished scholars nurtured by the state and held in reserve until they can be used change and follow foreigners, then truth will not be expressed and evil will therefore spread. It cannot but end after a few years by driving the Chinese people fully to yield to the foreigner. . . . It is hoped that the Emperor will decide independently to cancel the earlier decision at once, in order to care for the public well-being and stop unseen disaster. China would be most fortunate. (quoted in Biggerstaff, 1961, pp. 114–115)

Although important central authorities repulsed the attacks on the new school, its prestige suffered. Students chosen for Tong Wen Guan found themselves looked down upon by other Chinese because of their affiliation with a "foreign" school. They showed little interest in the new courses offered in language and science, concentrating instead on the traditional Chinese studies in the classics. They saw the new courses as impeding their professional opportunities after leaving Tong Wen Guan. Their concerns were well founded, as it was not until the 1890s that graduates of this school were granted official rank in the tradition of Chinese scholars who had passed the state examination. During the school's forty-year existence,

it had to face the stigma of offering an education perceived as dealing poorly with questions of moral character and inferior in its educational offerings (Biggerstaff, 1961).

In 1869, the school was near collapse. In one last attempt to build a strong program, Robert Hart convinced the Chinese authorities to name W. A. P. Martin, on furlough at that time in the United States, to assume the presidency of the school. He would also teach international law. After Hart agreed to handle the school's financial affairs, Martin accepted this proposal and returned to China (Covell, 1978). The Chinese, however, maintained control over the school. If Martin entered his presidency with any illusions on this score, they were quickly dispelled. Upon his arrival, his Chinese superiors gave him a test in mathematics to gauge his fitness for running a school involved in science instruction (Martin, 1900a).

Upon taking over as president of the school, Martin attempted to walk a fine line between Chinese sensitivities and his own perspective on what China needed. At some points, his pronouncements and actions clearly contradicted each other. Soon after arriving in China as a young missionary in 1850, he had said that "the first impulse in civilization came from the introduction of the gospel and every stage of [civilization's] future progress may be taken as an index of its influence" (quoted in Covell, 1978, p. 22). Speaking of his motives for being in China, Martin said his goal was to open "this mass of ignorance, pride, superstition and pollution to the entrance of Christian truth and knowledge" (quoted in Covell, 1978, p. 94). He saw his work at Tong Wen Guan as a new podium from which to pursue his missionary goals. Early in his years there, he stated:

Humbling is it not? Yet the logic of events was destined to convince China that not only in languages, but in everything that makes a nation great and strong, she would have to accept the teaching of foreigners. (quoted in Covell, 1978, p. 171)

While this attitude stayed with Martin throughout his years in China, he also knew how to maintain harmonious relationships with Chinese authorities. He went so far as to participate in Confucian rites. He did this partly out of respect for China's customs, but also as a calculated move that he knew would be appreciated by the Chinese. In his public pronouncements, he refused to attack traditional Chinese religions or the practices surrounding ancestor worship, Taoism, and Buddhism. This public posture, however, did not keep him from advancing his religious views whenever possible. Like modern missionaries who appear in later chapters, Martin (1900a), toward the end of his tenure in China, said, "Though the nature of the institution precluded the regular teaching of religion, I always felt at liberty to speak to the students on the subject" (p. 325).

In the final analysis, Martin decided that the best way to win converts to

Christianity was to train the future Chinese scholars in the ways of the West. If he could not spread the religion of his culture directly, he could spread the basic principles upon which it rested. His experience showed, he said, that this approach would gain more converts for Christianity than he could win as a traditional missionary working outside the Chinese system (Covell, 1978).

As the administration of the mathematics exam shows, Martin's power as an administrator was not all encompassing. He was given limited authority, but the Chinese authorities prevailed if differences arose. On the one hand, Martin was free to reorganize much of the curriculum. Soon after arriving as president, he instituted a five-year curriculum and an eight-year curriculum. The five-year plan included mathematics, science, political economy, and international law. The eight-year plan included English, French, German, Russian, geography, science, mathematics, and history. Those studying English were taught all classes in that language. Those studying other languages were taught all classes, except language, in their native Chinese. The Chinese authorities watched Martin's actions closely, however. At one point, they disallowed his appointment of a medical professor who had been hired to teach medicine and physiology. The Chinese would not allow Chinese students to engage in clinical practice of any kind (Covell, 1978).

By 1872, despite the ever-present differences between Chinese and Western authorities, Hart could point with pride to the strides made at Tong Wen Guan. He wrote: "I am glad to say that the college is going ahead. We have now over 70 Peking students, 12 Cantonese, and 7 from Kiangsoo and Chekiang, about 100 in all . . ." (quoted in Biggerstaff, 1961, p. 125).

By the end of the nineteenth century, Tong Wen Guan had established itself as a solid, if still somewhat unpopular, fixture on the educational scene in China. The fact that it never gained the acceptance it sought was highlighted during the Boxer Rebellion of 1898 when the foreigners affiliated with this school were treated no better than foreigners anywhere else in China. After escaping to the U.S. legation following the killing of the German ambassador, Martin (1900b) said of himself and his friend Robert Hart:

As we looked each other in the face, we could not help blushing for shame at the thought that our life long services had been so little valued . . . from my thirty years' teaching of international law they had learned that the lives of Ambassadors were not to be held sacred. (pp. 96–97)

After the Boxer Rebellion, Tong Wen Guan was re-opened but placed inside a new university established by Chinese authorities. This later became Beijing University. The new school was patterned in part after Tong Wen Guan and established in China a university of a new type, one fash-

ioned in many ways after those found in the West. In this way, at least, the school proved successful in influencing China to learn from the West (Biggerstaff, 1961).

In the final analysis, however, Tong Wen Guan achieved few of the goals desired by Martin and his foreign colleagues. As Covell says of Martin, "Despite the fact that his government position helped him accomplish some subsidiary goals, Martin's ultimate purpose that the T'ung Wen Kuan [Tong Wen Guan] would lead to a complete reform in the educational system was not realized" (Covell, p. 183). At the end of his tenure as president, Martin (1900a) lamented:

Unlike the Japanese, who adopted the Western system in all their schools from kindergarten to university, the Chinese were so well satisfied with their old style of education that they never dreamed of reforming or supplimenting it to any great extent. The college was established as a concession to the demands of a new situation to supply a limited number of trained officials, not to renovate the whole mandarinate. Deep and permanent as its influence must be, how much grander would be its destiny if it were made the starting-point of a new departure. (p. 327)

Martin saw that China worked from its self-interest at all times, even in its use of him and others in the school. He realized that China was moved to accommodate the West because of the "roar of the Western cannon," rather than the "sound of celestial music" (Covell, 1978, p. 95).

Martin's attempt to work within a Chinese institution did not appeal to most foreigners in China at that time. They desired more control over their schools' mission and curriculum, especially in the area of religious interaction and recruitment of faculty. By the 1880s, missionaries from various Western countries, especially the United States, were entering a weakened China to establish their Western-style schools. By 1890, such schools operated in Beijing, Shandong, Hangzhou, and other centers in China. Two of the most famous and enduring, St. Johns College in Shanghai and Lingnan University in Guangzhou, were established during this period. By the turn of the century, others, including Suzhou University and Fujian University, opened their doors under Western missionary direction (Fenn, 1976).

During the early years of the twentieth century, the Qing Dynasty lost control of the country. Changes were inevitable, and education was one area that began to change before the last days of this last dynasty. Reformers, fearful of stagnation on the one hand and foreign domination on the other, continued to advocate the development of a new educational system for all China, so that China could regain its prestige and strength. Zhang Zhidong, one of the leaders of the reform movement, advocated the implementation of a system based on that found in Japan (Abe, 1987). Japan had defeated China in the Sino-Japanese War of 1894–1895, and China watched as Japan defeated Russia in the Russo-Japanese War of 1904–

1905. It became clear to some in China that Japan's successes were in large measure due to its modern educational system, built with the help of foreigners during the Meiji Period of the 1870s. In 1902, Zhang was named head of the new ministry of education, a ministry modeled on that found in Japan. In 1905, the civil service examination, which had served China for almost thirty centuries, was abolished. The short but important era of Japanese influence in China's educational system began. For the next several years, Japan sent Japanese teachers and administrators to China, translated textbooks for Chinese schools, and accepted more than ten thousand students from China into Japanese schools.

During these years of Japanese influence, China's concern with how to deal with foreigners in its internal fabric remained paramount, especially in education. China chose a Japanese model not only because of Japan's great success on the battlefields and oceans of Asia and Russia, but also because both nations shared respect for Confucian ideas and feared and needed Western support. As always, China had to balance the two. In the introduction of the 1904 school regulations, the new Ministry of Education in China announced:

The principle idea in establishing any school is a basis in loyalty and filial piety. In other words, traditional Chinese learning must be the basis of education to form students' character. After that, the importance of Western learning is emphasized to enrich knowledge and to give technical skills to students. . . . (quoted in Abe, 1987, p. 65)

As Abe points out, this is patterned on the Japanese model of combining a Confucian-based moral education with an education strong in modern science.

At the time of the final collapse of the Qing Dynasty in 1911, Japan's influence had reached its peak. Abe points out that Japan's influence then began to wane due to several factors. First, the experiment of using Japanese educators in China proved successful in many ways. Chinese educators who had studied under the Japanese began to fill the positions held by their former teachers. This was true of both those Chinese who trained in China under the Japanese and those who journeyed to Japan to gain further training.

A second reason for Japan's decline reflects the low standard of teaching brought to China by many Japanese educators. Abe states that many went to China because they could not find equally prestigious and financially rewarding positions in Japan. Still another reason Japanese influence in China waned after 1911 had to do with Japan's growing desire to influence, then rule, that country. Between 1922 and World War II, the years when Japan exercised colonial rule over parts of China, many Chinese educators looked to the friendlier United States for educational ideas. This was due in part to the increased influence of educators from the United States during the early part of the twentieth century through the missionary movement and the opening of major universities, such as Yanjing University, Yale-in-China, and Qinghua University.

Wang (1981) notes that by the early twentieth century, missionary and YMCA schools had established themselves in China as prestigious centers of learning, influencing Chinese colleges and universities to such a degree that English developed into the proper language of instruction throughout China's institutions of higher learning. By the 1920s, as Japan's influence waned, an appreciation for Western literature spread, and students sought Chinese newspapers carrying English advertisements for foreign goods and films.

According to Wang, the use of English increased communication and personal contact between China and the West. New relationships built on these contacts, however, accentuated cultural differences between Chinese and foreigners as much as they brought the two groups together. Whereas the Japanese had at least shared a common Confucian heritage, educators from the West arrived with no such common philosophical perspective. Problems in classroom instruction highlighted this. Despite interest in Western ideas, cultural differences in teaching methods and classroom expectations sprang up whenever Westerners taught Chinese students. These students, steeped in a traditional learning style dependent on rote memorization, resisted Western teaching methods that encouraged their active classroom participation. Foreign teachers could not understand why Chinese students balked at their proven methods; the same methods educated Western students successfully. Speaking of the historical role of foreigners in China's classrooms, Wang argues a point that is as true today as it was in the nineteenth and early twentieth centuries. He writes: "It is not always wise to train teachers to use the same methodology without modifications in a country with a different historical and cultural background" (p. 657).

One of the most famous and intriguing examples of Western involvement in China's higher education movement began with a Yale University missionary movement. The early 1900s saw young men from Yale strike out for China to establish Yale-in-China, a Christian education movement set in Changsha, the capital of southern China's Hunan Province. Hunan's reputation as an antiforeign province, hostile to missionaries and other Westerners, drew them there. Upon their arrival, they found posters on the city wall greeting them with such slogans as "Let us kill foreigners and their officials!" and "Put to death the foreign students and foreign children" (Spence, 1980). Spence says that such pronouncements left Yale's first young emissaries undaunted and even more determined.

Holden (1964) reports that Yale-in-China first founded a middle school that taught English and emphasized, but did not evangelize, Christianity. It then founded a hospital and medical college, naming as its head twenty-nine-year-old Edward Hume. Sounding much like W. A. P. Martin of a generation before, Hume announced that he hoped Chinese would attend this medical college, where they would learn Western customs and the Christian religion. In this way, he argued, they could become true citizens of the world. The college enrolled few students and admitted few patients in its early years (Spence, 1980).

Hume learned much about China during his first few years in Changsha and slowly gained an appreciation for China's culture and its customs, even to the point of incorporating traditional Chinese medical techniques into the college's curriculum and practice. Chinese doctors trained in the West joined his faculty and, by the early 1900s, Yale-in-China had gained the confidence of the people, many of whom learned to depend on the hospital for their medical care. By 1910, when a new wave of antiforeign riots broke out in Changsha, Yale's reputation among the citizens of Changsha saved the college and hospital from destruction (Spence, 1980).

The longer Hume stayed in China, the more dreams he had for the country. He regarded the overthrow of the Qing dynasty in 1911 as an opportunity for China's Western-educated men to lead the nation. He encouraged China's nationalist mood by inviting Chinese to sit on the board of directors of the Yale hospital. This led to cries of outrage from many Yale supporters that Hume paid too much attention to China's problems of nationalism and not enough to spiritual matters (Spence, 1980).

Spence writes that Hume tried to integrate himself into Chinese life as much as possible and delighted in joining a literary society populated by well-educated Chinese. This experience turned ironic in later years, when Hume discovered that his presence had been requested to assure the safety of the other members, for this group in fact met to plot the overthrow of the government. Hume's presence merely protected them from police harassment; as soon as he left each meeting, the conspirators began their political intrigue. Actual integration by a foreigner into Chinese society, as Hume discovered, never happens and should never be assumed or anticipated.

Hume insisted that Yale's presence in China paved the way for great changes there. As much as Hume desired this, however, he ultimately misunderstood the country. As the medical college expanded, the earth beneath its foundations shook with the forces of civil war and revolution. By the time the fighting subsided almost forty years later, the impact of Yale-in-China, while not altogether negligible, appeared irrelevant to the Chinese (Spence, 1980). One young Yale idealist, reflecting Hume's optimism but equally naive in his understanding of China, said that men from Yale could teach the Chinese fair play and give them a high sense of honor, thus making China great. Like so many other foreigners, this young man, writes Spence, knew nothing of China and its starvation, infanticide, humiliation at the hands of foreigners, and fierce pride. Just as Western teaching methods proved awkward in Chinese classrooms, Western morals and a Western sense of honor fit uncomfortably in the lives of Chinese students in a Yale-in-China setting.

Spence paints a sad picture of Hume's later years. As he watched China's nationalist movement resist foreign domination and move China forward, Hume admitted that Yale might not be best for China unless China absorbed it. The university, he said, intruded on China and should at least restructure its presence to that of a guest. In 1925 he reported:

Foreign teachers who come to us from now on will have to face the possibility of being replaced as time goes on by qualified Chinese. And what has been said of teachers applies equally to administrative positions. We who come from the West are bound to feel that our service has been fruitful in proportion as we prepare our places for Chinese who shall make the interest of our institution and the progress of Christian education in China their controlling purpose. (quoted in Holden, 1965, p. 101)

This bold proposal, to replace foreigners gradually with Chinese, was not welcomed by many who financed and directed the program in New Haven. Spence reports that in the same year that he proposed more Chinese leadership, Hume asked Yale not to send young men to Changsha ignorant of Chinese culture. He grew impatient with teachers and staff who refused to adapt to Chinese customs and conditions. In 1926, frustrated and isolated in his views, Hume resigned. He departed a scorned man, rejected by many because they believed he paid too little attention to American and Christian interests. Spence asserts that these people failed to realize that the Chinese refused to see the foreigners as the foreigners saw themselves.

Hume's sensitivity to the need for Chinese to operate their own educational programs was not shared by most foreigners in China during the first two decades of this century. While many Chinese were eager to learn about education from the West, especially the United States, the concern over foreigners interfering in their educational programs was gaining momentum. Chung (1934) states that from 1900 to 1922 the Chinese people only tolerated foreigners in this role of educator. In 1922, however, Western educators in China faced compelling resistance to their presence and influence in Chinese society, due to an outpouring of antiforeign sentiment supported by the new ruling Nationalist party. Antiforeign sentiments were especially active in the government schools, of which there were thirty at the national level and forty-eight in the provinces. Such activity also occurred in the mission schools, though usually underground. While the movement did not take on the violence of the Boxer Rebellion of the turn of the century, it did disrupt the activities of foreigners in China, to the degree that by the mid-1930s only ten foreign institutions of higher learning could be found in China (Fenn, 1976). In 1923, according to Chung, there had been eighteen mission or foreign schools in China. Bastid claims that antiforeign sentiment proved so prevalent in China during the 1920s that by 1927 only five hundred of an original eight thousand missionaries remained in China.

To gain more control over their own country, Chinese educators developed what Bastid calls an eclectic approach to education. Educational leaders sought to integrate Chinese education into the international mainstream while maintaining autonomy and Chinese characteristics at the same time. The problems, Chinese educators insisted, was not that particular foreign systems were inadequate. The problem was that China had simply been copying these systems slavishly, without understanding how they might work in a Chinese context. While the United States system held more influence than others through the 1930s and 1940s, China made great efforts to create a new system, which, while borrowing from the West, retained Chinese characteristics and stayed under Chinese control.

To begin to meet this challenge, a national conference was held in Henan Province in 1924 that addressed the influence of foreigners in China's educational system. The final report stated:

a. Education is the most important function of the civil administration. Foreigners established schools without registration. This is an interference with the educational rights of a nation.

b. Each nation has its own policy for the education of its people. The policy of foreigners is contrary to our own educational principles.

c. The policy of foreigners in China looks like charity, but in effect it is really a form of colonization. The students trained in foreign nations will learn to love these nations. This will injure the patriotic ideal of Chinese students.

d. If we investigate the content of their work we will find that most foreigners who are doing educational work in China usually have as their purpose either religious propaganda or political aggressions. (quoted in Chung, 1934, pp. 173–174)

In 1926, the Nationalist government in Guangzhou issued regulations governing, among other things, the activities of foreign-administered and funded schools in China. In a move that placed these schools in a category parallel to Chinese-operated private schools, the government dictated:

a. Christian institutions can no longer be recognized as a special class, but are given the status of private schools and must be so designated.

b. The administration must be in the hands of Chinese. A foreign principal may continue in school where one is already functioning, but in such cases a Chinese vice-principal should be appointed and shall have charge of dealings with the government in educational matters. The majority of the members of the managing board, whenever there is one, shall be Chinese. The Nationalist requirements are that the principal must be a Chinese, that there must be a local managing board and that its chairman as well as a majority of the members must be

   Chinese. A foreigner may, in special cases, be invited to act as adviser to the
   administration.

c. The curriculum, inspection, etc., shall be the same as in other private schools,
   with the Nationalist Party requiring closer control of the institution by the educational authorities.

d. Religious propaganda shall not be introduced into teaching of other subjects
   but there will be no interference with the freedom to teach religion and hold
   religious services. Religious propaganda in class teaching is forbidden.

e. While freedom to teach religion and to conduct religious exercises is permitted,
   . . . students cannot be required to attend classes in religion or required to participate in religious exercise.

f. All private schools not yet registered must apply for registration within a prescribed period. (Chung, 1934, pp. 175–176)

As the final word on who controlled education in Nationalist China, the
government let it be known that any school not managed "properly" was
subject to closure by the government.

   The move to place foreign educational institutions under Chinese authority moved forward at the Second National Education Conference of 1930.
This conference, attended by 106 delegates from 21 provinces, argued for
the immediate registration of all private institutions of higher learning with
the Nationalist government. By 1934, writes Chung, practically all of the
Christian schools were under Chinese presidents and principals, and all religious formalities had been abolished. While some of the new regulations
proved of little concern to most foreign schools, the ban on religious teaching was a difficult policy to accept. After the Nationalist government implemented its new policies, many churches petitioned the Ministry of Education to repeal the restrictions on religious education and worship in
Christian schools. Their petition was refused.

   By the late 1930s, the foreign-operated colleges had been integrated into
the mainstream of the Chinese education system under the direction of the
Nationalists. Now working more closely with the government, their acceptance among the populace increased. By 1937, one-seventh of all students in
Chinese institutions of higher learning were enrolled in Christian schools.
Some of these schools, such as Yanjing University in Beijing, gained influence within government circles. One of the few Chinese professors at Yanjing left his post in 1933 to assume that of Vice-Minister of Education. In
1937, the Nationalist government's Minister of Finance became the university's chancellor.

   Because the late 1930s saw China gain control of its own system, a new
problem arose that had not been expected. China now needed more foreigners to teach than it was able to find. They were needed especially to teach
the sciences and English. At this time, however, China decided that it no
longer needed just any foreigner who could speak English to teach, like the

missionaries of years past. Now it wanted trained educators, especially those with doctorates. As will be shown later through interviews with modern educators in China, the problems and attempts at solutions facing China today prove strikingly similar to those of the late 1930s.

The years from 1922 to the late 1930s show a marked strengthening in the self-confidence educators in China took toward leading their own education system. Foreigners in institutions of higher learning found themselves in the uncomfortable position of reporting to Chinese administrators and giving way to Chinese who slowly took over positions on the faculty. In 1923, the ratio of Chinese to foreign faculty in China was one to one. By 1932, the ratio was two to one; four years later, it stood at four to one. By the end of the Nationalist era in the late 1940s, the ratio was nine Chinese to every one Western faculty member. A modern Chinese educational historian, Gu (1984) criticizes the Nationalists for establishing so few institutions of higher learning and for allowing the West to dominate the system so thoroughly. He says that in 1949 China had only 204 colleges and universities and, that over a period of 80 years, China graduated only 185,000 students. While his figures may be correct, the blame does not lie completely with the Nationalist party. Answering the call of many in China at the time, it took steps to reduce the role of the foreigner in Chinese schools and met the needs of the Chinese better than at any time prior to its domination of the political scene.

NEW CHINA

In 1949 the Communist party overthrew the government of the Nationalist party and set out to create a new type of socialist society. Education was a paramount concern. In an interview shortly after the new government came to power, Tsao Wei-feng (Cao Weifeng), Deputy Director of the Higher Education Department of East China, commented on the historical importance of diminishing the Western influence found in the new China's universities. He said:

Almost without exception the schools used foreign language textbooks. . . . Their materials referred to foreign countries. For example, in civil engineering they studied the large projects in America and England. America's Tennessee Valley Authority was always cited as the example in classes studying waterworks. In political science, economics, the social sciences, in education it was the same. Scarcely ever was an example from China used. One result of this was that students were often better informed on conditions and developments in America or European countries than they were on conditions in China. (quoted in Campbell, 1951, p. 8)

Tsao (Campbell, 1951) and Orleans (1960) state that of the more than two-hundred institutions of higher learning found in China at this time, one-third were private or missionary schools. The level of instruction was uneven, and the political outlook fostered in these schools of course concerned the party. The role of foreigners in these schools was also a matter of some concern to the new government, and they set out to change it as quickly and completely as possible. Tsao said, when speaking of the situation in and around Shanghai in the early 1950s:

East China is much better supplied with institutions of higher education than any other comparable section of the country. This situation holds true for the private missionary schools. Of the total of 14 such institutions throughout the country, 11 are in East China. Education in East China has also been more heavily influenced by foreign imperialism.

In the near future all the private schools and universities, including missionary ones, will be registered and will form new boards of directors. According to the decisions of the National Higher Education Conference, all properties which were originally held by the missions and all administrative jobs that were originally held by personnel other than Chinese will be taken over by Chinese. (quoted in Campbell, 1951, p. 10)

The U.S.-China Education Clearinghouse (1980) reports that even though all decisions governing education now rested solely with the Chinese, for the first time since the turn of the century, the problems of improving and restructuring the country's education system proved enormous. The Chinese realized quickly that China again needed foreign expertise to advance their ideas for a new China. This time, however, foreign assistance would not come from the west. Tsao acknowledged that the development of new schools, utilizing new teaching methods, textbooks, and administrative organizations, rested largely on the experiences learned from the Soviet Union (Campbell, 1951).

In 1950, five Soviet experts arrived in China to work in the Ministry of Education. Spence relates that between 1950 and 1960, 11,000 Russian advisors lived in China. Of these, the Chinese reported that 861 assisted in restructuring the higher education system (Price, 1987). Soviet reports say the figure stands at 1269 advisors and teachers (Orleans, 1987). In the first few years of this involvement, educators translated 1,400 textbooks from Russian into Chinese. These replaced out-of-date Chinese texts and filled expanding university libraries around the country with hundreds of thousands of new volumes. Orleans (1987) reports that after 1950, the Soviets increased their influence at both the national and provincial ministries of education. Chinese educators have told me of Soviets sharing equal power with their Chinese university presidents during this period.

By 1956, the relationship between the Soviet Union and China in the areas of education and cultural affairs was formalized in the "Agreement Between the Union of Soviet Socialist Republics and the People's Republic of China Concerning Cultural Cooperation." Signed in Moscow, this document, in part, states:

Article 1. The Contracting Parties shall strengthen and develop cooperation between the two countries in the spheres of science, technology, education, literature, art, public health, physical culture, journalism, publishing, broadcasting and television, and in other cultural spheres.

Article 2. The Contracting Parties have decided: (1.) To strengthen direct relations between the scientific research institutions of the two countries, to exchange the results of scientific research, and to provide for exchanges of visits of scientists and their participating in scientific conferences and joint scientific research work; (2.) To promote and to develop direct relations between higher educational institutions and the exchange of pedagogical experience, teaching materials, and publications; (3.) To dispatch professors, writers, and artists, literary and art organizations, and workers in the fields of education, public health, journalism, publishing, broadcasting, television, and the cinema to visit and inspect each other's country, to participate in conferences, to give academic lectures, and to conduct art performances; (4.) To exchange students, graduate students, and teachers who wish to improve their qualifications.

The Soviets, Spence reports, assisted in reorganizing academic departments, developing research institutes, and creating specialized studies in nuclear physics, chemistry, engineering, and biology. Following the suggestions of their Soviet advisors, the Chinese established specialized colleges and universities emphasizing science and technology (U.S.-China Education Clearinghouse, 1980). Gu states that the shift to science and technology relegated the study of the humanities, which Western education had emphasized, to obscurity.

Special attention to practical nation-building goals and Communist party politics dominated in higher education circles during the 1950s. Results favorable to society, not the individual, dictated educational policy (U.S.-China Education Clearinghouse, 1980). J. Scovel (1983) and Orleans (1987) state that this Russian-Marxist education model fit well in a Chinese setting. Teachers shifted to texts developed by the state, never departing from their content. Whereas Western instructors had encouraged spontaneity and creative expression in the classroom, Chinese teachers, like their Soviet advisors, now followed their own cultural and political realities. Classroom materials included those with safe political messages and short, concise lessons that were easy to memorize. If a teacher memorized a lesson and taught his or her students to do the same, no one risked criticism for voicing unorthodox views on a subject. Everything taught and learned depended on what the authorities published. In some ways, this fit the ancient Chinese custom of memorizing the approved classics. Most Chinese responded favorably to this style of teaching.

One outcome of the new relationship with the Soviet Union was a de-emphasis of English and an elevation of Russian as the most important second language in China (Wang, 1981). Crook and Crook (1979) and J. Scovel (1983) report that new students shied away from English during the 1950s because of its association with imperialism and the American-supported regime defeated by the Communists. The English teaching that remained depended on texts drawn from Communist newspapers from English-speaking countries and from English translations of Russian books. Crook and Crook stress that this hardly suited the Chinese situation, for the literature, especially the Russian texts, rested so heavily on foreign cultural bias that students grasped the examples and tone of the lessons with only limited success. Wang's admonition to appreciate cross-cultural problems while teaching in a Chinese classroom seems to apply to socialist brothers as well as capitalist intruders.

The role of the Soviet advisors, not surprisingly, eventually ran the course of other foreign educators. Fundamental problems between Chinese and Soviet advisors arose after only a few years. Spence and Orleans (1987) assert that the Chinese expected the Soviets to help modernize China at an unrealistic pace. One Soviet advisor claimed that the Chinese wanted "every Soviet specialist to be a sort of magician, capable of giving them the one correct answer to all sorts of complex problems . . . in a few minutes" (Klochko, 1971, p. 477). At the same time, the Chinese distrusted the Soviets' motives. Though both Marxists, the Chinese feared that the Soviets wanted the Chinese to follow their lead, not help them lead themselves. During the Great Leap Forward in 1956, Chinese leaders began to limit Soviet influence in education. While official pronouncements of harmony and appreciation continued, Soviet suggestions were ignored and tensions increased (Orleans, 1987). By 1957 Chinese political leaders publicly voiced concern that China relied too heavily on foreign countries. In a speech delivered in 1958, Mao Zedong stated that China's adoption of the Soviet education model had proved disappointing and that China should look more closely at the models developed in the liberated areas of China before 1949 (Price, 1987). In 1960, the Soviet Union's advisors, including all those placed in colleges and universities, abruptly left their posts and returned home (Spence, 1980).

For the first time since the late nineteenth century, China found itself alone to run its educational system. The foreign imperialists were forcibly removed in 1949 and the foreign friends were bidden good riddance in 1960. In what direction would China's colleges and universities now move? What role, if any, would foreigners play in this new era?

Between 1960 and 1966, China struggled with the issue of which direction education should take. Zachariah (1979) writes that during this period China's colleges and universities held to the course that the Soviets helped establish, at least in the style of administration. Gu agrees with this analysis, stating that by 1966, China's post-1949 educational policy was in place and stabilized. Louie points out, however, that by the early 1960s, Confucian ideas on education were again being mentioned directly and in a positive light. This was due in large measure to the failure of the Soviet-Chinese political relationship, a relationship that had reinforced antiforeign sentiment and a deep cultural bias to look inward for the improvement of the country. People yearned for more traditional, China-centered, ways in all aspects of life, including education. President Liu Shaoqi and Foreign Minister Chen Yi even referred to Confucius as a positive example for the nation's youth. Not all of the Chinese leadership agreed with this return to traditional examples of good education, however. Most notable in his criticism was Chairman Mao, who looked to Yenan as the model. Confucius was far from his ideal.

THE GREAT PROLETARIAN CULTURAL REVOLUTION

During the years between 1955 and 1966, Chairman Mao proved unrelenting in his criticism of Confucian thought and, more importantly, the actions growing out of traditional Confucian habits. At the same time, he continued his criticism of Soviet education and renewed his call to learn from the education of the liberated areas. One of the most important conflicts raised by Mao in the mid-1960s concerned the issue of manual versus mental labor. Traditional Confucian ideas separated the two clearly. Soviet-style education did little to break Chinese away from this mentality. Mao wanted to build a society that combined the mental and the physical, as he remembered from the days in Yenan's guerrilla base. In large measure because of this philosophical conflict, the year 1966 saw Mao call on the young people of China to make their own revolution against the old ways still prevalent in China and to sweep out those who held to these ways. What followed this call were ten years of turmoil that came to be called the Great Proletarian Cultural Revolution (Louie, 1984).

The young people answering Chairman Mao's call, many of whom joined groups making up the newly formed Red Guard, criticized all ideas of the past and were bent on breaking China away from its old culture, ideology, and customs. One of the most forceful ways to attack someone during this period was to tie him or her to Confucian thinking. Education, insisted the Red Guard, should be based on egalitarian, not traditionally elitist, principles. Confucius was attacked as authoritarian and antilabor, the antithesis of modern, revolutionary principles (Louie, 1984).

In August 1966, the Central Committee of the Chinese Communist Party in effect closed all schools and, following Mao's lead, encouraged the country's young people to make revolution and attack the "four olds": old ideas, old customs, old habits, and old culture. Leading the pack of those accused of upholding the so-called four olds were the educators. Educators came under fire for allowing students to graduate who possessed only theoretical knowledge but no practical skills. They were, it was reasoned, training students to be elitists over peasants and workers (Montaperto, 1979). Not surprisingly, they were also the group most closely identified with foreign influences and known to have developed foreign relationships.

The primary and middle schools reopened in 1967. Universities, however, stayed closed until 1970. When their doors opened again, students found a very different educational environment. The number of years needed to graduate from senior middle school dropped from twelve to ten—five years of primary, three of lower middle school, and two of senior middle school. The curriculum took on a decidedly political tone, with great emphasis placed on Marxist classics, especially the works of Mao. School and society melted together through the concept of open-door education, an experiment that saw students substituting several hours a week in a factory or agricultural setting for time previously spent in the classroom. It was here that the problem of elitism was attacked, as theory and practice came together.

Administratively schools took on a radical new look, as "revolutionary committees" formed to run them at all levels. The plan was to create a "three-in-one combination" of workers and peasants, revolutionary cadres, and teachers and students. Admissions policies changed as the children of workers and peasants gained entrance to universities over the previously admitted children of intellectuals and old capitalists. Yet before even these students entered university, they had to spend several years in the countryside or in a factory "tempering" themselves and learning from the workers and the peasants before they could be selected. For the first time, the universities had little to say about who would be admitted, as the workers and peasants with whom the young people toiled now decided who would represent them in institutions of higher learning. Formal examinations, both as a requirement to enter universities and as class requirements, disappeared from China's education system for the ten years of the Cultural Revolution (Montaperto, 1979).

Summing up the Red Guard's position on these new policies, the Peking University Educational Revolution Group (1972) stated:

Through practice of the recent work of student enrollment, we deeply realize that reform of the system of student recruitment is an important link in the proletarian revolution. Whom should the university serve, and for what class should it train successors? This is the focal point of the struggle between the two classes, the two roads, and the two lines on the educational front, and it takes form first of all in the question of school enrollment. After the Great Proletarian Cultural Revolution, the university has opened its doors to workers, peasants, and soldiers. It is a great victory for Chairman Mao's revolutionary line. (p. 6)

Concerning the use of examinations, the same Peking University Educational Revolution Group argued that only people holding old ideas favored examinations for the selection of students. This method worked only to bar children of workers and peasants from universities. On the other hand, the new system "resulted in the selection of outstanding elements for enrollment in the university to the satisfaction of the workers, peasants, and soldiers" (pp. 7–8).

During this period, China not only tried to rid itself of traditional Chinese values, but it also worked feverishly to rid itself of all foreign influence and to concentrate on learning from within. The negative experiences with both the capitalist West and Soviet Russia, together with China's historic distrust of foreigners, drove China to this new phase of isolationism (Hayhoe, 1984).

The Cultural Revolution proved a difficult period for the few expatriate foreigners living and teaching in China and for Chinese educated in the West. Butt (1979) tells of several foreigners spending years in a Chinese prison only because of their foreign backgrounds. He also tells of Chinese intellectuals persecuted because of pre-1949 ties with the West.

During the Cultural Revolution, criticism of anything foreign measured redness, or revolutionary fervor, in the eyes of many. As Wang, Gu, and Spence point out, from the first years of foreign involvement in China's educational system, concern to preserve China's culture and national essence against outside penetration and influence prevailed. The Cultural Revolution proved that whether the concern rested on traditional values or revolutionary principles, the Chinese have remained capable of fierce attacks on foreign residents and foreign ideas (U.S.-China Education Clearinghouse, 1980).

THE POST-MAO ERA

In 1976, after the death of Chairman Mao and the arrest of the radical Gang of Four, the Cultural Revolution ended, ushering in a more moderate political climate. The changes affected colleges and universities almost immediately. Cleverley (1977) reports that throughout the country, radical leaders in higher education left their posts, and more moderate administrators and teachers regained their lost positions. The change for most Chinese educators proved dramatic. For a while, foreigners and foreign ideas remained suspect, however, and anti-Western propaganda continued to dominate English texts. When foreign teachers prepared new and original materials for their classrooms, they found most of it censored before it reached the students. A few Chinese educators proposed that ties to the West re-open, but 1976 and 1977 saw few developments in this area (Cleverley, 1977). Rebuilding the country demanded immediate attention, and consideration paid to foreigners came after solving more pressing problems.

Not until 1981, Kormondy (1982) reports, did the Higher Educational Research Institute open in Beijing to carry out research on higher education in China and abroad. By the early 1980s, foreign journals and newspapers were reappearing in China's university reading rooms and libraries. In

1981, English reclaimed its position as the most important foreign language in China (Zachariah, 1979).

Hayhoe reports that following the reconstruction of its higher education system, the Chinese moved quickly to establish ties with the West in educational matters. Today cooperation and exchange in the field of education are at their greatest since 1949. Cooperation and change, however, do not override a continuing fear of the "cultural contamination" brought by outside relationships.

In 1979, Jiang Nanxiang, then Minister of Education, stated that institutions of higher learning should follow the road of socialism and not transplant everything from colleges and universities in the West. He argued:

It goes without saying that we should earnestly study the experience of foreign countries . . . but to blindly follow the way schools in capitalist countries are run or, as some people have suggested, to let foreigners come and run the schools in our country is obviously not practical and not compatible with China's specific conditions.

Schools are different from factories. . . . In the case of a factory, the equipment and technology, which are classless in nature, can be imported. But schools are part of the superstructure and they should train students, who have a class character, to work wholeheartedly for the cause of socialism. (quoted in Beijing Review, 1979, pp. 8–9)

In 1982, Deng Xiaoping, the paramount leader in China, stated his policy governing the opening to the West with these words:

We will unswervingly follow a policy of opening to the outside world and actively increase exchanges with foreign countries on the basis of mutual equality and benefit. At the same time we will keep a clear head, firmly resist corrosion by decadent ideas from abroad, and never permit the bourgeois way of life to spread in our country. (quoted in Hayhoe, 1984, p. 41)

This statement, reminiscent of the 1904 proclamation of the Qing Dynasty ministry of education, makes clear the attitude that Westerners face as they enter China today. Deng's remarks warn foreigners that academic exchange holds some interest for the Chinese. Life-style exchange, however, remains unwelcome. If anyone ever doubted Deng's determination to stick to this policy, the suppression of the student strikes in June of 1989 should speak clearly to those doubts.

In 1981, about 180 American teachers and 50 research scholars lived and taught at Chinese universities. Today there are hundreds more. All of these new foreigners naturally reflect American life-styles and political views. This unwelcome but unavoidable side effect of inviting foreign educators to China worries many of China's leaders. Heeding Deng's warning, many Chinese still shy away from personal contact with foreign teachers, except to learn specific bits of knowledge useful in their work or study. Hayhoe writes that they fear accusations challenging their patriotism and political views. For foreigners living in China, the problems raised by such attitudes present unexpected dilemmas and make circulating among and understanding the Chinese a complex, bewildering web through which to maneuver. This certainly holds true for teachers of English, who constitute the majority of foreigners now in China's colleges and universities. Trained primarily to teach English, many of them have little knowledge of Chinese culture or history and enter China ill-prepared for what awaits them.

Murray (1982) recounts that when he first entered China to teach English in 1981, walls dominated his initial impressions. The Great Wall stretches across North China; walls circle cities and colleges. Such walls offer no threat. Walls, however, also enclose the living quarters of foreign teachers. These walls, Murray argues, confront the foreigner in China and imply distrust. The wall surrounding the foreign compound at Murray's college is locked at night, keeping Chinese out and foreigners in. Foreigners have no keys to the gate. Murray has the impression that while the Chinese approve of the transfer of specific knowledge, the life-style of the foreigner remains off-limits. The Chinese believe, Murray states, that polite behavior is acceptable, but not to the point of exposure to the disease of decadent Western behavior.

Relationships based on such attitudes maintain a psychological wall between Chinese and foreigners that requires more adjustments for the foreigner than the physical walls. Murray shares the experience of welcoming eager students to his office for long discussions, only to find the students disappear for several weeks because college leaders criticized them for spending too much time with the foreigner. Students, Murray discovered, even report on the activities of their foreign teachers to the college authorities. Westerners rarely, if ever, learn to accept such behavior. Summing up his response to this, Murray exclaims, "What the practice of putting up walls did to the foreigners themselves, I can be more definite about. It drove us nuts" (p. 56). Some foreign teachers grow so paranoid and restricted in their relationships that they retreat into their isolated, individual worlds until they leave the country (Murray, 1982).

In addition to the walls in social relationships, Murray discovered, as have many others before him, that the Chinese style of learning creates additional walls between Chinese and foreigners. The Chinese teacher has historically played the role of the sage, pouring out wisdom to his students. As noted by Wang and J. Scovel (1983), students resist attempts to make them voice an opinion in the classroom. Murray suggests that this reluctance is caused by fear of embarrassing the teacher (by not knowing the answer) and by fear of ridicule from fellow students. These fears find a basis in traditional Confucian mores. The instructor should never lose face before his or her students by finding a student ill-prepared for class. A student always avoids the loss of face before classmates. Ridicule that follows the loss of face can influence a student's career if the ridicule turns to official criticism by the college authorities, who assign students their jobs upon graduation.

Like Wang, Spence, and Hayhoe, Murray recognizes that such physical and psychological walls existed in China long before the 1980s, and he sympathizes with the Chinese who must tolerate foreigners unfamiliar with China's culture and language. He cannot help voicing frustration, however, when his students respond with silence and disinterest as he teaches them Robert Frost's "Mending Wall," which emphasizes the importance of breaking down walls between people.

Observations by other foreign teachers of English on their role in Chinese universities in the early 1980s support Murray's contention that foreigners now entering China must face ambiguity, pain, and frustration in their academic and social relationships. Maley (1983), for example, points out that in the classroom, Chinese teachers of English and their Western counterparts face several problems concerning language usage. They have different meanings for the same important words. When referring to the word "book," Chinese speak in tones of reverence. For them, a book possesses absolute authority. A Western educator usually refers to a book to stimulate discussion, debate, or to seek interpretations of a point of interest. The word "test" is another example. A test in China usually decides a student's future. Tests judge absolutely and are not open to further interpretation. Foreigners usually employ a test to gauge a student's progress; to most foreigners, nothing absolute rides on a test grade.

In terms of a foreigner's social life, Maley voices the same frustrations as Murray. Foreign teachers are treated as machines to impart knowledge. Foreigners want to make Chinese friends, but they live in isolated quarters cut off from the Chinese physically and psychologically. This problem dampens the enthusiasm of most foreign teachers and creates bitterness in some. Maley notes one encouraging sign among those foreigners who stay a second year to teach. The second year proves easier for the foreigner and the Chinese. Perhaps, Maley suggests, the foreigner needs at least one year to prove himself or herself to the Chinese.

T. Scovel (1983) perceives the problem of expectations as irreconcilable. The Chinese assume that Americans arrive in China wealthy and fully knowledgeable about modern technology. Echoing Klochko's comments concerning Soviet frustration in the 1950s, T. Scovel says that the Chinese expect Westerners to furnish new state-of-the-art machinery in their universities and to upgrade programs and institutions in unrealistic and probably impossible time frames.

T. Scovel also points out that Westerners hold misconceptions about their Chinese hosts. Most foreign teachers find China's culture intriguing, but some expect to change their little part of it by introducing new teaching methods developed in the West. These methods usually emphasize individual-centered learning. China discourages individualism and encourages action by the collective. Again, Wang's comment on the importance of adjusting methodology to China's culture supports T. Scovel's observation.

T. Scovel, like Maley, views the relationship between Chinese and foreigners with guarded optimism, however. Because so many of the foremost English teachers in China received their early education at the hands of foreigners in the 1920s, 1930s, and 1940s, a common academic language exists that allows room for greater understanding and compromise in classroom techniques. If young teachers on both sides can learn from the experiences of their elders, there is hope of resolving academic contradictions. It is the deep-seated cultural problems that present the greatest obstacles to overcome.

The Chinese view cross-cultural misunderstanding in the classroom differently, as described by Wu (1983). Because of social, political, and cultural differences, foreigners find life in China difficult. Wu argues that foreigners are at least partly responsible for their own problems. She suggests that foreigners should enter China with a more realistic assessment of their new responsibilities. China's teachers use old teaching methods and know little of new methodologies because they have not mixed with foreign educators for decades. Both parties must realize that changes come slowly. Foreign teachers should show patience toward their Chinese colleagues and strive to bridge the gap between their new methodologies and Chinese reality (Wu, 1983).

Ultimately, Wu argues, the foreigner's strength in a Chinese English-language classroom lies in the command of his or her native language and knowledge of modern linguistics and teaching methods. Foreigners, however, lack sensitivity to Chinese culture, and no amount of linguistic training can overcome extreme cases of this. Wu states:

In the foreign language classroom we sometimes find situations like the following: A foreign teacher starts a conversation class with a topic or a series of questions which in his own culture arouse the interest of the students and start a lively discussion. But because the topic or the questions are inappropriate in the students' culture or area outside their experience, the students fail to respond, or even feel uneasy about the teacher's intention. Topics like sexual promiscuity and what to do with sudden wealth are examples of such topics in the Chinese situation. Teachers who expect the students to participate in such class discussions will be disappointed in the outcome. (p. 113)

Even when a topic holds cultural interest for the students, Wu agrees with Murray's analysis that classroom participation comes slowly for Chinese students. Foreigners must not expect Chinese students to move comfortably from a teacher-dominated class to one actively engaged in classroom discussion.

Wu stresses that the foreign teacher should look upon his or her Chinese colleague as an equal. Many problems promise easy solutions, if the foreign teacher but asks a Chinese colleague for advice. The Chinese teacher knows the particular problems that Chinese students face in learning English and can explain them to foreigners, if they want to hear. Each should learn from the other's strengths to offset their own weaknesses. The foreigner knows his or her language, while the Chinese knows his or her culture. Working together with this attitude can produce more profitable results.

CONCLUSION

The concerns expressed by Wu and others in this study reflect upon a surprisingly short period in Chinese history. China practiced education for twenty-nine centuries before the West made any inroads there. Once a door opened to educators from the West, however, they made their presence felt in important and controversial ways. When Western educators entered China in the mid-nineteenth century, they brought with them a sense of intellectual and moral superiority that prevailed until 1949. The foreigners failed to understand one important element in Chinese thinking, however. They failed to see that the Chinese looked upon them as the inferior ones. In Chinese eyes, foreigners entered as uncivilized intruders. The experiences of Martin at Tong Wen Guan and Hume in his later days at Yale-in-China characterize the problem well. The difference was that Martin altered his view little, while Hume finally realized that Yale had forced itself on China. The Chinese perceived Yale not as a savior, but as a trespasser.

A study of foreign involvement in China's colleges and universities indicates that research on social relationships between Chinese and foreigners dominates the literature. A piece of literature that begins by pointing out the problems of teaching in a Chinese classroom usually ends by discussing the problems foreigners face in relating to and being accepted as colleagues and friends. On the one hand, foreigners historically have found appreciation for the knowledge they bring to China, but at the same time have expressed frustration and outrage at the social isolation imposed upon them by their students and colleagues. The deep-seated distrust of foreign motives and the fear of contamination by foreign culture kept Westerners isolated in China at the turn of the century and continues to isolate them into the modern era. Whether feudal mores or socialist principles impose the isolation, the result remains the same.

The following chapters continue to explore this cross-cultural relationship between foreigners and Chinese in their interaction in China's colleges and universities. The preceding discussion approached this relationship from its beginning through the early post-Mao years. What follows relates to contemporary perceptions of foreigners and Chinese as discovered through interviews in China and the United States from 1987 through 1989.

The Role of the Foreigner in China's Colleges and Universities: Chinese Perceptions

TEACH YOUR DISCIPLINE AND EXPLAIN YOUR CULTURE

Following the completion of the Cultural Revolution in 1976, only China's most prestigious colleges and universities cautiously opened their doors and invited small numbers of foreigners to teach on their campuses. By 1979, however, schools throughout the country were inviting foreigners into their classrooms. In those early years, from 1976 to about 1981, most foreigners arrived to teach basic English courses. This proved the case whether the school served as a teacher-training institution, a multipurpose university, or a special technical school. Hong says that in the late 1970s, when foreigners began to arrive in China, the level of language learning among students and teachers was low at all schools, even in her highly regarded Foreign Studies University in Beijing. Middle school students entered university ill-prepared for language study, and Chinese teachers proved unable to teach the most basic courses adequately. Even today, says Ma of the State Education Commission, English teachers make up almost half of all the foreign educators in China.

In terms of teaching language, Chinese students and teachers agree that the primary role of the foreigner in China's classroom is to explain in detail the uses of the language and to impart information about the culture in which the language operates. Xie outlines seven areas where the foreign teacher of language might best play a role: (a) expose Chinese to "true" native language; (b) teach foreign culture; (c) teach the use of idioms; (d) explain contextual meanings of words; (e) teach "vivid" use of the language, as opposed to Chinese teachers' dependence on direct Chinese translation of words; (f) teach natural pronunciation and accent; and (g) present lectures to improve listening skills and explain the culture of foreign countries. Some or all of these were listed by the other Chinese interviewed who deal with language training. Some of the Chinese, including Hu, Wu, Tao, Yuan, and others, emphasize the importance of teaching writing skills as well, especially for those going abroad to study.

In recent years, some major universities and language institutes have had foreigners teaching courses besides those in basic English. Today these schools desire what Hong calls more content-oriented classes, rather than skill-oriented classes. By the mid-1980s, she says, new students arrived on the more prestigious campuses better prepared in language. By this time, the Chinese teachers, through training by foreign teachers, had advanced to the point that they could teach the basic skills, such as listening comprehension, conversational speech, and writing.

As pointed out by Shang at Beijing's Foreign Studies University the foreigners' expertise at the more advanced and prestigious institutions is now used in areas such as linguistics, American culture, sociology, and Western civilization. At this point, says Shang, the Chinese are unable to teach such courses, so they must call on foreigners for assistance. At the Foreign Affairs Institute in Beijing, a specialized school that trains diplomats, foreigners also teach courses in political science and international economics. (Dong, chair of the foreign languages department, points out, however, that because of a shortage of qualified Chinese teachers of English even there, foreigners are reluctantly asked to teach some basic English courses.) At Beijing University's department of Oriental languages, only new language offerings, such as Filipino, Indonesian, and Hebrew, have foreigners teaching basic skills. As the years go by, says Liang, chairman of the Oriental languages department, the goal remains to have foreigners offer more in-depth language, linguistics, and literature instruction, while the Chinese teachers become better qualified to take over the basic teaching of these courses.

At prestigious schools like Beijing University, the Beijing Foreign Studies University, Beijing Normal University, and the Foreign Affairs Institute, the Chinese now invite teachers with greater academic diversity and higher levels of professional preparation than comparable teachers invited only a few years ago. Authorities at all of these schools point out that competition among foreign educators for these positions is fierce, as the college leaders scrutinize résumés and references much more closely than before. Most foreigners in these institutions possess doctorates. The challenges they bring to the older students and teachers appear sufficient to hold their interest and broaden their knowledge. The trend, at least at these major universities, shows that the foreigners' role will include less teaching of English as a Second Language (ESL) and more content courses. This recalls the 1930s, when the Nationalists invited foreigners with doctorates and lessened their dependence on unqualified foreigners whose only skill was an ability to speak English.

While the more prestigious and wealthy schools change how they use their foreign teachers, other less attractive, less wealthy schools content themselves with inviting foreigners much as they have since the late 1970s. At Henan Teachers' University in Xinxiang, Henan Province, the only difference between 1979 and 1987 involves whom the foreigners teach, not what they teach. Today in Henan the foreigners teach only students. This contrasts with my experience in this school between the years 1979 through 1981, when I spent most of my time teaching Chinese teachers. Cai, a young teacher there, says the change developed because the foreigners attracted to such provincial schools rarely hold advanced degrees and are capable of teaching only basic language skills. She says that these courses proved helpful to teachers in the early years of foreign involvement, when she and her colleagues were starved for any knowledge from outside China. Now she finds these courses uninteresting, however, and looks enviously on those schools inviting foreigners to teach other, more specialized courses. Based on discussions with other Chinese and on my own observations as an instructor, researcher, and visitor there, I concur with Cai's perspective. The foreign teachers in Henan today either are trained in ESL or, some Chinese say, are not trained at all. "They can't teach us," Cai says, "in the areas of sociology, economics, political science, the hard sciences, and so on. Frankly, there is little more the teachers or seniors can learn from them. That is why we do not attend their lectures or ask for special classes with them."

Pointing to the differences between the prestigious schools in the major urban centers and those found in the provinces, Mao, an administrator in the foreign languages department in Henan, tells the story of inviting a Ph.D. from a major university in the United States to teach linguistics. The foreigner, a dean of academic affairs on a one-year sabbatical, accepted the school's offer, and the students and faculty at Xinxiang awaited his arrival anxiously. Finally, they thought, the teachers will learn new content and receive a high level of instruction from which to learn new materials and teaching methods. Shortly before the arrival date, Mao received a letter informing him that the professor had accepted another position at a large university in Shanghai. "I don't blame him," laments Mao, "because the living conditions in Shanghai are much better than here." The disappointment, however, shows when he explains that the college was forced to accept an alternate application from an ESL instructor who could offer him and his colleagues nothing new, but would continue to teach basic skills to the lower level students. In addition to offering knowledge in their area of expertise, most Chinese interviewed say that an important role for the foreign teacher is introducing new teaching methods into the classroom. Eagerness to learn in the abstract does not always translate into appreciation or willingness to imitate, however. In line with the arguments of Wang (1981) and Wu (1983), Mao in Henan points out the difficulty of presenting new teaching methods. He says, "We want new teaching methods, but we still ask the foreigner to teach in a style the students and teachers are comfortable with. It is a problem." Hong, a middle-aged teacher from Beijing's Foreign Studies University, points to the complexity of this. She says:

Sometimes the Chinese students, especially a few years ago, said that they expected their foreign teachers to come in and talk the whole fifty minutes. The American way of teaching to get the students, you know, involved in the class, to have a lot of give and take. The students are not used to that and half of the time they ask, "What is this?" They think they are not learning because they are talking. I think this is because the traditional way of education between these two is different. . . . [However,] I think it's good that the foreign teachers are coming in and bringing their new methods, to try to get the students more involved—to discuss things.

Yi, a middle-aged teacher from Henan, says she was initially eager to learn Western teaching methods. After exposure to foreign teachers, however, she grew disillusioned and decided that the foreigners with whom she is familiar simply do not know how to teach well. A majority of Chinese involved in this study agree with her, at least with regard to the initial years of learning under foreigners. For example, Zeng, dean of the English department at another foreign language institute in Beijing, says that from 1979 to 1982, they employed foreigners whose only skill was the ability to speak native English. The problem, she says, was that most could not teach well. Zeng continues, "Now we depend on other foreign teachers we respect and our own Chinese teachers who have been abroad to recommend good teachers." Ye, one of the vice-presidents at Beijing Normal University, agrees. He states that in the early years of 1979, 1980, and 1981, they invited as foreign teachers almost anyone who could speak native English. Now, he says, "We have paid the tuition and have learned better how to invite foreigners. It took several years and cost us a lot of money, but we have learned over the years."

Although most Chinese concur that the first few years in the post-Mao period brought many unqualified foreign teachers to China, there also is the growing opinion among some, including Yi, Dong, Mao, and Hong, that part of the problem lay with the fact that the foreign teaching methods which they and their colleagues initially desired to learn proved unattractive when actually implemented. As much as she wants to experiment with new teaching methods, Yi simply cannot appreciate them. This is true even of the methods of those foreign teachers whom she considers well qualified. She says that the new methods may be fine for the foreigner, but not for her.

Dong, professor at the Foreign Affairs Institute, says that most of her students await their first foreign teacher eagerly. After a period of sitting in their classes, however, they tell their leaders that they learn little and want only Chinese teachers. She attributes this problem to a teaching style that the students find uncomfortable and to a perception that many of the foreign teachers just "muddle along" without planning their lessons well or taking their teaching seriously. Ling, a colleague of Dong's, voices the generally held opinion that "Foreign teachers can teach as they wish. Policy is not to interfere with teaching method. However, we will meet with foreign teachers if it seems they are not serious." The problem, as pointed out by the comments of Hong, Yi, Zen, Mao, and Dong, lies with deciding what is different and what is simply poor or uncommitted teaching.

Disenchantment with foreign teachers and teaching methods is not unanimous, however. Pei, a young college teacher in Henan, voices one of the few unqualified positive attitudes toward foreign teaching methods when she says:

Foreigners bring a new world outlook to the Chinese students. They help the students think in different ways. When the foreigner brings new teaching methods, they encourage the students to think and analyze, not just memorize what the teacher says to memorize. The foreigners help us to see the text in a broader, more human way.

A graduate student, studying under American professors at the new Nanjing University-Johns Hopkins University Center for Chinese and American Studies in Nanjing, attempts to strike a balance when she remarks:

First, American professors do not give you teaching materials, nor do they give you outlines of their classes in the Chinese way. All the assigned reading materials are considered reserve books. These are the books you can get in the library and read there. Each time you have three hours in which to read. If no one else wants it, you can then borrow it for another three hours. This facilitates book circulation. Each week's reading assignment is rather large. This puts much pressure on those Chinese students not used to American professors' reading assignments. Each day, outside of mealtimes and sleep, most time is spent reading in the library. Some courses begin at one o'clock in the afternoon, as American professors do not have the habit of a noon nap. So, while nodding off you do not clearly hear what the professor is saying. Even strong tea cannot restore your spirits. Topics brought up in the professor's reading assignment can be discussed in the next class or may be the subject of a written quiz. The good point of this method is that with questions in mind while reading, it strengthens the student's analytical ability and the professor can concentrate in the classroom on key or especially difficult matters. At the same time the student is encouraged to raise questions, to begin discussion. This makes for a lively atmosphere. In any case, this methodology can contribute to our educational reform. But at the same time, in my opinion, this methodology also has shortcomings. The professor rarely writes on the blackboard, the student does not get teaching materials to keep, and it is difficult to take well organized notes on the basis of understanding and comprehension. While the grade is given at the end of the semester, outside of this grade all that the student receives is in the mind. Even if your memory is strong, there are limits, so that later when you want to review, you do not have books to use. This is very inconvenient! I believe in this matter both Chinese and American teaching methodology have strong and weak points. As time goes by and exchanges increase, there will be possibilities for both sides mutually to improve. (Qin, 1986 pp. 3–4)

The conflict between the teacher-centered, Confucian-rooted, rote style of learning and the more student-active, inquisitive style of the foreigners is far from being resolved. Although the Chinese say they want new methods, they usually avoid their use when they gain access to them. Ruan, a noted scholar with the State Education Commission, says that even though there is a "national resistance" to learning new teaching methods, the introduction of a more lively Western style of teaching is a positive contribution by foreigners in China. "Gradually," he says, "some are beginning to appreciate this new style." It will be interesting to watch future developments in this area as more young people like Pei gain positions of responsibility. The conflict between styles may then take place between the generations in China as much as between Chinese and foreigners today.

A unique experiment in teaching meets this problem head on. Hong and Tao, both at prestigious schools in Beijing, mention cross-cultural team teaching. This approach pairs a foreign teacher with a Chinese teacher in the classroom. The foreigner imparts knowledge in his or her field, and the Chinese assists the foreigner in getting the message across when language and/or cultural differences get in the way of understanding. It has taken about ten years, says Beijing University's Director of Foreign Affairs Tao, to settle into this teaching method. Yi points out that in provincial Henan, they are experimenting with this method, though it is a recent innovation and the Chinese still play a small role in the team aspect of the teaching.

In summary, during the years immediately following the end of the Cultural Revolution, colleges and universities, regardless of location and prestige, saw foreigners teaching mostly basic language skills, with some reference to Western literature, culture, and pedagogy. Foreigners were expected to teach little else; indeed, at that time, China needed little else. As pointed out by Ma, "English is the international language of commerce and trade." Establishment of a language base to import new technology and science was the goal in these early years of studying English.

Over the past few years, this role has remained basically the same as in the early years, except that at the more prestigious, largely urban schools, foreigners now teach fewer courses in basic English and more in-depth content courses. Additionally, team teaching, which recognizes the importance of placing a new language or discipline in a Chinese context, also finds a place in some of these major universities. The less prestigious schools, like that found in Henan, still recruit basic skills teachers for their classrooms. The role of the foreigner at these schools remains almost the same as in the late 1970s. In the final analysis, however, regardless of how successful or disappointing the outcome, regardless of the type of institution served, and regardless of what course is taught, Chinese educators say that the role of the foreign teacher in the classroom remains merely to teach his or her discipline, impart knowledge of a foreign culture, and contribute new ideas on teaching methods.

GO TO THEM WHENEVER YOU HAVE A QUESTION

The role of the foreigner outside of the classroom is as important, say Ling, Shi, and others, as the role played in the more formal atmosphere of the classroom. This is stated explicitly by Ling and Shi, and implied in comments by others. In fact, as Wong, Lan, Sui, Su, Cai, Pei, Mao, Jin, and others stress, the role outside the classroom differs little from the role played inside. In both places, the role is to teach. Whether this takes place in the foreigner's home, on a stroll around campus, or in a restaurant sharing a meal, the foreigner's primary responsibility is to continue teaching. This teaching may take the form of simply going over texts used in class. It may, as Xie, Shi, Pei, and Yuan point out, find the foreigner organizing informal educational activities, such as plays and songfests. Pei and Yuan also discuss the recent development of "English clubs" led by foreigners. This involves foreigners holding regularly scheduled yet informal discussions in English with anyone, including young people from other departments and even from outside the university.

Two telling statements about the importance of this informal teaching role come from Ling, an official with the Office of Foreign Affairs at the Institute of Foreign Affairs, and Sui, a young teacher from the Second Foreign Languages Institute. Ling, responding to a question on the activities of the foreign teachers outside the classroom, states, "We keep them busy because we want to exploit them as much as possible. Partly we do this because they are, by Chinese standards, paid highly." Sui, commenting on this from the perspective of one who studied under foreigners rather than supervised them, says:

We were encouraged [by Party leaders] to use them as much as possible. We were told that since they are here and they are paid by our department $800 a month, you should go to them whenever you have every question, even very, very silly questions. Just try to make good use of them. We took them totally as academic figures rather than human beings.

Realizing that this use of foreigners appears cold and overly pragmatic to many foreigners, Zhou points out that these expectations are similar to those about Chinese teachers. Before foreign teachers arrived on his campus, Zhou says that he and his fellow students never thought the foreigners would be treated very differently from Chinese teachers in terms of access. Outside the classroom, the teacher, whether Chinese or foreign, always remains a teacher. Chinese teachers answer questions while walking across campus, buying vegetables at the market outside the college gate, or during the evening in their apartments. The only difference, he says, is that the foreigner, due to his or her special knowledge and high salary, is expected to engage in this even more than the Chinese teacher. I know from my observations and experiences as a teacher in China that Zhou's description of the role of the Chinese teacher outside the classroom is accurate.

This outside-the-classroom, informal teaching role allows the foreigner to share more with China than a narrow knowledge of an academic subject. It is here that discussions about foreign culture find an open forum. Yi, Cai, Geng, Shang, Ling, and others stress the importance of this. As Shang says:

The foreigners' "unofficial role" is to bring in from abroad characteristics, values, and ideas beyond strictly academic subjects. It is good for Americans, for example, to bring openness, sense of equality, discussion of political rights, and the work ethic to our students. This has an impact by undoing stereotypes.

Geng and He, a young teacher and a student in Henan, say that discussions about culture may cover areas as diverse as the nature and character of Western philosophy to the life of students in foreign countries. Geng even stresses that foreigners may actually act as role models outside the classroom through their everyday behavior. For example, she says that Chinese should emulate foreigners in their broad-minded and polite interaction with others, their trait of following through with promises, and their "good custom of not spitting" in public.

This desire to understand and present foreign culture to the rest of China takes unique shape at the major universities that develop foreign language texts and dictionaries. At Beijing University, professors used to compile language texts and dictionaries without foreign assistance and without knowledge of the culture behind the words. Now these are jointly written with foreign experts to bring into full play both the linguistic and cultural aspects of the meaning of words and phrases.

Such eagerness for a knowledge of Western culture was not always stressed so explicitly. Sui and Xie indicate that when foreigners first appeared at their schools in the late 1970s, they were suspected of being spies. As one who taught in China during that era, I hold a particular memory of walking past a classroom building on a Sunday afternoon in 1980, only to have a student from a fourth-floor window direct the words "spy, foreign spy" at me. Mao explains this attitude by describing the mentality of those leaders responsible for inviting foreigners to their campuses during those years. He explains:

Premier Zhou [Zhou Enlai] once said, "There is no small thing concerning foreign affairs; you should ask your superiors everything relating to this." He was, of course, speaking of government issues, but in the late 70s provincial, city, and college leaders took it to mean foreign teachers as well.

With this mentality, Mao says, foreigners confronted skepticism and built-in distrust upon their arrival in China. Every issue dealing with foreigners had to be sent to higher authorities. Chinese were told to stay away from them except to improve their English. I remember discovering in 1979 that the few students who had recently spent time with me in my office inquiring about my culture, found themselves criticized by the college leaders. I also remember being told that I could not leave the college grounds for any purpose without first getting permission of the college authorities. The perception of many Chinese at that time appears to have been that teaching in the classroom was fine, but what transpired outside class had to be watched closely.

By all appearances, this attitude changed dramatically by 1989. Sui and Xie point out that in the late 1970s they were told to view the foreigners as possible spies. By the late 1980s, however, that attitude had all but vanished. In Henan, Xie says, "We don't know where they go. It doesn't matter. People outside the college can visit [the foreigners] and vice versa. This shows how much thinking has changed."

One role the Chinese desire the foreigner to play more often is that of a bridge between China and the West. As noted by Jin, president of a provincial university, this role was not anticipated in the early years of the new era. Now, however, with the growing number of foreign teachers needed in China and with the impressive numbers of Chinese going abroad, the role of bridge takes on vitally important dimensions. Liang at Beijing University, Ye at Beijing Normal University, and Zeng at the Second Foreign Languages Institute explain that they now depend on foreign teachers who have taught at their university previously to recommend new teachers. Liang points out that a recent Japanese instructor, upon returning to Japan, wrote that, "My home is Beijing University's office in Japan." Foreigners are counted on to send books, teaching materials, and even to set up scholarships for Chinese students to study abroad. Jin and Mao at Henan, as well as Shi at Beijing University, emphasize the importance of foreigners' assisting their students and teachers to go abroad to study, attend conferences, and publish articles in journals. At Henan, two former foreign teachers have either directly arranged for teachers to study abroad or have initiated the establishment of sister school relationships between Xinxiang and American universities. As Ma, an official in the Education Commission, says, "The bridge is terribly important."

Other outside roles mentioned by Chinese include sharing films, tapes, and books borrowed from foreign embassies and giving lectures to institutions and programs not affiliated with their own schools. More intangible offerings include bringing in new ideas (called by two of those interviewed "fresh air") to the country and generally to foster friendship between China and foreign countries. Finally, He and Hong say that some of the foreigners prove "safe" friends with whom Chinese can share deeply held personal or political opinions that cannot be shared with other Chinese. These foreigners, they say, can usually be trusted to listen to the Chinese young people's opinions without sharing this information with others. Some foreigners act as important and trusted confidants, holding the information they share within these "safe houses."

Ruan of the Education Commission, Mao in Henan, and Shang at the Foreign Studies University state that although foreigners are well received today in China, the role Chinese expect foreigners to play outside the classroom is sometimes still marked with uncertainty. Shang says that while discussions outside the classroom now enjoy a greater free exchange of ideas, some Chinese authorities still encourage these discussions only in the areas of language and the hard sciences. In areas of the social sciences, the topics of discussion are best kept in the more limited and formal arena of the classroom. Ruan states that many Chinese leaders discourage free discussion of sensitive internal subjects like the 1986–1987 student strikes. This is certainly true in the provinces, although Ruan argues that such attitudes are also common in Beijing and other urban areas. He acknowledges, however, that such views expressed by the leadership have less and less influence over people's thinking and actions in Beijing, while in the provinces the words of the leaders still carry substantial weight.

Ren, an official in a college in Shanxi, reports two instances when some leaders in her college and province attempted to curtail contact between foreigners and Chinese. One instance in 1981 bore a striking resemblance to the views expressed by Qing dynasty officials in the previous chapter; several members of the college community, including the director of the foreign affairs office and professors in departments outside the foreign language department, actually advocated inviting no more foreigners to their school. Foreigners proved to be more trouble than they are worth, they said. "What is the role of the foreign teachers that it costs us so much money?" they asked. "We can do without them, the college can go on." The consensus among these college authorities was that foreigners brought the college too much trouble by spending too much time with Chinese in informal, unstructured conversations, by "snooping around" trying to find out information about China, and by generally disrupting the normal flow of events at the college. Following the line established by the Qing emperor a century before, however, the national and provincial leaders stated clearly that foreign teachers were now important to China's development. Those dissatisfied lost their argument.

Ren recounts another episode involving a foreign teacher at her school. Upon completing her third year of teaching, she asked to remain for a fourth year. The provincial authorities told Ren that the foreigner could not stay. They feared that in another year she would begin to understand too many of the subtleties of Chinese life and be able to explain to new foreigners how to get around in China without going through the proper, bureaucratic channels: "They were afraid she would understand China too well." Ren told the teacher that the province had a policy forbidding foreigners to teach in that province for more than three years. "Of course," she told me, "there is no such policy."

In instances like these the differences between Beijing and a provincial city emerge clearly. In Beijing, the Chinese leaders of several schools have encouraged their popular foreign teachers to stay for several years. During a visit to Beijing in 1987, I encountered several such foreign teachers. This difference was made clear to me, however, when, after recounting the story of the teacher who wanted to stay at the provincial university, two Chinese in Beijing told me the provincial attitude was "stupid." "That is only in some provinces," one of them said. "You would never hear that in Beijing."

The Chinese perception of the role of foreigners outside the classroom is thus twofold. First, no matter how much teaching he or she does inside the classroom, the foreign teacher is never finished teaching. Questions about the text, the use of idioms and colloquial sayings, and cultural matters follow the teacher wherever he or she goes. Some topics of conversation outside the classroom may alarm various Chinese leaders, but the importance of this informal teaching is attested to by almost all Chinese studying under foreigners. Second, the foreigner, especially in recent years, is viewed as one who can help build a tangible bridge between individual schools and further educational opportunities and resources.

Activities that stray from these two approved roles meet uneven resistance, depending on the location of the school and the mindset of the school's leaders. Both of the approved roles were highlighted to me in a memorable exchange during a trip to China in the summer of 1987. Visiting the college where I had taught from 1979 to 1981, I was standing alone in the courtyard of the foreign teachers' compound when a familiar middle-aged teacher approached me. We had not been particularly close when I had lived there and had not seen each other for more than six years. He greeted me nervously with the customary "How are you," then proceeded to pull a standard English text out of his book bag. Pointing to a section of that book, his next words were, "Mr. Porter, I am teaching this text in a few minutes. Can you please look at this and tell me why the preposition *of* is used here instead of *at*?" After I responded to this question, he then asked, "Mr. Porter, I have been trying to go abroad to study for several years. Do you think you can assist me in this?" It was as though I had never left the school. Even though he knew I was there only to conduct research and visit my old colleagues, my role in his eyes had changed not at all during the past six years. I was at once a teacher and a potential bridge for him. My sense is that in his eyes I played no other role in life. While this man may have acted in a more forward manner than some, he certainly put in perspective how many Chinese view the role that foreign teachers play in China.

ADVISORS MAYBE, ADMINISTRATORS NEVER

Except in a a few isolated and unique settings, none of the Chinese cited here knows of any current example of foreigners acting in an administrative role in a Chinese university setting. One exception is at Beijing University's department of Oriental languages, where the only teacher of Filipino, a woman from the Philippines, also holds the title of department chair of the Filipino department. Liang, dean of the Oriental languages department, says that her duties in the department include editing texts and teaching. While arguing that she is considered more like a colleague than a foreigner, he admits she does not attend administrative meetings with other department heads, but meets with Liang regularly to be informed of policies and to receive feedback on her teaching. The reason for her absence from the meetings, he says, lies in her inability to speak Chinese.

A second instance of administrative activity on the part of foreigners can be found at the experimental, foreign-sponsored Yellow River University in Henan Province. A study of this university highlights the possibilities and problems involved in foreigners playing an administrative role in a Chinese institution of higher learning. As outlined by Zhu, a Chinese teacher and administrator who spent two years at this university, in the early 1980s, an American overseas Chinese educator named John Chen approached leaders in Beijing and Guangzhou with the idea of setting up an American-style graduate university in China. Courses taught, mostly by overseas Chinese professors, would include computer technology, American studies, and economic management. The newest American texts and standard American teaching methods were to be employed. At first, Chen received no encouragement for his idea from those major cities. Leaders in Henan Province met with him, however, and the two sides came to an agreement. The provincial governor and Communist party secretary agreed to donate a government villa (once used exclusively by Mao Zedong) as a campus for the school and to construct additional buildings. The Americans said they would purchase equipment and books, secure funding, and recruit and pay the salaries of the foreign teaching staff. This concept was presented to central leaders in Beijing, where it met some resistance but finally gained approval.

From the beginning, says Zhu, the overseas Chinese who funded the operation desired administrative responsibility at the school. The Chinese and the foreign educators arranged for a joint board of trustees to oversee the school officially. Zhu says this board is the only one of its kind in China. Its members include seven Chinese and seven overseas Chinese from the United States. Zhu says, however, that the experiment is not working as the foreigners originally envisioned. The overseas Chinese want more administrative input, for they realize that this board is more a formality than a real maker of policy. As Zhu says, "Theoretically, they make decisions about the college and about the funds, but in fact it is not so easy." The foreigners have told the Chinese that they want to chair academic departments and hold positions as high as vice-president. Even though Chen and other Americans meet regularly with provincial leaders to share their desires and other opinions about the school, none of the foreigners holds an administrative position. The Chinese authorities say that the board of trustees, an American concept, should serve their desire for administrative power sufficiently. The attitude, says Zhu, remains: "The foreigners do not know China's policies, so they cannot run a Chinese campus."

Zhu projects that this school will continue in the same fashion for as long as the foreigners raise enough outside funding for the school to survive. It proves a workable, if difficult, experiment to continue. Whether foreigners will continue to accept their role as teaching and funding parties without meaningful administrative powers and whether the Chinese prove satisfied with the level of funding will determine the future status of this school. If the Chinese at any time feel that the problems of working with foreigners in this environment outweigh the benefits, Zhu says that they will merely change the role of the foreigner and incorporate the school into the mainstream provincial educational system.

A third exception is the Nanjing University-Johns Hopkins Center in Nanjing, a graduate program established jointly by the two institutions. This center is run through a joint and equal administration, at least as stated in the agreements that established it. In a later section of this book, the problems inherent in this endeavor will be discussed more fully.

Most Chinese say that foreigners currently have no role to play in their educational administration. While some Chinese teachers find nothing wrong with the idea of foreign administrators in principle, none considers that a possibility now. They realize that it will take new reforms to bring about such a role in Chinese education. One reason that many Chinese teachers think this change unlikely is the attitude of their leaders. Discussing a possible administrative role for foreigners, Yang in Henan speaks for several of the young teachers when she says, "Even though [foreigners are] capable and in some cases even more responsible than some Chinese leaders, it will not be allowed. The leaders find it too threatening, too dangerous. They want the power and would never give it up to a foreigner." Cai and Geng agree with this, each stating that while some foreigners may be capable, it is up to the local leaders to implement such a policy. Geng says it would take exceptionally "progressive leaders" to allow such a role for foreigners, while Cai doubts whether many leaders have ever thought of this. He, a senior student, says flatly that foreigners cannot play an administrative role. "They can teach but will never be chair of a department. You

GOSHEN COLLEGE LIBRARY
GOSHEN, INDIANA

know, in China the Communist party exercises leadership in everything. They will never allow that." Following this, Yuan, a middle-aged teacher, voices an opinion not unlike that of his younger colleagues and his students. He explains:

Even though we are disappointed in the present situation we can do nothing because the leaders are only interested in their own benefit. They are afraid of what high leaders will say. But some teachers would welcome this. The relationship between Chinese and foreigners is very close. Many teachers trust foreigners.

Wong notes that some of his younger colleagues point with hope to an experiment recently tried in Wuhan where a German manager took control of a large factory. This made an impression on his colleagues, and some wonder if higher education might not learn from this. Those in leadership roles, such as Mao, Ruan, Jin, and Shi, often mention this example when discussing foreigners in administrative roles. They hold, however, a different view from Wong. Mao, dean of a foreign language department, states that in a factory setting, a foreigner could perhaps play the role of an administrator. There, production and the economics of profit and loss can be judged quickly. In education, he says, the outcome is not so quickly or easily calculated. Jin agrees, saying that in a factory where goods are produced, production laws are clear. In education, where people are produced, the environment is more complicated. How, he asks, can foreigners deal with unexpected problems springing from political and cultural dynamics not their own? The practical problem here, says Jin, relates to the role of the Communist party committee that oversees the work of the college at all levels. "A foreigner," says Jin, "could not be given access to even some of the reasons that go into making certain decisions about the school. How could a foreigner make clear decisions based on too little information?" Concluding his remarks with this question, Jin agrees with young teacher Cai's comment, doubting that any leaders in his province have even considered the possibility of foreigners being involved in educational administration. Both Jin and Mao agree with Ye of Beijing Normal University when he says, "Foreigners are not now, will never be, administrators in the future. In factories it may be okay. They produce things. In a university it is not okay. They produce people."

In addition to the politically sensitive problems involved in foreigners acting as administrators, many Chinese point out cultural and social differences difficult to reconcile. Two problems, say Pei, Geng, Shi, Liang, and Xia, concern language and length of stay in China. Without a knowledge of Chinese and a desire to live for a long period in China, no foreigner can hope to accomplish anything meaningful as an administrator. Shang believes that foreigners cannot make administrative decisions relating to the important issue of personnel because they can never understand one important cultural trait. In China, he says, almost every decision dealing with personnel must be based on information relating to a history of personal relationships, especially the nuances found in these relationships. Job performance constitutes only one part. *Guangi,* or personal relationships, play just as important a role in Chinese society. No foreigner would ever know the depth of this. Shang says, "The foreigner, as administrator, would want to be deeply involved in decision making, but the Chinese would not imagine there is any reason to tell the foreigner much of the information needed to make a good decision." Shang adds that "this would not be like a real secret, but they would ask, 'Why should they know this?' " Lan, a departmental vice-chair at a university in Beijing, comments on the political and cultural problems of this issue with this observation:

Higher education is considered part of the most important propaganda branch. It is regarded as a very important area, ideologically, that is strictly controlled by the party. They appoint those people who can follow the present policy. The departmental leadership follows, because it is the only way they can climb up. This situation will not change in the near future, or longer. Never.

Finally, summing up the opinion of many, Hu says that foreigners simply do not understand the Chinese way of dealing with problems and cannot adjust their administrative techniques to fit Chinese society. He states, "Foreigners are not used to it and don't understand it. So they should not say anything about it."

While Chinese voice skepticism about foreigners actually playing an administrative role in a Chinese university or college, most agree that they can act as advisors. Today, at the Beijing Foreign Studies University, a British couple who have taught at the school since the 1940s hold official positions of advisors. Shang, admitting that they are a rare case, states that the leadership weighs their opinions carefully and more deeply than those of ordinary Chinese of senior staff status. They have no decision-making power and no authority, but they serve as advisors in a very real sense.

Aside from this example, none of those involved in this study know of any official advisors operating in a Chinese university. Ye, Jing, Ruan, and Ling, all administrators, welcome informal and solicited advice from certain foreigners. Ling states what appears to be the leadership position on this question: "There is certainly not an official role for a foreign advisor here, but I would solicit advice on how best to teach spoken English." Most of the teachers interviewed, including Hong, Geng, Sui, Pei, Xia, and Xie, welcome foreigners' advice. Cai and Geng point out, however, that even as advisors, the attitude of the leaders affects how much advice is welcome. Yi, while welcoming advice, says that even if a foreigner gains the formal title of advisor, such a title in fact "means nothing." While the attitude toward foreigners acting as informal advisors remains tolerant, Zhu, Xie, Sui, Hong, and others point out that this advice is welcome only in the area of curriculum development and teaching methodology.

Hu points out that even as advisors, many foreigners tread in areas not deemed appropriate, especially when the advice is unsolicited. He relates the story of a marketing professor from Canada who publicly criticized the Chinese practice of allowing students to attend colleges and universities free of charge. He doubted that the Chinese students could stay motivated in their studies if they received their education with no financial sacrifice. Hu points out that such an attitude ignores the reality that Chinese students study very hard and also the reality of Chinese perceptions of education. Such advice is not appreciated and shows the problem of foreigners unfamiliar with Chinese culture playing any role in administrative or official advisory roles. Suggestions in technical matters, he says, such as how to computerize student records better, might prove practical and appreciated. Still, he points out, to say as some foreigners have, "You should change your leaders," is useless. "I don't mean it is really dangerous. I mean it is not useful. It is meaningless."

Chinese find the possibility of a foreigner playing an administrative role in a Chinese college or university unlikely at present and, indeed, in the foreseeable future. The political control that the Communist party exerts over this important ideological institution, coupled with the cultural differences between China and the West, make such a possibility not only impossible, but impractical. This problem applies equally to the role of formal advisor, except in the rare cases in which foreigners have lived in China for decades. Informal advice appears to be appreciated by most Chinese, but it is best offered in areas of curriculum and teaching, not in areas of personnel and administration. The only chance that this may change, assuming that no dramatic changes take place in the political structure in China, rests with the possible rise to authority of the mostly young teachers who desire more input from foreigners. But when they achieve positions of responsibility, two questions will remain: (a) Will they follow the pattern outlined by Lan, climbing up to power by following present policy, or will they be the "progressive" leaders Geng now wishes for and (b) Will they decide that in fact China and the West are, as Ma says, "just too different" and admit that the role of the foreigner should be separate from any decision-making responsibilities outside of teaching and curriculum development?

Chapter 4

The Role of the Foreigner in China's Colleges and Universities: Foreign Perceptions

FREE TO TEACH

The foreigner's perception of his or her basic role in China's classroom differs little from the Chinese perception. While the subject taught or the method of teaching varies from teacher to teacher, all agree that the central job remains imparting specific information about the subject to the Chinese students. Agreeing with the perceptions of many of their Chinese hosts, Bill, Frank, Ian, Matthew, and most of the other language teachers see their most important role as representing "native speakers" in the classroom. Jason, an American teaching at Henan Teachers' University, says that his role is in some sense that of "a warm body who speaks English as a native language." Michelle, a professional ESL instructor from Australia, finds that her role is tied to the difficult task of explaining colloquial and slang expressions. Her biggest problem with this, she says, is that American culture so dominates the view of the West in China that most Chinese have little time or interest in her culture. Jason and Mark, a colleague of Michelle's at the Second Foreign Languages Institute, say that part of their role includes teaching writing, since the Chinese are afraid to teach this. Ian, from Ireland, believes that his role is to utilize his native-speaking understanding of vocabulary and grammar and to "push those words into their heads." All of these approaches to teaching English rely on a native understanding of how the language operates. As Frank says, "Many of our Chinese teachers have an excellent command, or more accurately, knowledge of the language, but it's a command largely from books, and it's largely through the eyes rather than the ears." Summing up how many language instructors perceive their role in China, Matthew, an untrained language teacher before going to China, notes, "I feel that even if my methods are not that good, whatever you do as a native speaker you are not going to lose a whole lot. Even if you bomb out, at least they have heard English." This attitude seems to support Wang's view that the only contribution many foreign teachers make is their ability to speak their native languages. As seen above, for many Chinese this is no longer sufficient.

In most cases, the foreigners see the importance of teaching Western culture as well as their academic subject. While this comes naturally with teachers like Lawrence, who teaches American government and politics at the Foreign Affairs Institute, and Scott, who teaches American history, politics, and culture at another Beijing University, it also holds true for most of the language teachers. The few exceptions include Victor, a translation teacher, Gladys, a professor emerita of linguistics who says that discussion of culture has no place in her classroom, and Yukio, a Japanese instructor of Japanese language who avoids discussing Japanese culture, due to sensitive Chinese feelings about the past Japanese occupation of China and Japan's envied economic development on the world scene.

While most foreigners say that discussion of culture develops inevitably through discussion of the texts, Debbie relates that in her classroom, teaching culture takes precedence over English. Not only does she enjoy this more, but she also says the students encourage it. Jason relates his bewilderment upon first arriving in Henan at discovering the "way out" ideas his Chinese students held about the United States. To overcome this, he utilizes short stories to explain his culture to them. Some foreign teachers, including Bridget and Kate, spend much of their time preparing students to study abroad. Teaching culture and social interactive processes becomes central to their teaching.

None of the foreigners feels constrained at this time about discussing any issue relating to his or her culture. This stands in contrast to the experience of Karen, a young teacher who entered Henan Province's Zhengzhou University in 1979 and was told directly that she could teach anything she wanted, except that she could not "discuss religion." Today, whether in the provinces or the urban centers, foreigners appear to encounter few such restrictions. Frank, a British national who has taught in Beijing's Foreign Studies University for over forty years, says of the current environment, "I've included lectures on world religions—Buddhism, Islam, Judaism, Christianity, and so on. And I've often said to the students, yeah, go ahead, go to church, and see what it's like. . . . I think that is a healthy thing to do."

On the question of foreigners sharing new teaching methods, foreign teachers agree with their Chinese hosts that this is an important contribution they can make. Unlike some of their Chinese colleagues, most of the foreigners expect this contribution to have an effect upon the Chinese. Kate, teaching in Henan, states that her primary goal in teaching is to impress the students with her Western style of teaching. She says:

I was trying to teach something about Western liberal education and a more permissive classroom. I think that it is not different from most of us here [in China], whether we think of it consciously or just do it unconsciously. For example, I was appalled that when I walked into the classroom the first day the monitor gave a signal and the whole class got to their feet and said "good morning teacher," and I said good morning back to them warmly, and said please sit down. And then I got them to stop doing that, and I told them that that made me feel very uncomfortable, and I wanted to foster them feeling free to discuss, which was very difficult for them. . . . I would say that over a period of a year my classes relaxed. This was a conscious priority in my teaching.

This concern with opening the students up to a Western-style discussion also finds favor with Lawrence, who says his primary role is to "tell them what I think may be true and hope they give me back some ideas. My role is to learn while I teach. It is the same as in the States. The way to do this is have them talk." As pointed out by Hong, Chinese students think that if they are talking, they cannot be learning. To hear an American instructor say that his primary role in China is to learn rather than teach certainly brings out the difficulties inherent in taking a Western view of liberal education into a Chinese classroom.

As an indication that a desire to share new teaching methods in China is not only a Western trait, Yukio from Japan states that his primary role is to improve teaching methodology in teaching Japanese. At present, he says, the method is too rigid. He has tried to introduce a "coaching" style of teaching, in which he encourages the students to speak as much Japanese as possible. His biggest concern is that after he leaves, the teaching methodology he has introduced will be abandoned.

Bridget, a Belgian teacher of French with over twenty years of experience in classrooms around the world, argues that the Chinese method of teaching foreign languages is completely wrongheaded. She sees her primary role as encouraging the Chinese to utilize new teaching methods, especially new "communicative" methods using computers and audiovisual equipment. She admits that this proves a difficult task, as she learned one day after giving a workshop for her Chinese colleagues on how to use a microcomputer for self-study. After watching and listening attentively for the duration of the workshop, she was told politely that this was of no help, since no one in the school had access to a microcomputer. She says she is determined to buy computers for the school herself. She desires to make the Chinese classroom as much like a continental French classroom as possible.

Some of the more experienced foreign teachers criticize the Chinese for moving them and their foreign colleagues into higher levels of instruction and away from the lower, first- and second-year levels. Bridget complains, "I told my Chinese friends that the books for beginners are very bad. It is only reading material. They need to speak also in the first year." The Chinese method of learning, she laments, rules out speaking in the early years and this is difficult to overcome later. "Foreign teachers," she says, "should be at the lower levels teaching with Western methods rather than at the higher levels they place us now." Frank, in China for over forty years, agrees, arguing that teaching courses like linguistics to undergraduates is "absurd." The most important thing, he says, is for the foreigner to teach native language and culture. "There is an overemphasis on linguistics and on literature, and generally not contemporary literature. I think the current emphasis in many universities, where on the whole they are doing a very good job, has this shortcoming."

Rachel, an American who has been in China for ten years and now teaches at the prestigious Beijing Foreign Studies University, acknowledges that the Chinese are indeed moving away from the position favored by Bridget and Frank. She says:

In '79 foreigners were just beginning to come who were not coming in on the basis of political recommendations. They were beginning to look for people who had had some sort of special training. At first they were looking for people trained in ESL. Very quickly they didn't want those people. They wanted people who had had experience teaching English to native speakers and the higher level universities were beginning to ask for new types of teachers. A M.A. was not enough, they were beginning to ask for Ph.Ds. What they were demanding from the foreigner was completely different. They were demanding excellence and experience. . . . They were after prestige and they were after something more than the nitty gritty of ESL.

Steve, also in this institute, says that to his knowledge all of the foreign teachers invited to his school with full salary and benefits hold a doctorate and teach in areas outside traditional ESL courses.

As one can see from the previous discussion of how Chinese view this shift, those in the provinces, like their Beijing counterparts, desire more advanced and experienced instructors but cannot attract them to their locations. Most foreigners in the provinces, therefore, continue to teach in the ESL field rather than in narrowly focused but more prestigious fields. The situation poses a paradox, as foreigners like Bridget and Frank wish their prestigious institutions in Beijing would employ foreign teachers more as they are used in the provinces, while the provincial institutions desire the more specialized sort of foreign teachers found in Beijing. Foreigners clearly see that the trend in China is moving away from the basic ESL instructor toward the specialists in single, more prestigious disciplines. Most of the foreigners outside the ESL field voice no opinion on this matter, accepting that their very presence in China speaks to the direction that China is taking in the classroom. Those in the ESL field sense the change coming and, not surprisingly, oppose it.

Mark, Bill, Kate, and others also note a conflict between the Western concept of academic rigor and the Chinese concept of academic advancement with or without serious effort. Bill, an overseas Chinese from Canada, says that his role, at least in part, is to present a different academic point of view. In one of the more direct statements made by a foreigner in this study, he argues:

I have been criticized for being too strict, too demanding, and unbending. When I say I want a piece of work done by a certain time, they have to get it in. Or they get "what for." Well, nobody talks to these babies that way, because traditionally they don't fail. I soon discovered that what they really want for a teacher is Mary Poppins. I told them, after I figured this out, that their ideal teacher is someone who is amusing, is accommodating, will not work them too hard; someone who will take the place of their doting parents and will wipe their noses for them. And if he or she is good looking, it will help a lot. What they really want is a babysitter.

This problem of academic rigor comes up daily in one of the most unusual attempts at Western-style teaching in China, the Nanjing University-Johns Hopkins University Center for Chinese and American Studies. Since opening its doors in 1986, this center has brought Chinese graduate students into classrooms to study under American professors, while American students are taught by Chinese instructors. Terrence, a professor with twenty-five years' experience in the classroom and one of the first Americans at this experimental school, states that he and most of his American colleagues find their Chinese students uninterested in many of the courses offered and rarely motivated to pursue a rigorous academic program. Only 10 to 20 percent of the students, he says, approach the academic level of students found in graduate programs in the United States. Surprised to find this low level, Terrence and his colleagues have had to lower their expectations of their Chinese students.

Agreeing with other foreign teachers, Terrence acknowledges that part of the problem lies with the different teaching methods used by Chinese and American educators. Presenting the problem from the perspective of the professor in a graduate classroom, he says:

Contrasting Chinese and American styles have their greatest impact, in my judgment, on the balance between adherence to received wisdom and criticism, revision or supersession of that wisdom. Chinese papers and exams consist largely of material reproduced from readings and lectures. Set phrases or formulas that represent a larger argument are popular, often used by almost everyone referring to that argument. Criticism when offered is often perfunctory ("I believe the argument is basically correct") or a truism ("We can find exceptions to this generalization" or "Each country has its own special characteristics"). Discussion of independent work often revolves around the students' effort to discover what the professor thinks the project should be. American graduate students are expected to show that they know the received wisdom by the accuracy and pertinence of their references to its key elements, and by the relevance of their criticism of it, *not* by extensive or literal summa-tion of its content. The professor assumes the student knows the basic material assigned and challenges the student's command of it only when there is evidence it is not fully understood. The interest of professor and students alike centers on the stu-dents' efforts to go beyond the material in their independent analysis and assessment of its significance. Whereas American students have been encouraged to do this since secondary school, or at least since their undergraduate courses, most Chinese stu-dents in my courses seemed puzzled by my proddings in this direction; some seemed uncomfortable if I pushed too hard, usually saying they didn't have enough back-ground to do the job.

Unlike some Westerners (like Victor, who insist that the Chinese conform to the Western approach to learning), Terrence acknowledges that the strug-gle may be too difficult either to maintain or win. The Chinese, he argues, support each other in their adherence to the traditional Chinese method of teaching and their rejection of new methods introduced by foreigners. This collective resistance, however, can be turned to a useful, if not very West-ern, teaching method. Terrence suggests that the Western teacher allow the students to work collectively on a critical analysis of a problem and arrive at a group opinion. While individual papers may be required, the students know before they turn in their papers that they are not taking issues outside the mainstream of their class as a whole. When commenting on this option, Terrence acknowledges that he has not tried it, but offers it as a possible alternative for the future.

The issue of academic strictness remains difficult for most foreigners. Victor speaks of the problem a Western teacher has with Chinese students cheating, and Ian and Jason speak of the poor efforts given by many in their classes. Kate acknowledges that she passes her students, even though they may not pass her examinations. In this way, she says, she has given in to Chinese methods and repressed her Western bias. Terrence says grading remains one of the most difficult problems to address. The Center in Nan-jing, he argues, cannot follow the Chinese wish that all the students pass. Minimal standards must be maintained, so the standards should be ex-plained to the students at the beginning of the academic year. Grades and regular attendance in class cannot be abandoned. Terrence is open, how-ever, to changing the grading system to an honors, pass, fail system.

An experience I had while teaching in China highlights the problem of transplanting a Western approach to a Chinese setting. In 1980 I presented a final examination to a group of young teachers at the end of the semester and passed their grades to the departmental administrators. While no one received a pass or fail, they were graded numerically. The young man with the lowest mark lost much face before his colleagues and throughout the foreign language department. The night he received his mark, he returned home with a great sense of shame. He took his frustration out on his wife, beating her and screaming that she had interfered with his study time and was responsible for his poor showing. Such a response makes an impression on a foreign teacher who thought he was doing his job properly—that is, as he would have done in the United States.

The foreign teacher in China's classroom sees his or her role as three-fold: first, whether teaching basic language skills with a M.A. in ESL or American economics with a Ph.D. in American studies, impart information on the subject at hand; second, share knowledge of one's culture with the students when appropriate; and third, use and advocate Western teaching methods, including the introduction of standards of rigor and grading not inherent in most Chinese classrooms. Most foreigners involved in this study agree that these three roles are important, and in this, they echo their Chinese counterparts. The only point on which they disagree are the importance and appropriateness of using new teaching methods in a Chinese setting and grading Chinese students as strictly as foreigners would grade at home. As Wang (1981) argues, when Western educators enter a Chinese classroom, cultural differences in teaching methods and classroom expectations exist automatically, as they have historically in China, dating back over a century.

TEACHING MACHINES AND MISSIONARIES

In many ways, the foreigners' perception of their role outside the classroom also differs little from that of the Chinese. Foreigners agree that teaching rarely stops just because class ends. This responsibility may take the form of opening one's home in the evening to engage in "free talk" about Western culture, as is practiced by Mark, Matthew, Michelle, Jason, Helen, Ian, and others. It may involve organizing songfests, as Michelle does, or dramatic presentations, as advocated by Frank and practiced by Mark. It also takes the form of assisting students to set up school newspapers, as Bill and Kate volunteered to do. Betty, speaking of her teaching experience in a province from 1979 to 1981, says: "Outside office and classroom, I don't know where the personal and the professional is divided, because as foreigners we are always educating and being educated." Mark, teaching in Beijing in 1987, says:

It seems to be a Chinese way of thinking that teachers are always teachers. I've been asked to do many, many different things relating to the class work outside the classroom. [For example,] "Could you help me with this letter, could you help with this translation? We're putting on a play in English, could you come and help with the English?" These things are not at all required.

Some of the foreigners, such as Jim, Michelle, Sally, Victor, Matthew, Yukio, and Lawrence, welcome this constant interaction with their students. Lawrence says that he makes no distinction between inside and outside, as he enjoys entertaining in his home and sightseeing with his students.

Yukio says that his classes offer too little time for him to teach as fully as he desires, so he welcomes the informal coaching sessions in his home that take place almost every evening. Sally and Betty argue that, without this interaction, they might never have enjoyed a social life with the Chinese. In some ways, the Chinese need of round-the-clock teaching meets the need for social interaction on the part of the foreigners. I know that my experience in China from 1979 to 1981, when I was one of only two foreigners in a medium-size Chinese city, supports this view.

This constant demand on the foreign teacher's time, while enjoyed and welcomed by most, also evokes concern expressed by some of the foreigners. Ian, from Ireland, says, "There is more expected of you than I thought. Your oral class begins outside the classroom. This takes a lot of your time, and when they come to your house every night, it gets to be a bit much." Mark says that sometimes the requests for further help demand just too much of his time. In those instances, he begs off by saying, "I'm sorry, I'm busy, etc., etc. I make excuses. Because I really do need private time and space, I don't really encourage people to come over all the time. But they do come over quite frequently to ask my help."

Even those who enjoy the teaching role outside the classroom express various levels of cynicism about how the Chinese use them. Betty and Sally mention that even after living in China for more than two years, they never felt fully appreciated outside their role as teacher. Betty states, "If they could have encapsulated English teaching in a machine, that is what they would want." Sally supports this view when she says, "Some thought we were just teaching machines and couldn't envision us as human beings." Gladys, who also has experience in setting up cross-cultural exchanges with China, argues that if the Chinese leaders thought knowledge from the West could be gained without the presence of foreigners in their country, they would certainly prefer it.

Two of those interviewed say that they have no teaching role outside the classroom. Gladys says that she has no time for teaching outside if she is expected to be prepared for the next day's class. Larry, who enjoys Beijing's "counterculture" social life frequented by young artists and actors, distinguishes clearly between his personal and professional life. "Once I've finished with the class, that's the end of my teaching," he explains. In the final analysis, however, whether teaching in Beijing or one of the provinces, and whether teaching English or history, most foreigners understand that their role outside the classroom remains that of teacher.

Another important role that both Chinese and foreigners stress is for foreign teachers to act as a "bridge" between China and the West. Mark, Steve, Kate, Bridget, and Victor acknowledge that the Chinese desire to use them as a way either to foster formal exchange programs or to assist individuals in gaining entry to a Western college or university. Steve outlines what he says is a typical scenario relating to this role. He explains:

I come here, have a good time, and go back to my university. Three months later, I get a letter from my good Chinese friend which says he has been approved to study in the States but he doesn't have a school to accept him. I go to my Dean and say, hey, this is my buddy. Let's have him over. It'll be fun. So what's happened? Good things have happened for the school and ultimately for the student.

Instances such as this appear to be widespread in China, as more foreign teachers try to assist their friends and colleagues to study abroad. There are also cases in which teachers assist their Chinese institution to set up ongoing sister-school relationships with American universities and colleges.

Another manner in which this role manifests itself is through simple advising to students who want to study abroad. Bridget, who teaches young scientists going abroad to study, says that such advising is as important in her work as her teaching. Lawrence, at the Foreign Affairs Institute, agrees that this is one of his most important activities outside the classroom. Victor notes that when he first arrived in China, several of his students approached him to ask for his assistance to study in the United States. Since Victor had taught outside his home country for several years before moving to China, his contacts proved too weak to be of significant assistance to them. He says, "I was approached a number of times but once they realized who I was and what my limited connections were they lost interest. When it was found that I was not a very strong bridge, I didn't have those people pulling at me."

It is interesting to note that few foreigners expected acting as a bridge to be a role for them before they arrived in China. And only when asked specifically about the concept do they agree to its importance. The Chinese volunteer the importance of this quickly and see it as more important, it seems, than do the foreign teachers.

Some foreigners, like some Chinese, perceive that they play an important role as a confidant or counselor to their Chinese students and fellow teachers. This role can manifest itself in discussions relating to personal problems or sensitive political issues. In this way, the foreigner's residence becomes a "safe house." Jason says that he and his wife act as counselors for several students. Most of this counseling deals with problems of girlfriends and boyfriends. Jason explains:

They come over because we are safe. Maybe they think we have a more humane way of dealing with people problems. For example, this year we had two suicide attempts. My wife and I visited the girls in the hospital. We had also visited them in their dorms, so we did not think this was unusual. I don't see Chinese teachers doing this.

Kate, a middle-aged teacher at the same school, says that she has opened her home up to women teachers to discuss personal problems. Most of the discussion deals with marriages and children. Explaining why this takes place, she says, "I think I am safe as a foreigner. Partly this is because they could couch [problems] in terms of comparison. They could ask, 'How is it in the West?' "

One foreign teacher in Beijing acknowledges that during sensitive political periods, such as the December 1986 student strikes, her house has been used as a place where students could freely discuss the issues at hand. "They knew I would not discuss their comments made here," she says, "and so they felt safe to come here to talk. Sometimes we act as ears." At the same time, she points out that she offers very few of her own ideas to the students. She merely allows them to discuss these sensitive issues safely in her house. In some ways, this recalls Yale-in-China's Hume, who allowed political discussion in his "safe" house during the days of the revolution against the Qing dynasty. The difference between the two is that Hume acted unknowingly, while modern foreign educators in China appear to recognize their homes as potential safe houses.

The role outside the classroom has an added dimension for three of the foreign teachers involved in this study. Ruth, Debbie, and Matthew each traveled to China under the auspices of a Christian-sponsored, English-language organization. Their underlying goal involves opening doors for Christians to influence China. Matthew says that, aside from teaching, his most important role is "as a Christian." He continues, "I want to relate to people as they come to me with questions, as they seek information. And maybe to encourage other Chinese Christians that happen to be here." Ruth, who taught in a provincial university in 1986, carefully selected literature for use in and out of the classroom that presents Biblical phrases, names, and concepts. Ruth states, "We had an agenda, to contact people who might be Christian." She invited students to her apartment to listen to tapes of great literature, such as *The Red Badge of Courage* and *Moby Dick,* each of which uses Biblical references. She hoped to elicit questions relating to those references so that religious concerns could be broached. Matthew displays three modern and artistic religious posters in his living room, where he invites Chinese to evenings of discussion and further study. He says that if they ask questions about the posters, he has an opening to bring up his Christian beliefs. Debbie says she opens herself up to discussing her religion also, but, like Matthew, rarely initiates the subject unless given an opening. She agrees, however, that her goal is to make lasting contacts that might lead to a greater Christian presence in China. She wants to draw people to her through what she calls her "principled Christian life-style." "Teaching," she says, "is the tool to get this across."

The organization with which these teachers are affiliated has an arrangement with China that appears to be an honest one. The Chinese, all three acknowledge, know the organization's motives for entering China, while the foreigners traveling under this organization's auspices understand that it is illegal to proselytize while in China. The Chinese, they say, gain much from them, however, even given the self-defined mission of these teachers. Debbie explains, "They want Christians because our morals are higher, and we're more serious about our work. Additionally, we pay our own way to China and receive no salary from them beyond room, board, and in-country travel." Debbie adds, "The Chinese know how to get what they want." Through my observations and discussions in China during the summer of 1987, I can say that, at least in the provinces where foreign currency is scarce and foreign teachers still fall into the category of basic English teachers, Debbie's assessment proves accurate. Jim, a Jewish foreign teacher in Shanxi Province who has taught with Christians from this organization, also supports Debbie's claim. He explains, "They need teachers so badly, they just look the other way."

As one who taught in China in the early days of this new open-door environment, I was surprised on my return in 1987 to learn that these modern-day missionaries now move about China openly espousing their beliefs. That would have been unthinkable in 1980. Each year, several hundred of these Christian teachers go to China at the invitation of the Chinese authorities. The reason for the invitation seems to rest partly with Debbie's claim that Christians, at least those from her organization, prove more dependable morally than other foreigners and are cheaper. Inviting these Christians also shows a sense of self-confidence on the part of the authorities, for they exhibit little concern about any influence on their students. This is shown by Matthew when he says he found to his surprise that his students, for the most part, possess only an intellectual interest in Christianity. "They are surprised that someone who is educated could believe in God. The Christians here are mostly from the lower economic levels. I think maybe they come from the countryside mostly." The Chinese leaders apparently feel that the advantages of cheap, moral teachers outweigh any danger of China's educated young people following this Western-based religion. This self-confidence stands in stark contrast to the criticism of foreign educators and their foreign religion expressed in the 1920s.

The role played by foreigners outside their Chinese classrooms, as perceived by those foreigners themselves, can thus be seen as four-fold. First, they continue to teach, if somewhat informally. Second, they act as a tangible bridge to the West for their schools and for the individuals with whom they teach and work. Third, some view themselves as confidants and counselors with whom the Chinese can share problems and views that cannot be shared safely with most other Chinese. Fourth, a small yet growing number of them enter China as Christian missionaries and see their role as promoting Christianity. These roles are perceived similarly by the Chinese as outlined previously, except that the Chinese appear to stress the idea of the bridge more than the foreigners do and the foreigners appear to emphasize the counselor role more than do most Chinese. Additionally, while the new missionaries entering China see their role as models for Chinese to follow, most Chinese see them as competent teachers who act properly in their personal lives and who cost them little in foreign currency.

POLICY MAKERS NOT WELCOME

As shown above, there exist two types of universities in China where foreigners now teach. Most foreigners teach in the national and provincial schools operated exclusively by the Chinese government. The other, more experimental in nature, are those schools such as the Yellow River University in Henan and the Nanjing-Johns Hopkins Center in Nanjing. Each of these schools, through official agreements, operates through an administration that is officially equal and jointly responsible for decisions related to all matters at the school. We will first review the more traditional schools and the possible administrative role that foreigners can play there. Following this, the jointly run programs will be reviewed.

Foreigners who teach in the state-run universities agree that Chinese colleges and universities make no room for foreigners as administrators. This proves true even at the Foreign Studies University, where foreign teachers acknowledge that they are treated as genuine colleagues. Larry, after completing one year of teaching there, says, "Even at this very liberal school they exclude us from policy making. It seems very unlikely that foreigners will ever have an administrative role here." Rachel, who has taught at this school for several years, says that while her opinions on subjects relating to classroom assignments and student projects appear welcome, she will "probably not" play any administrative role in her institution. She continues, "It's hard to know where all the decisions get made in the administration, it's hard to know anywhere." Bridget, who taught at this school in the early 1960s and returned in 1986 for another engagement, says there is much doubt about such a possibility at this school.

Several foreigners at less progressive schools discount emphatically the possibility of engaging in any administrative role. Victor, when speaking of his tenure as an instructor of translation in Tienjin, argues:

In my own experience I would say that would be damn near impossible. We were pretty much kept out of meetings of any kind involving policy. We were simply told what the policy was. We were almost never invited into the administrative framework. There's one foreign expert who's been at my institute for five or six years and his position was no better than mine as far as being in the decision-making process. They make a very clear distinction.

Victor says that he knows of one American in Harbin who reportedly holds the title vice-dean of a foreign language department, but he doubts if it is more than an honorary title. I know of a foreigner who has taught in a provincial Chinese university for thirty years. She now holds the position of chair of the foreign language department. Chinese and foreigners tell me, however, that she holds little real administrative power outside that of curriculum reform. Echoing the comments of Yi and He, Victor explains that there remains:

a problem about the Party, Party members, Party secretaries on campus. They're the ones who really are heavily involved in the decision-making process, who really call the shots. And you are not going to be able to rub elbows with them much. There are certain barriers within the system.

Yukio understands the Chinese reluctance to admit foreigners into the decision-making process. The Chinese will never allow this, for they are, he says:

too proud. In Japan we have the same situation. There are no foreigners in an administrative role there. We never think about it. Foreigners are ignorant of too many domestic issues and can too easily mess things up through ignorance of the culture.

Some of the most insightful remarks concerning this question come from Frank, who has been with the Beijing Foreign Studies Univeristy since the late 1940s. At one point, soon after the Communist victory in China, Frank actually held the post of deputy head of the English department, a position that entailed administrative responsibilities. It proved an awkward role for him to play, however. He explains that, because he was a Communist, the Chinese authorities felt that he could work well with them, since there would be no question of following the party's line in educational matters. However, because of his still-limited knowledge of the written language and of subtle matters of cultural interaction, he finally found himself relieved of his duties as an administrator. He says:

It was not appropriate for a foreigner to be in a position of leadership in administration. This is an extremely complex society, very difficult to understand. Part of that is the language problem. And there are many things that are found we can't cope with. For example, I remember a meeting that was to be held involving all the teachers in the department. And one of the party members came to me a day or two in advance and said, "Now what do you think about the questions we're going to discuss?" So I said, "Well, we're going to have a meeting to discuss it. Let's not waste time doing it now." See, this was totally divorced from a Chinese traditional practice in which you have prior consultations and sound out people, and then by the time you get to the meeting, you stand a better chance of having some degree of unity and equal understanding. Another time we were discussing something, and I finished announcing a certain decision and then I said, "Well, any questions or suggestions?" So, I waited about half a minute, saw there were none, and called the meeting over. Very un-Chinese, you see. If you want people to talk, you've got to draw them out.

So that again shows ignorance of the working of the Chinese mind and the history of Chinese society.

Moving to the two experimental schools in Henan and Nanjing, we find that through negotiations between the two parties, joint Chinese-American administration exists, at least on paper. In 1981 Nanjing University and the Johns Hopkins University signed "An Agreement for the Establishment of the Nanjing University-Johns Hopkins University Center for Chinese and American Studies." On the question of administration, the agreement states:

The Center shall operate under the supervision of Nanjing University, and its day-to-day operation shall be conducted by a Chinese and an American co-director. The co-directors shall be appointed separately by Nanjing University and the Johns Hopkins University from faculty members they appointed at the Center. (Nanjing-Hopkins Agreement, 1981)

John, one of the first professors to teach at the school, entered the program with the understanding that the program would actually be run through a joint and equal administration. He soon discovered otherwise. First, he says, he was surprised to find that none of the Chinese administrators in this program were from the field of international relations, which was "the supposed thrust" of the program. The Chinese co-director was a professor of linguistics, while the academic dean came from the English department. A French teacher, who also held the position of party secretary for his department, was named assistant director for administration and another English teacher was named head of the foreign affairs office.

While the selection of Chinese administrators was a surprise to John, an even more disturbing outcome of the Chinese approach to administration was the manner in which actual decisions were made. John explains:

Decision making supposedly was made at the Center level by the Chinese co-director and the American co-director. In practice, decisions were made by neither the Chinese nor American co-director. The party secretary and the director of the foreign affairs office made the decisions. Then the co-directors found out what the policy was to be and told their colleagues."

The Americans felt most deeply disappointed with the unsolicited and unannounced decisions made by the director of the foreign affairs office. Several episodes took place, such as when the desks of Chinese employees of the Center were moved to allow them a better view of the activities of the Americans, to keep a closer eye on them as they interacted with Chinese, some Americans believed. In response, one American professor drafted a letter to the president of Johns Hopkins outlining the anger felt by the Americans toward this Chinese official. To maintain a workable relationship with the Chinese, however, John and others more familiar with Chinese sensitivities persuaded the professor not to send the letter.

Lawrence, a guest lecturer visiting the Nanjing program, supports John's view by observing that the Americans teaching there understand that while Johns Hopkins holds joint and equal administrative responsibilities with Nanjing University, "it hasn't worked out that way. While there are presumably co-directors, if there is real disagreement it will be done the Chinese way. At all times, in fact, Chinese authorities are in control."

The Yellow River University in Henan, as noted by Zhu, theoretically operates from a joint administration as well. Jason, familiar with this university through visits and discussions with his American colleagues teaching there, argues:

On paper Yellow River looks absolutely wonderful, but it goes against the way the educational system works. I think the way of decision making is deeply entrenched and the Henan officials run it like a Chinese university. I know that before coming the American administrators and teachers had different ideas of what it would be like and became very, very disappointed once they got here. Yellow River is a good example of an attempt at foreign input into administration where an idea was born and laid out in the wind to die.

When discussing the possibility of playing an advisory role, most of the foreigners agree that this proves more likely than administration. There exist differences, however, in perceptions of how eagerly such advice is solicited or received by the Chinese. Ian, at the provincial university in Henan, says that his advice has never been sought. "Therefore," he says, "I've never offered. It seems here that they don't want any." Others, such as Matthew in Henan and Larry, Mark, and Michelle in Beijing, also show little eagerness to advise their Chinese colleagues and leaders. For Matthew, the reason is that he personally feels uncomfortable and shy approaching the Chinese about his views, even though he holds opinions about how foreigners could better serve in China. For the others, the reasons lie with their perception, like Ian's, that the Chinese care little for their advice anyway, so why discuss things with them?

Some foreign teachers, however, feel compelled to offer advice. For example, Kate argues that if enough foreigners spend enough time advising on one issue, some suggestions actually turn into policies. She supports this view by reflecting on a provincial meeting organized by the authorities to hear the foreign teachers' suggestions on improving their work. She says that at this meeting she brought up the problem of students having little or no access to the English library in her department. She discovered that this same point had been brought up at the meeting one year before and that all the foreigners wanted to discuss it again. Following the meeting, the schools in the province opened the library to the fourth-year students. While she admits it would be "arrogant" to say that the change came only because of the foreigners' advice, she maintains that such a move would have been less likely had she and others in the foreign teaching camp not suggested it.

Kate admits that this is an isolated case of affecting Chinese decisions, however, by pointing out that this meeting and the subsequent actions hardly prove that the Chinese authorities care much for the opinions of the foreigners. In fact, she admits of the meeting that "This was just window dressing. They gave us a nice banquet, and they took us to an opera. It was a very fun kind of thing. . . . I think they wanted to know what we were thinking. The better to keep an eye on us or to know where dissension is."

Even though Kate says she recognizes that the Chinese care little for her advice, she is the kind of Westerner who feels compelled to advise them on various issues. At one point, she says, she "used all my influence" to convince the college president to transfer middle-aged couples in her department back to their home towns so they would be happier in their work. She also says that whenever possible she tells her Chinese students and colleagues that they should rid their culture of the preface word *Xiao* [little] when addressing someone their junior. It is, she argues, too demeaning to use in addressing adults. Both of these comments, in the first instance attempting to influence such a serious and complex issue as job assignments in China, and in the second criticizing an unquestioned and endearing salutation traditional through centuries of Chinese personal interaction, appear to support Hu and Frank's view that foreigners know so little of Chinese tradition and culture that they should have little or nothing to say about how China runs itself. Certainly neither suggestion was taken seriously, and both undoubtedly fall into Hu's category of "meaningless" suggestions made by foreigners. Another foreigner who would like to influence his school but has been frustrated in his attempts is Jason. Understanding the Chinese lack of interest in his opinions, however, Jason expresses his frustration at this by stating he and his wife have "made suggestions and they've asked us in a very patronizing way to give suggestions, and we have done that on several occasions. Afterwards, we've always been told 'that's a very good idea,' but we never saw any follow-up, even in teaching methods where I wanted to help them."

In Beijing, some of the foreigners engage in more formal and informal advising on policies than they do in the provinces. Lawrence, at the Foreign Affairs Institute, says that the school invited him to write a proposal creating a new American history and culture curriculum through the use of video tapes and transcriptions of tapes. Bill, at the Tourism Institute, has been asked to supply examination questions, although he says that his suggestion of using materials not possible to memorize proved "too much work to grade and perhaps politically difficult to judge." His suggestions were rejected.

The most open environment for the role of advisor apparently exists at the Beijing Foreign Studies University. Rachel, at this institute for several years, reflects on the differences between her first teaching position at another school in China and her present one:

It was pretty hard to make any kind of impact on the administration at my first institute. There was a very definite effort to keep me isolated and separated. There was an impact on policy only where it was allowed and in the interest of somebody or another to be able to use my authority as a foreign expert to back their arguments. But as far as my own impact there was virtually none. Here it's been much more collegiate. So that if somebody comes and says we are thinking of changing the number of class hours required for graduate students, well I am glad to hear that you are in agreement or what are your objections. So that I have a feeling that what I have to say is taken into account probably as often at the same level as other experienced [Chinese] teachers are taken into account.

To show the difference between her institute and others, Rachel points to Frank, the foreign teacher who has taught at her institute for over forty years and now serves in the formal capacity of advisor to the leadership of the university. His views, she says, prove important to the leadership and are often solicited. In fact, because of his unique history and place in the institute, she agrees with Shang that his opinions carry more weight than those of many of his Chinese colleagues.

The foreign teachers interviewed in this study share the opinion that the Chinese show no interest in inviting a foreigner actually to administer a program in a Chinese college or university. Even in programs that allow this in theory, such as the Yellow River University and the Johns Hopkins University program in Nanjing, the reality remains that the Chinese operate the schools in China. The only example of a foreigner truly administering a program, as when Frank served as a leader of the English department of the Foreign Studies University in the 1950s, ended in failure. He admits this and says the experiment proved a mistake. A foreigner, at least for now and in the near future, cannot hold a position of administrative authority in a Chinese institution of higher learning. This is true whether in Beijing or in the provinces.

With regard to to the role of advisor, it appears that in some schools, mostly in large urban areas like Beijing, Chinese authorities invite the suggestions and opinions of their foreign teachers. Most of these suggestions involve questions relating to curriculum. The genuine desire to solicit and take under advisement the foreigners' suggestions, however, is not found in all institutions. In many places, foreigners perceive that their suggestions are not desired at all. In these places foreigners find that their advice is sought only in a polite yet meaningless manner. Foreign teachers' responses to this prove mixed. Having no problem with this situation, Betty argues, "We are foreigners in a Chinese institution and we're only a very small part of the institution. We should not try to change it. American institutions would not like that." Others, however, desire to produce change through their own suggestions, or at least to exhibit their Western prerogative to say what they think. Jason, speaking from this perspective, believes that the reason Chinese do not want to listen to foreigners' views on how to improve the institution is that "They are too damn lazy. It's too much work. When I leave I'm going to sit down and give suggestions for improvements and make a few recommendations, if only to satisfy myself."

Chapter 5

Why Foreigners Go to China, Why Chinese Invite Them

FOREIGNERS IN CHINA FOR ADVENTURE AND ROMANCE: CHINESE PERCEPTIONS

When discussing what they think motivates foreigners to teach in China, Chinese say that most foreigners come to China, in part if not primarily, to travel around the country and experience this "mysterious" culture. Wong, Zhou, and Lan speak for several of their colleagues when they point out that the reasons foreigners come to China include a desire to have a "China experience," find adventure, have fun, go to the seaside, and just enjoy themselves. Other perceived motives include a desire to share Christianity, establish relations for future business ventures, prepare for a field in Chinese studies, spy on China, and learn to speak Chinese. Several, both in Beijing and in the provinces, mention that some foreigners come to China to "marry a Chinese girl." Clearly the Chinese perceive that most foreigners are motivated to teach in China for reasons far removed from the arena of the classroom. As Mao says, "The foreigners are realistic. They are mostly interested in China, and teaching is the best way to get here and see it."

Chinese educators are not so cynical as to believe, however, that all foreigners teaching in China hold only ulterior and personally selfish motives for being there. Pei says that some, though not many, come to China because of their dedication to teaching. Yi says that other perceived motivations include the desire of many foreigners to encourage cross-cultural friendship. Yang and Cai, Yi's colleagues in their provincial university, Liang in Beijing University, and Ma with the Education Commission agree, pointing out that some foreigners enter China because they desire friendship with the Chinese people and want to help them improve academically. Dong says that "about one-third of the foreign teachers love teaching, especially teaching abroad. China is now interesting and mysterious, so they come here." Those foreigners motivated primarily by this ideal carry with them, says Shang at the Foreign Studies University, a "sense of mission that China needs teachers and they can contribute."

One motivation appreciated by the Chinese involves that of the overseas Chinese. Hu insists that most overseas Chinese are motivated by their desire to serve "the Motherland" and contribute to China's development. "They are all very conscientious in their work," he says. Ruan and Ma, both with the Education Commission, say that their experience supports this view. In addition to the desire of overseas Chinese to contribute and discover their own family roots, Ma adds that some children and grandchildren of former missionaries in China return for the same reasons as many overseas Chinese: to serve the land so dear to their families and to discover this part of the family heritage.

One difference between perceptions in the provinces and Beijing lies with motives related to personal academic advancement and employment on the part of the foreigners. In Henan Teachers' University and other provincial schools, the Chinese say that one of the primary motivations for foreigners who teach in their country is their inability to find work in their own countries. Yang, Cai, Mao, He, and others argue that this proves one of the most important motivations drawing foreigners to Chinese colleges and universities, if not the most important one. Such a perception falls in line with the opinion of many in the provinces that they are unable to attract the best foreign teachers, due to poor living conditions, isolation from major urban areas, and lack of foreign currency. Basically, they perceive that all they can get are rejects from American academic institutions. A few Chinese educators in Beijing, Dong and Ling at the Foreign Affairs Institute, and Shang at the Foreign Studies University, also mention this as a motivation, though there it has been more a problem of the recent past than of the present. Dong says that for young teachers such an experience "looks good on their resume" when they return to their native country. In most schools in Beijing, however, this perception appears much less prevalent than in the provinces.

In contrast to the provinces, the more prestigious universities in Beijing find that the foreigners' academic motivation relates to research opportunities. Almost all of those interviewed in Beijing say that now that they are inviting more highly educated and senior educators from abroad, they find that upon arriving in China these foreigners bring with them an interest in taking something academically tangible and rewarding back with them. Many, say Ye at Beijing Normal University and Dong at the Foreign Affairs Institute, are on sabbaticals from their universities and use this opportunity to collect two salaries while also collecting firsthand information on which to write articles and books. Some of these senior scholars may, says Ruan of the Education Commission, engage in research with the aim of reporting their findings to the American government.

On the one hand, the Chinese educators involved in working with and supervising these senior scholars are pleased to have them, if for no other reason than that they bring specialized knowledge and extra prestige to the institution. On the other hand, because the visiting scholars' motivation is first to engage in research and second to teach, the results disappoint many of the Chinese. Dong says:

Some of those whose motive is to do research are good teachers. But some are not serious in their teaching and only want to research their scholarship. They come here to collect material to write books and create new relationships so they can be invited back later to write more books.

Su supports this impression. When she first heard that her university in Shanxi Province had invited its first foreign teacher, she became quite excited. After a short while in the foreigner's classroom, however, she grew disappointed in the foreigner's lack of attention to teaching. To her surprise, Su learned that her American teacher had entered China primarily to collect data for her dissertation and taught only to support herself.

Institutions that desire senior scholars but find them lacking in classroom enthusiasm face a dilemma. As an example, Dong shares the success story of a middle-aged women who held only a B.A. degree. This woman, an American motivated in part by her Christian faith, proved so conscientious and knowledgeable in her teaching of English that the students and teachers held her up as the model foreign teacher in that school, despite her lack of an advanced degree. The difference between her and the newly arrived teachers, Dong says, is that she desired to succeed primarily as a competent teacher. With the new movement away from those with less than a doctorate, however, she says that such people are rare in today's classrooms.

Hong at the Foreign Studies University confirms this impression, noting that one of the best teachers of English at her institute was the wife of a senior scholar who came to teach but preferred to spend time on his research. The wife found that when given the opportunity to teach in China, she was well received for her diligent approach to her work. In the end, she gained more appreciation than her husband as a teacher and desired to stay in China after his contract expired. Her motivation, says Hong, centered on the positive feedback from her students and the school leaders, and on her newly found prestige independent of her husband's reputation. Unfortunately, says Hong, the future for such teachers finding appointments in China without their scholar husbands is not a promising one.

Provincial colleges and universities complain that they can draw only lower-level teachers motivated by the inability to find employment in their own countries. The large prestigious universities complain that when they draw the more senior scholars from abroad, too many arrive motivated to engage in research rather than teaching. The pattern is set, however, and no solution to the dilemma appears on the horizon.

To conclude, the Chinese say that several motivations draw foreigners to China. Some motives they obviously appreciate more than others. It is clear, however, that in the final analysis, foreigners' motivations to teach in China prove of secondary importance to most Chinese educators. The Chinese attitude toward those arriving with various motives, whether they come as senior scholars, recent graduates of an undergraduate school, or ESL globe-trotters who happen to be in China this year, finds its most forthright assessment expressed by Ye, vice-president of the Beijing Normal University: "The motivation is not important as long as they teach well and abide by the law."

INVITE THEM TO MODERNIZE THE COUNTRY: CHINESE MOTIVATIONS

The motivation for inviting foreigners to teach in China cannot be separated from China's desire to advance in the realms of science and technology. Among others, Shang, Ma, and Ye in Beijing, and He, Cai, and Yang in Henan point out that if China is to develop in these areas, it must learn from advanced Western knowledge. None of the Chinese interviewed voice any disagreement with this serving as the most important motive in inviting foreign teachers to China. At this time, even in Beijing, the primary expression of this is through study of English, the acknowledged international language of science and technology. Jin, president of a provincial college, says that the need to learn from the West cuts across all disciplines and now focuses, at least in his school, on inviting English teachers to train his science students.

In addition to raising the academic level in language, science, and technology, several other perceived motives enter the picture. One is the desire to use foreign educators as a bridge to foreign university programs and faculty. As pointed out by Jin, this role for foreigners was not anticipated in the early years of this new era. Now, however, with the growing number of foreign teachers needed in China and with the impressive numbers of Chinese going abroad, the role of bridge is taking on vitally important dimensions. Liang at Beijing University, Ye at Beijing Normal University, and Zeng at the Second Foreign Languages Institute explain that they depend on foreign colleagues who have taught at their university previously to recommend new teachers. Liang points out that a recent Japanese instructor wrote upon returning to Japan that "My home is Beijing University's office in Japan." Foreigners are expected to send books, teaching materials, and even to set up scholarships for Chinese students to study abroad. Jin and Mao at Henan and Shi at Beijing University emphasize the importance of foreigners assisting their students and teachers to go abroad to study, attend conferences, and publish articles in journals. At Henan Teachers' University, two former foreign teachers have either directly arranged for teachers to study abroad or have initiated the establishment of sister school relationships between that university and American universities. As Ma, an official in the Education Commission, says, "The bridge is terribly important."

Another motive concerns the national and self-image of an institution. Mao, chairman of the foreign language department in his provincial university, says that even though his school is unable to attract foreigners who hold doctorates, his foreign language department must have foreign teachers to consider itself a legitimate university in today's China. Yuan, a teacher at this school, and Jin, president of the school, agree. Xie mentions that even though he finds fault with the quality of the teaching he receives from the foreigners, at least the prestige of the institution stays high if foreign teachers reside on campus.

Another motive for inviting foreign teachers relates directly to the results of the Great Proletarian Cultural Revolution of 1966–1976. Because of the disruption of academic institutions during those years, a generation of teachers was, in effect, lost to the country. To make up for this loss, educators such as Dong, Shang, Yuan, and others stress that the foreign teachers are "filling the gaps" created by the political turmoil. Dong says she wishes that she could have her foreign teachers concentrate on their own specialties, but because there are so few qualified Chinese teachers and so many students, the foreigners sometimes have to teach classes that she wants taught by Chinese. Yuan agrees, stating that the foreigners are invited partly because "we just need more teachers. There are not enough Chinese teachers now, especially in writing and listening."

Like foreign language departments and foreign language institutes, some specially oriented schools hold self-defined motives for inviting foreigners to teach in their institutions. At the Foreign Affairs Institute, for example, foreigners are invited to teach students who will become diplomats in the Chinese foreign service. These students need specialized courses in foreign culture and international affairs to prepare them for their future careers. Therefore, the school is motivated to invite foreign teachers with expertise in these areas.

Shang in Beijing and Zhu in Henan both say that, due to the political upheavals of the past thirty-five years, certain disciplines in the social sciences, like psychology and sociology, have been criticized and ignored in the classroom. Now that China is expanding its role on the international academic scene, it must invite foreigners to fill the gaps of knowledge in these and other areas that have been untouched for so many years. Shang agrees with Zhu that at some point in the future, Chinese teachers, especially those having studied under foreigners in China and those returning from study abroad, can take the place of the foreigners. At this historical juncture, however, Shang and Zhu believe the foreign presence is important. Zhu points out that the teachers invited from abroad also assist China by filling in the gap between the old Chinese educators, who where familiar with the

West before the Communist victory, and today's generation, who know almost nothing of the West. "The leadership," Zhu says, "desires its young people to know of certain things foreign and inviting foreigners to China gives them this opportunity. Before now, only a few in the older generation, those now in their seventies and eighties, knew much of the West. This fills the gap in both numbers and quality."

One last reason to bridge this gap in knowledge of other cultures is expressed by Cai in Henan. By knowing how foreigners think, she says, and by having foreigners begin to understand how Chinese think, it becomes more difficult to maintain hostility between countries. "This way," she explains, "there is less chance of war." Ruan says he is certain that the leadership has this in mind as it tries to create a more modern country as well as a more internationally peaceful and politically stable political environment for China. He gives an example from the early life of Deng Xiaoping to back up this claim: "Deng Xiaoping's experience in France in the 1920s [when he was a student and worker] must have influenced him to see the need for an open door."

The Chinese people desire above all else the rapid advancement of their nation in the areas of science and technology. To achieve their ambitious goals, they know they must gain knowledge from the West. For this reason, their central motivation to invite foreigners rests with their need to learn English and the science and technology presented to them through this language. They invite scholars in many fields, develop bridges through them to allow their students and teachers to study abroad, and use foreigners to fill in the gaps of knowledge lost during the past thirty-five years of isolation. The Chinese interviewed for this study express no doubt that the motives to invite foreigners are legitimate, and all hope ferverently that foreigners will continue to come. Ruan states categorically, "In China today there is no turning back to self-imposed isolation." Dong, by contrast, while expressing confidence in the future, serves warning to Chinese leaders who might be tempted to return to those old days. She warns, "I swear, I will leave if the open door policy ends. If it ends, I will leave any way I can. Or if I can't, I'll just be very quiet and very selfish." As long as the motives for inviting foreigners continue to revolve around opening China to new technology, science, and ideas, Dong's threat need not be carried out. The current motives for inviting foreign teachers appear to serve the needs of both those Chinese who want to learn as much as they can about the West and those leaders who see their duty to build a modern China.

IN CHINA FOR ADVENTURE AND CONVERSIONS: FOREIGN PERCEPTIONS

The motivations driving foreigners to teach in China prove strikingly similar to those perceived by the Chinese. Each foreigner entering China as a teacher comes with several motivations, usually one primary motivation and several secondary ones. Except in rare cases, few foreigners enter China out of a commitment to their field or area of expertise. Even then, the motivation to teach their subject proves only the primary, not the only, reason to teach in China. The first exception is Bridget, a Belgian teacher of French whose passion for teaching has carried her to many countries. She holds a unique place in her institute, because she had taught in the same Chinese school in the 1960s. She remembers from that early experience the enthusiasm of her students, and she desired to return to China for several years to share new knowledge with these eager students. She also returned to set up an exchange program between Belgium and China. The second exception is Lawrence, who entered China to teach in his specialized field of international relations. He says that his American university would not allow him to teach courses in his academic field, so he took a sabbatical to teach these courses in China. He recognizes, however, that other factors motivate him to teach in China. One is the desire to watch China as it changes in this new era. The other is to engage in research, though he states, "First of all I am a teacher, and if research comes of it, that's fine."

The two experimental schools, the Nanjing-Johns Hopkins Center and the Yellow River University in Henan Province, provide unique studies in motivation. On the institutional front, John, an instructor at the school, says that the motivation of Johns Hopkins University rests in its desire to strengthen the China program on its home campus and to hold its own "China card," adding to its prestige as a unique institution in the field of international relations. One can see how Johns Hopkins views its role in this new era of Chinese-American relations by noting the perceptions of its president, Steven Muller, on the eve of the establishment of this program. John says that Muller predicted that the Nanjing-Johns Hopkins program would be seen not only as a historic new development in Chinese-American educational ventures, but also as a historic landmark in Chinese-American relations overall.

Martin, a professor in this program in 1988, enthusiastically supports the historic mission of the Center as outlined by the administration at Johns Hopkins. He says that the very existence of the program makes it the "most important" educational joint effort in China. Echoing the president of Johns Hopkins, Martin predicts that the Nanjing-Johns Hopkins program will be seen as "something of a breakthrough in the history of U.S.-China relations and in the fascinating and rapidly evolving story of China's opening to the outside policies of the past several years."

In more utilitarian terms, Johns Hopkins University and Nanjing University, in the 1981 agreement establishing the program, stipulated that "The purpose of the Center is to train advanced professionals" (Nanjing-Hopkins Agreement, 1981). A further goal, as expressed by John, is to foster interpersonal relationships between Chinese and Americans that will improve international relations between the two countries for the lifetime of those relationships.

Martin and Terrence, however, while appreciating the Johns Hopkins experiment in China and agreeing with the institutional motive that took them there, voice concern that the motivation fits poorly with the reality found in Nanjing. Each argues that while the school advertises itself as a graduate program, the Chinese students they teach, many of whom originally studied English rather than international relations as undergraduates, are not at the the the level of graduate students they expect. While early motivation may have centered on taking a Johns Hopkins style of education to Nanjing, Americans find the actual experience centers on a struggle to redefine the original intent of the program into terms understood by both the Chinese and the Americans. Commenting on his concerns, Terrence says:

The criticism is that I feel I should know what the Center's mission is, that in fact I don't, and that I don't think my ignorance and confusion is my fault. The problem stems from differences between public image of the Center, as expressed in various university and public relations statements, and what goes on in the Center. Is it a graduate center or not? A research center or not? An emerging degree program, or joint credit program or not? A center for "future leaders" or not? And is it a center for professional training, international studies, Chinese and American studies, or some other combination of academic disciplines? It may be impossible to resolve such questions in the first year or even the first few years, but it is also desirable to keep confusing and contradictory messages to a minimum.

John, while ackowledging the lofty ideals of colleagues who teach at the Nanjing-Johns Hopkins Center, echoes others when he admits that the underlying motivation that takes most Americans to China as teachers, whether in Nanjing or in another city, has little to do with teaching. "The motivation to teach in China," he says, "is still the dream of seeing China."

Several of those teaching in China, including Jason, Mark, Michelle, Ian, and Gladys, have trained professionally as English as a second language (ESL) or linguistics instructors. When speaking of their reason for going to China, however, none mentions a commitment to teach in this area as the primary or sometimes even a secondary motivation for entering China. Jason says that he gained his master's degree in ESL out of a desire to live overseas. Teaching seemed the best vehicle to do so and China the best place to be at this time: "There's something about going to China to live; it's exciting. It's an adventure. And few people ever get the opportunity to go." Mark echoes Jason by saying that the only reason he studied ESL in college was to enable him to live abroad. He confides that his major motivation was "to experience this mysterious and intriguing country." Michelle, an Australian who had previously taught ESL in Thailand, argues this position best when she states:

One thing I'll recognize straight away is that it's more selfish on my part. You know, there's none of this idea that I'm going over there [China] to impart knowledge to these people, 'cause that's rubbish. You learn a hundred times more than you ever, ever give them. Teaching ESL is a horse to ride. I knew it was a pretty good way to get a job overseas.

As can be seen from comments of Mao and other Chinese, the fact that a desire to teach in China is tied only loosely to training in ESL is well known by the Chinese.

Ian, a well-traveled Irishman trained in linguistics and ESL, says that although he enjoys teaching, it is not out of any love for those fields that he came to China to teach. It was, he admits, out of curiosity. He says, "I'm getting a bit old to hop around the world, so I decided to try China or Japan for my last big gallivanting around. I got no response from Japan, but here they wanted someone with a linguistics background." Gladys, a professor of linguistics, proves the ideal visiting faculty member from abroad. She is a senior faculty member from a prestigious university, specializing in an area of interest to Chinese language teachers throughout the country. When asked if she went to China because she desired to share her knowledge of a field so important to Chinese teachers, Gladys says that was not why she went. "I went," she explains, "because it was a chance to see China without expense."

Rachel, with a doctorate in Chinese history, entered China as an ESL instructor. Knowing that she wanted to live in China, she pursued a teaching position in the area of ESL and gained employment in Beijing in 1979. She still resides there. Her motivation, she explains, was:

my academic interest in Chinese history. I had a deep interest in China, a desire to know more about the country. The English teaching was incidental and it didn't occur to me that it would be a challenging academic subject. The English teaching was the vehicle. So I came with an interest in learning more about China and in being part of a developing country.

Similar academic interests in Chinese culture motivated Kate and Betty to enter China as ESL instructors, Victor to come as a teacher of translation, Yukio to teach Japanese, and Steve to accept a position teaching American studies. Speaking for many of the foreigners teaching in China, Steve says, "I like being in a place where I learn something new every day."

Several foreigners support the Chinese perception that many foreigners come to China to teach, at least in part, because they cannot find jobs in their own countries. Kate admits, "My job had been eliminated in a special program in my college and I was in a very bad state. I was looking for another job when this happened." Jason applied for the position to teach in China while he was applying for other positions. One of the reasons he came to China, he says, was that "very seriously, it was a job offer." Jim, with a master's degree in journalism and no job offer, went to China to teach English through an arrangement made by his mother, a professor involved in cross-cultural programs with China. His motivation, beyond gainful employment, included the opportunity to publish stories on his experiences upon his return to the United States.

Another motive to teach in China revolves around the high prestige a foreigner attains in China versus that held by the same person in his or her own country. Rachel and Frank, the two foreigners interviewed who have lived in China the longest, point to the high academic, social, and economic status foreigners hold in Beijing. Rachel recounts the story of a fellow foreigner who criticized the Chinese teachers in her department for not working hard. The college leaders immediately met with those teachers, quoted the foreign teacher, and told the Chinese teachers to begin improving themselves. Rachel says, "We really do not know what power our words sometimes carry." Bridget says that this prestige factor is one of the reasons she returned to China after a twenty-year absence. Steve explains the attraction in this fashion:

I move in at the top salary level. I move into the top prestige level at the university. I don't have much committee work. And look at this great apartment. This is the best apartment I've lived in in my whole life. One of the reasons I want to stay here is I don't have to run quite so fast here to be at the top of the heap.

Larry argues that after two years in China, he feels more personally secure than at any other time in his life and is making no plans to return to the United States soon. As one who taught for two years in China, I can attest to the attraction, even seduction, of living at a high prestige level with access to easily gained favors not afforded to most of those around you. Leaving such an environment and re-entering a familiar situation in which one encounters much less esteem and privilege in daily life increases the attraction of entering and staying in China.

One intriguing point to raise here is that many of the same people who comment on the comfort of the prestige and security of China also conform to the Chinese stereotype of men who enter China "to marry a Chinese girl." Both Steve and Larry married Chinese women during their tenure, with Steve saying, "From early childhood I'll have to admit this. I have always believed Chinese women to be the most attractive in the world." Larry says that from his earliest days in Beijing, he sought Chinese female company and has had several "girlfriends" since arriving there; he married the most recent one. Additionally, Rachel is married to a Chinese-American who feels at home in China, and both enjoy the comfort and security of their privileged life-style. While the questions this raises demand further research, it appears that those who most readily recognize and accept the privileges and prestige given foreigners also most readily appreciate intimate social and personal relationships with the Chinese people.

Ruth, Matthew, and Debbie entered China with the primary goal of making contacts and creating an environment that might lead to a greater Christian presence in China. All state this clearly. Their goal is to win people to their religion. Matthew states, "In the past years I had prayed often for the church in China, the Christians in China. I thought if I came here I could be useful to God somehow." All of them feel that they are following in a rich tradition of missionaries in China, although Matthew now admits that after living in China he sees that Chinese Christians must lead their own movement; Westerners have little or no leadership role to play in that country's Christian church. There is no question, however, that at this time several hundreds, perhaps thousands, of Christians teach in China through their motivation to "witness" to the Chinese people. I met several of these teachers while traveling in China and was told by Chinese authorities in one provincial school of scores more whom they had invited for the future.

One other motivation mentioned by foreigners, usually expressed as a secondary one, remains that of helping the Chinese people improve themselves and building better bridges between their nations and China. Jason, agreeing with Shang that some foreigners come out of a sense of improving Chinese academics, says that this is "a time English teaching is needed here and perhaps a difference can be made here." Bridget is motivated in part by this desire to assist China in its academic development. Sally, a politically active "friend" of China during the 1960s and 1970s, says her primary motivation for going to China in 1979 was to improve relations between China and the United States. "For three years," she says, "I felt like an informal diplomat representing my country."

One final motivation of foreigners is mentioned by Ma. Several overseas Chinese and the children and grandchildren of missionaries desire to teach in China in order to discover parts of their family history. Bill, a Canadian-Chinese with many family members still living in China, says of his motivation, "I've always wanted to come back to China. It's a matter of finding roots, really." Steve, an American, is the third generation in his family to live in China. His grandfather was a missionary and teacher in China. As a child, Steve heard stories of China that left lifelong impressions from his father, who was born and educated in China. After his father died, Steve says:

I went through a personal odyssey of twenty years or so in the States looking for my father. And I couldn't find why he was the way he was in the States. And so, I figured it out. His life was here. If I wanted to understand my father better I had to come here.

In many ways, Steve proves the best composite of the foreigner who enters China to teach. This is because within this one person lie several motivations for going to China, most of which can be found in other foreign teachers. He wants to experience more than can be found in his own culture, so he strikes out for China, one of the most intriguing places in the world at this time. He enjoys the prestige of the foreigner in China, and he had hoped that he would meet and marry a Chinese woman. Steve also has roots in China that he yearns to discover. Though not himself a Christian missionary, he understands through his heritage that motivation to enter China. He feels a new sense of mission, however, in helping China to modernize, thus finding another motivation in building bridges between his native culture and that of his father and grandfather. We can see that for most foreigners there exists more than one motivation to enter China as a teacher. For most, there are several motives, with the most popular one remaining the desire to see that great and mysterious land that was closed off to us for such a long period of time. The motivation certainly does not lie in a passion to teach. As Michelle states, teaching is simply the best horse to ride to get there.

INVITED TO MODERNIZE THE COUNTRY: FOREIGN PERCEPTIONS

All of the foreigners interviewed for this study perceive that the desire to modernize is the primary motivation for the Chinese to invite them to China. Steve says, "I really think the Chinese motivation to invite us is to join the twentieth century." Kate agrees, explaining, "There is a feeling of awakening like Rip Van Winkle from a long sleep and discovering we are really behind." Jason, Ian, and Frank perceive that they are in China teaching English because the Chinese need to gain technological knowledge, and they agree with their Chinese hosts that the best way for China to begin this drive is through the teaching of English and other foreign languages. Jason says, "They need English for practical, economic reasons. If friendship ties come out of it, all to the good. But mostly this is a business decision." Bridget, Yukio, and Matthew, all language teachers, agree that the Chinese motivation to invite them lies with the need to have teachers who are native speakers and who can teach from that perspective. Bridget states, "They have to have the skills we bring for development of their modernization."

This motivation causes Kate and Michelle to voice disappointment over their perceived notion that the Chinese invite them only to get exactly what they want and not return anything to the foreigners. Michelle says, "I get the feeling that it's selecting what they like about you and then rejecting what they don't like." Kate says that she was "crushed" when she realized that this was why she was invited to China. She hoped to be part of a joint venture where "we'll expand everybody's horizon." She says she found, however, that the motivation to invite her was only to get certain bits of knowledge about the English language that could help the Chinese in their modernization drive. Expanding horizons was not a consideration in inviting her, she acknowledges sadly.

Agreeing with Mao, Yuan, and Jin from the provincial university in Henan, Matthew, Bridget, Victor, John, and Mark point to the importance of their presence in raising the prestige of the institution in which they teach. John, speaking of the motivation for Nanjing University to engage in the special international relations program with Johns Hopkins University, argues, "The motivation for Nanjing University was to put Nanjing on the map." For the leaders at this university, he continues, "The presence of the Center is bigger than what goes on there. Nanjing needs the Center more than Hopkins does." Matthew says that this is especially true in his provincial institution. Without foreign teachers in China today, he argues, that school would not be able "to build up the status of the university." Bridget notes that at a foreign language institute like hers the Chinese must maintain their high prestige by having the best-qualified foreign teachers available. Victor and Mark, both in large institutions in urban areas, voice the same opinion, but find their situation somewhat distasteful. Mark says that on his "bad" days in China, he thinks:

The motivation is our usefulness as window dressing. They just want to prop us in a corner and say—here we have X number of foreign teachers at our school. This means our foreign teaching is much, much better than the other schools who have fewer teachers.

Victor agrees with this assessment when he comments:

I sometimes think we are frosting on the cake for them. They like having foreigners around who can help them out with linguistics problems. Exactly how much the students profit from it I'm not real sure. But surely the administration and the reputation of the school are elevated by the fact that they have a number of foreign experts.

Taking his argument further, Victor explains that in his view the Chinese want the warm foreign bodies for prestige more than they want to accept the responsibility for taking care of the warm bodies once they are on campus. He continues:

All too often I've heard stories that when you come they pull out the red carpet for you and when you leave they just treat you like dirt. This happened time and time again. Really good people who threw themselves into their teaching. When we first arrived in China the whole staff came out and emptied the truck and moved everything into our apartment. When we left they wouldn't so much as lift a finger. One foreign expert had a bad leg, another [was] near pneumonia. They were done with us and didn't owe us a thing.

While none of the foreigners interviewed ignores the importance of modernization as a motive for the Chinese inviting them, a few emphasize more eclectic perceptions. Larry, a professor of literature, says that the reason he was invited to China was simply to upgrade the academic level of teaching literature. Because he has little interest in the politics or history of China, he says that he has thought little about the modernization drive as motivation to invite him. Lawrence, following his earlier comments that he went to China to learn, transfers his motivations to the Chinese. He states, "I was invited here because my school was willing to receive ideas as well as language." Matthew, motivated by his Christian calling, likewise places his motivations on the Chinese when he says, "I wonder if there are some key people here, knowing we are from a Christian organization, who might be Christians and maybe they worked some things to get us here, because I'm surprised they invited us here knowing this." Even Mark, who previously voiced his "bad day" perception of why he was invited to China, also voices a "good day" perception. He says, "On a good day they really ask our input in how to bring more order to the chaos in the country. They ask us to introduce new ideas and new techniques. And they respect our access to Western knowledge and information." The perception of Chinese motivations takes a personal turn with Steve, the grandson of a missionary to China, when he states that he was invited through the personal intervention of former students of his grandfather. He explains:

They were fulfilling an obligation to my grandfather. I had nine teaching offers in China through this network. In the Chinese system if you do something for me, I'll do something for you. For thirty years they haven't had a chance to do something.

In reviewing the motivations of the Chinese to invite foreign teachers to China, the foreign perceptions show both similarities and differences from those of the Chinese. All agree that the foreign presence is needed to assist China in its modernization drive. Additionally, most agree that the presence of foreigners raises the prestige of the university, whether it is a small provincial university or a major institution in Beijing. Without foreigners, a college or university has little or no prestige.

In other areas, the foreigners perceive none of the motivations mentioned by many Chinese. They do not see themselves being invited so that they can act as a bridge for their Chinese colleagues and institution after they leave. It is not that they are unwilling to perform this service. It is simply that they do not perceive this as one of the reasons they might be invited. Another difference is that most foreigners going to China are unaware of the shortage of qualified teachers there, so they do not fully appreciate their role as "gap fillers" during this period so soon after the Cultural Revolution. The only foreigner to comment on this is Steve, who is a student of Chinese culture and more familiar with Chinese history than most foreign teachers in China.

It is also interesting to note that several foreigners believe that their invitation to China has little or nothing to do with the Chinese desire to promote friendship and international understanding. This is in contrast to expressions of Cai and Ruan, who say that this is an important Chinese motivation. As Jason comments, if warm relations follow that is fine, but it seems to him that the Chinese place little importance on such a motivation.

In the final analysis, it appears that most foreign teachers in China believe that they were invited primarily to speed up the modernization drive, to play the role of just another machine to move China forward. While some say they were invited to play more creative roles, the majority see their hosts using them to their own benefit during this historic period. Larry, reflecting on this question, states, "Chinese teachers have told me that as more Chinese become qualified, they'll phase us out. There is no long-range goal to assimilate us into their educational system."

Chapter 6

The Future

KEEP THE DOOR OPEN AND INVITE MORE SCHOLARS: CHINESE PERCEPTIONS

When reflecting on the future, Chinese predict that foreigners will continue to play an important role in their higher education system, at least in the near future. Most anticipate that the future of foreign involvement in China's colleges and universities will be at a higher level than that found now, and they predict that the relationship will be more equal in substance. Jin, president of a provincial university, states that over the next few years more scholars possessing doctorates, in contrast to the current ESL teachers, will be invited to his school. He hopes to bring scientists, preferably overseas Chinese who speak Chinese as well as English, to lecture in their fields. Over the long term, he hopes his science students will learn enough English to attend lectures given by Western scholars who do not speak Chinese. He also sees foreigners visiting his campus to engage in joint research projects, with the language barrier falling year by year. Reflecting her president's optimistic view, senior student He states proudly that after China has caught up with the rest of the world, "perhaps China will send some of her scholars to help foreigners."

Mao, Zhu, and Yi, all Communist party leaders in their provincial university, see the day in the future when the relatively low-level foreign language teachers they invite now will disappear and teachers in specialities like literature, linguistics, history, and science will arrive. Zhu looks forward to the day when "world prestigious professors" will bring "new fresh air" to their campus. To attract such world-class scholars, they admit, the economy of the country must improve and the benefits must filter down to isolated institutions such as theirs. Yang, He, Cai, and Lan, teachers and students in this school, also desire more prestigious foreign teachers. They sense, however, that in a provincial institution like theirs this remains unlikely. Accepting this, but still grateful for the foreign teachers she has, He says, "In the short term the numbers will increase. The old reasons for needing foreign teachers will exist for some time. We will still need native speakers."

Zeng, chairman of the foreign language department at her Beijing institution, and Ye, vice-president of another Beijing institution, have specific plans for the future involvement of foreigners in their schools. Zeng says that her goals include inviting foreigners to her program as consultants and, like Jin, engaging them in joint research projects. Ye says that in the science fields, the future emphasis rests with short-term contributions in specific fields. His school is about to embark on the first such activity. Ye states, "We invited an environmentalist to teach in our newly formed Environment Protection Institute. He will teach in English and be interpreted into Chinese." In the area of language, Ye hopes to invite teachers for up to five years at a time. Until now, no language teacher has stayed longer than thirty months. Like Jin in Henan, Ye looks forward to the time when the relationship between his university and those in the West rises closer to equality. One way to accomplish this, he says, is for his institution to offer master's and doctoral degrees to foreign students. Currently, foreign students cannot earn a degree at his institution, although some reside on campus as they work on their theses or dissertations.

While bringing in scholars of higher status, the Chinese also want to insure that those invited arrive with new and varied backgrounds. Shang at the Foreign Studies University looks for more specialization in American studies. Shi at Beijing University hopes to see the numbers of foreigners increase in the politically sensitive disciplines of the social sciences. Like Ye, he sees many of the future foreign teachers holding high academic status and staying for shorter periods of time. Ma and Ruan from the Education Commission also look forward to more exchange of high-level scholars in new and varied fields and, like Ye and Shi, anticipate that these exchanges will be short-term engagements. The reason, they say, reflects financial considerations. Ma notes, "The material incentives are just too weak to attract high-level scholars for long-term periods." The Chinese remain optimistic about their future, but they recognize the problems involved in bringing the higher caliber of educator to their campus for long periods of time.

Some Chinese expect that the long-range future will find fewer foreigners teaching in Chinese colleges and universities. Geng, Shi, Dong, Zen, Ling, Shang, and others comment that the reasons for this are two-fold. First, foreigners have taught in these Chinese institutions for several years, so many of the young Chinese teachers have reached a higher level of competency as a result of their teaching. Chinese can now take over some of the lower-level courses previously taught by the foreigners. Second, over the next several years thousands of Chinese students will be returning to China after several years of studying abroad. Their contribution is expected to be substantial as they take over the role played by many of the lower-level foreign teachers now found in China. This prediction has a historical precedent in the role played by Japanese educators in the early part of the twentieth century.

When discussing the possibilities of a long-range future for foreigners in China's colleges and universities, Chinese educators give mixed signals. On the one hand, there are those at high levels of responsibility, like Jin, Ruan, and Ma, who insist that the future is secure and the relationship will grow. Ma argues, "This is a program of longevity, even though this will alter our system to a degree." Ruan, in a vehement defense of the present open-door policy, states:

This is a long-standing policy. It is not a matter of expediency. We will not close the door when we have gained so much. Some leaders may look at it as expedient, but too many Chinese have too much experience with foreigners both here and abroad to change people's minds to the old way of thinking.

Other Chinese, more skeptical of the intentions of their own leadership and all too familiar with the changes in policy of the recent past, reflect a different view of the long-range future involvement of foreigners in their institutions. Mao, when asked what shape he though the long-range future of this relationship might take, initially responded with laughter. "China," he shares, "is too unpredictable. After Deng Xiaoping who knows who will be the leader? And what will be the policy?" Yang says, "I seldom predict the future now. Things always change in China. I just look at what's now." Cai, Xia, Ye, Shang, and others echo these concerns about the direction and stability of the political situation and the quality of the future political leadership. They join others in their desire for further involvement, but they do not join Ma and Ruan in their certainty in its development.

The future role of foreigners in China's higher education system rests, as it always has, on the political decisions made at the highest levels of government. Some, having felt the sting of changing political tides before, offer no guarantees of future developments. They say what they think will develop if the trend continues, but add that they are not certain if the trend will in fact stay on course. Others, mostly at high levels of authority in the educational structure, assert that China has now entered a new age. The fact that so many openly express their views of the future to a foreigner goes some distance in making this claim valid. Whether it is a radically new day that allows China's door to remain open or to open even wider, however, remains to be seen. Those are the mixed signals received from the Chinese. Such signals emanating from Beijing after the supression of the spring movement for democracy in 1989 shows this clearly. The government expresses its desire to keep the door open, but at the same time cancels newly signed contracts that would bring in Peace Corps teachers of English and criticizes foreign teachers for interference in Chinese affairs. Skepticism appears to be the logical view of the future.

WATCHING THE SWINGING DOOR:
FOREIGN PERCEPTIONS

Most foreign teachers feel that the number of foreigners involved in Chinese colleges and universities will change little over the next few years. Some think the numbers will increase. Agreeing with many of their Chinese colleagues, Steve, Larry, Bridget, Victor, Jason, Matthew, and others see that China's drive for modernization depends too much on foreign knowledge at this time to decrease the numbers of foreign teachers. Steve says that over the short term, he and other foreigners will "continue putting our thumbs in the dike." The knowledge gap, he says, especially in areas such as the sciences and technology, demands so much attention that the Chinese cannot do without foreigners if they wish to continue speeding up their modernization drive. This also holds true, he says, for professional fields like law and medicine. Larry envisions little change either, especially in the provinces. There, he says, they will continue to invite as many foreign teachers as they can, until "they join the twentieth century." Victor argues, "I think the status quo will probably go on for a number of years to come until they feel that they don't need them anymore. But I feel they still feel they need foreign experts here. They still serve a good purpose."

While the numbers may stay the same or increase slightly, Mark, Rachel, Bridget, and others see the actual role changing in most schools. Mark sees more teacher training led by foreigners, while Rachel foresees even more foreign teachers being brought in to teach at the graduate level. Agreeing with Geng and other Chinese, Rachel states, "The Chinese are developing some really good, strong Chinese native speakers who are fluent in English and are very good teachers." These students, she continues, are trained by foreign teachers in China or return from study abroad. Bridget expects that, in the near future, some of her students will go abroad and then return to China more knowledgeable about new teaching methods and new laboratory equipment available for teaching foreign languages. Although her preference remains that foreigners should teach lower-level language classes, she sees the returning Chinese being assigned to these lower-level classes and the foreigners moving into the specialized areas at the graduate level. Frank, who has seen firsthand the use of foreign teachers through decades of change, agrees with Bridget in both her desire and her prediction of what will actually happen. No matter what the role, however, he holds to the view that if China is to develop, especially in language study, it must invite foreigners. He says, "To put something across in a foreign language with understanding is hellishly difficult, and they've got a long way to go, so I think there will be a future for the foreigners in China in the field of language."

One way the role may change in the short term relates to China's new freedom to branch out in entrepreneurial endeavors. Ian, sitting in a province, says that in the future, foreign teachers may moonlight by giving private English lessons, as ESL teachers do in most other countries. Currently, he says, his contract forbids such activity. Victor, in Beijing coordinating a language program for American students, says that this is already taking place there, as native English-speaking teachers and exchange students are enticed to make extra money on the side. He says:

We have this one old guy who is constantly pestering us to have [American exchange] students leave the school and teach. Now these kind of [private] schools are rampant in Taiwan. They are all over the place, and the entrepreneurs who run these are making a lot of money. Well, this guy's doing exactly what his brothers have been doing in Taiwan for years. . . . I would say this is another thing that's going to develop rapidly.

In terms of the long-range future, most foreigners agree with Mao and stress China's unpredictable history with foreigners. Rachel states:

When we came in 1979, I thought we had about five years before the door would swing shut. I thought it was going to swing shut in 1983 with the spiritual pollution campaign. But that stopped in a hurry. I think my guess is the next twelve months are going to be very crucial in determining what the role of the foreign expert is going to be. Changes in leadership, changes in emphasis among the leadership toward foreigners can go either way and I think it's in the balance right now. . . . Those of us who know Chinese history know how often the door has swung shut after it has swung open.

Ian agrees, stating, "There is no long term in China. The political situation can change and foreign friend can become foreign devil again."

Betty, Sally, and Ruth agree with this; each expects periodic shifts in the numbers of educators entering China and the freedom allowed them in teaching and interacting with the Chinese people. Betty calls this China's "loosening and tightening, loosening and tightening." In this way, teachers prove no different from all other foreigners, as China at all levels responds to what Sally calls "the fluctuating political currents found on the national level." While expressing confidence in the short-term involvement of foreigners in China's colleges and universities, Ruth says she fears that China will either open up more to Western ideas and educators as a long-range policy, or else will shut down completely. "Something," she says, "will give one way or another."

Steve, a foreign educator who is also a student of Chinese history, ventures a look into the long-range future with these words: "The long term? We're going to be phased out." This will happen, he says, in all areas except language instruction, where the native speaker's ability will always be needed. He continues:

The primary reason to phase out foreigners is because there are still leaders around in China who fought the urban bourgeois elements who had formed a coalition with Western elements to oppress the overwhelming majority of the Chinese people. We represent half of that coalition because we're the foreigners. As we formulate relations with younger Chinese students and scholars, it is going to look to them like the people who went out into the streets in December [student demonstrations of 1986] are going to be that urban bourgeois liberal class that's going to get its ideological alliances not from Marx or Mao, but from de Tocqueville and Locke and so on.

Making this phasing out of foreigners practically possible, Steve says, are the numbers of scholars returning from abroad who will hold Western-granted doctorates. In the nation's leaders' eyes, these returning scholars prove as well trained as the foreigners and infinitely less expensive to maintain.

The future role of foreigners in Chinese colleges and universities can be viewed from the short term and the long term. In the short term, most foreigners agree with many of the Chinese interviewed and think that a foreign presence will continue. There remains too much knowledge to gain from the West to think of breaking off this relationship at this time. The numbers will remain about the same, or may increase. The role played, however, will change as narrower disciplines will be required by the Chinese as their own knowledge and experience grow. Taking up the slack from the lower-level teaching previously offered by the foreigners will be Chinese teachers who have studied under foreigners either in China or abroad.

About the long term few foreigners speculate authoritatively; one who does voices the opinion that most foreigners will eventually be asked to leave China. Most foreign teachers in China refuse to speculate about long-term foreign involvement in China's colleges and universities without first expressing their uncertainty about Chinese policy holding to its present course. Based on China's past, this appears to be a realistic appraisal of their position. Summing up the opinion that many foreigners hold of their presence in China and the future of this presence, Larry says:

If it was any other country I would say there will be a certain number of foreigners who will stay and become assimilated into the staff and into the city and community they live in. But in this country I have serious doubts if there will be any kind of assimilation by foreigners. . . . If this is true, the long term will probably be pretty much like now, with short-term experts.

Chapter 7

Conclusion

When beginning this look at foreign teachers in post-Mao China, I was confident that the conclusions reached would duplicate in large measure those presented by Spence in his work, *To Change China* (1980). Spence argues that historically the Chinese have invited foreigners into their country to accomplish specific tasks for them, but want them shut out of any meaningful interaction within the Chinese culture. He argues further that foreigners entering China have done so with a sense that they represent a culturally and technologically superior civilization. Accompanying this attitude has been their desire to have the Chinese adopt their standards and world view. The actual conclusions reached here, however, show that Spence's findings prove only partly applicable in this new era of Chinese-foreign relations. On the one hand, China still invites foreigners to carry out narrowly defined tasks; this has changed little from previous generations involved in this relationship. On the other hand, there is convincing evidence that the days when foreigners enter China to change it into their own image are all but over.

It appears as accurate today as in preceding generations that China invites foreigners to its institutions of higher learning for narrowly defined reasons. Foreigners teaching in China are expected to teach not only in the classroom, but also during their free time outside the classroom. Ling says they are to be "exploited" as much as possible, and Sui says that as a student she was told by her leaders to go to the foreigners at any time to ask anything. Use them as much as possible before they are sent home, she was told. Hu argues that contributions outside their role as teacher prove "meaningless" in a Chinese context.

When foreigners enter China hoping to have administrative input, they find disappointment and confusion. Even where administrative roles are shared through joint boards of directors, as at the Yellow River University experiment in Henan, foreigners expecting to have important decision-making power over the programs in China find themselves shut out of any meaningful administrative roles. Even in the role of advisor, most foreigners find their contributions limited or nonexistent, as seen by the frustration of Jason and Kate when they complain that their suggestions are accepted politely but rarely if ever acted upon. This follows Spence's comment in reference to foreigners in China during the late nineteenth and early twentieth centuries. He writes: "Chinese refusal to accept the validity of their goals, and the Chinese rejection of their advice, were met with Western bewilderment or anger" (p. 290).

This narrowly defined role expected of the foreign teacher comes as no surprise when the motivation the Chinese have for inviting them is understood. In all cases, the Chinese involved in this study understand that the reason to invite foreign teachers to China lies in the need to modernize China as quickly as possible. Secondary motivations, such as promoting world peace and learning about foreign culture, prove important but always secondary. When so much remains to be done and so much advancement rides on the knowledge of the foreigners, the Chinese desire to get as much out of foreigners as possible in as short a time as possible. This attitude, coupled with a history of distrust toward foreign involvement in Chinese society, continues the traditional desire to use foreigners in narrow roles while keeping them out of meaningful interaction in the community. Larry expresses this well with his comment that China seems unprepared to assimilate foreigners in any real sense into their community. Such a limited role facilitates what Victor and Steve see as the eventual phasing out of most foreigners in China's institutions of higher learning once the Chinese gain the knowledge they desire.

Exceptions to this limited role for by foreigners can be found. At Beijing's Foreign Studies University, with its history of foreign involvement since before the Communist party victory in 1949, foreigners play what they call a collegial role. Some even act as official advisors to the leadership on matters dealing with school policy, especially as policy relates to curriculum reform. Chinese and foreign teachers at this school agree, however, that this school proves unique even in Beijing. Ruan, a senior-level leader with the Education Commission, says this new era is not just of an "expedient" nature, although he admits that some Chinese leaders view it as such. He says, with Ma, that the tide has turned, and there can be no turning back to the old isolationist period. Foreigners, he argues, are in China to stay. While their role may be limited for a long time to come, they will not be phased out but will continue to make contributions to Chinese modernization and scholarship.

Comments such as those of Ruan and a few other Chinese show signs that this new era may be an important historical turning point in the role foreigners are allowed to play in Chinese institutions of higher learning. A more popularly held opinion comes form Mao, who, when asked what the future role of foreigners will be in China, answered with laughter and then responded that the future of such relationships is too unclear to predict. China changes, he says, too much to venture such a guess. As in other periods in Chinese history, the future of the relationship depends, he says with others, on the quality and direction of the country's leadership.

The second part of Spence's argument proves largely invalid in today's China. Except in a few instances, most foreign teachers enter China showing little interest in bringing a new sense of order or morality to the Chinese people based on a sense of superior Western culture. As seen in the discussion of foreign motivation to enter China, most foreigners are pleased just to have a chance to experience Chinese culture. Michelle admits that her reason for teaching in China is selfish and that for anyone to hint that her reasons are to bring great knowledge or a better cultural perspective on the world to the Chinese is "rubbish."

There are exceptions. Bridget finds fault with Chinese teaching methods and has a sense of mission about imparting new methods. Jason and Kate show great frustration with Chinese decision-making processes and insist on advising the Chinese leadership through their Western-oriented outlook. Both entered China with the idea that at least part of their mission was to explain their own culture to the Chinese so that they might better understand Western ways of thinking. George says part of what he wants to see in China is more of what he calls "humane" interaction with students, a trait he says he and his wife show but which he fails to discern on the part of his Chinese colleagues. The most obvious exception are the Christians, whose primary motivation for entering China is to spread the word of their faith. They engage the Chinese in discussion about their faith less directly than their predecessors from the pre-1949 era did, but their goal remains the same. They prove most like those Spence writes of, who enter China with a sense of superior moral self-righteousness and a desire to make the Chinese more like us. Yet even these modern missionaries admit, as seen through Matthew's comments, that today's China needs a Christianity that is Chinese oriented and led. It was a rare pre-1949 China missionary who admitted to this, as seen through Hume and his Yale-in-China experience of the early twentieth century. It is also true of these new missionaries that they have little interest in changing the Chinese in any other way than in their religious preference. An example is Ruth's comment that she and other foreigners have no right to suggest to the Chinese how they might better operate their colleges and universities. We would not want them to tell us how to change ours, she reasons, so why would we expect them to desire our views on changing their programs?

It is this attitude of respect for Chinese institutions that points to the biggest change in the attitudes of foreign teachers in China from the days before 1949. With the Chinese Communist party victory in 1949 came a renewed self-respect spoken to by Chairman Mao Zedong when he stated at the founding ceremony of the People's Republic of China, "The Chinese people have stood up." Before 1949, foreigners could enter China almost at will. Since 1949, foreigners entering China do so at the invitation of the Chinese themselves. They must follow Chinese law, and their presence is at the pleasure of the government. As one who lived and taught in China for two years, I can attest to the fact that the Chinese people feel a strong sense of self-direction. I can also attest that no foreigner lives long in China without realizing that he or she makes little or no impact on the Chinese people without permission to do so from those same people. In today's China, unlike the days before the Communist victory, the foreigner does what the Chinese want him or her to do, and little else. This point became clear to me one evening when I argued with my Chinese interpreter over the bureaucratic tangles involved in getting a foreign teacher in our school to the hospital. I told him angrily that he and his leaders took too long to make these arrangements. Indignant, he told me that the days of foreigners telling Chinese how to run their business were over and that I and all other foreigners would never have control over their decisions again in China. Furthermore, he argued, he was a member of the Chinese Communist party, which I would never be, and as such he represented the Chinese people in a special capacity. I should never, he insisted, speak to him in such a manner again. The point was made. While as a foreigner I disliked the way he and his superiors made some of their decisions, I realized that in fact I could do practically nothing to influence their behavior.

China has changed since the years when foreigners went there to remake it in their own image and to act in a manner that looked down upon the Chinese. Today in China this fact seems to have impressed itself on the foreigners living there. Thus, Spence's (1980) argument that foreigners go to China consciously to fashion it into their own image proves in the main incorrect, at least in institutions of higher learning. Most go there, as Michelle, Lawrence, and most others state, more to learn than to change.

The official Chinese position on the attitude that Chinese take toward foreigners in their country is expressed by Deng Xiaoping in the 1982 statement referred to earlier. It is worth repeating again. Sounding not unlike officials from the Qing and Nationalists eras, he says:

We will unswervingly follow a policy of opening to the outside world and actively increase exchanges with foreign countries on the basis of mutual equality and benefit. At the same time we will keep a clear head, firmly resist corrosion by decadent ideas from abroad, and never permit bourgeois way of life to spread in our country. (quoted in Hayhoe, 1984, p. 41)

The interviews for this study show that there is no reason to believe Deng's sentiment will not hold sway in the near and probably distant future. It certainly rests on sound historical footing. Foreign teachers will continue to enter China and play the role assigned to them by the Chinese. It is a narrow role, and if they attempt to step outside that role, they will be reminded of their place. Few foreigners will try to change China, as their predecessors of decades ago did, because they know the Chinese people are too strong to tolerate that attitude now.

In the final analysis, one finding in this study emerges that was not antici- pated at first. The Chinese get from the foreigners what they want, through the knowledge needed to modernize, through educational bridges built to foreign universities, and through the prestige gained by individual campuses by having foreigners present. The foreigners, at the same time, get what they want, by being invited to live for an extended period of time in China at little or no expense. Ye says the motivation of the foreigners entering China matters little to the Chinese, as long as they teach well and obey the law. Likewise, the motivations of the Chinese to invite foreign educators prove unimportant to most foreign teachers, as long as they get to see the country and have an exciting China experience. It is this equally opportunis- tic use of the other's offerings that marks the difference between the pre- 1949 era and the present. The days of arrogant foreigners telling the Chi- nese what to do are over. The days of *hu xiang bang zu* [helping each other] or, in some cases, *hu xiang li yong* [using each other] have arrived.

Historical Documents Relating to Foreign Educators in China

INTRODUCTION

Official agreements between Western and Chinese institutions of higher learning date to the early part of the twentieth century. In 1913, Yale University and the Hunan provincial government signed such an agreement. This agreement, in effect until the overthrow of the Nationalist government by the Communist party in 1949, followed several years of unofficial Yale involvement in Hunan. The agreement established, among other things, the respective responsibilities of Yale University and the Hunan government in setting up the Siang-ya (Xiangya) Medical Educational Association. As seen in the document, Yale agreed to build a new hospital and staff it with Western-trained teachers, physicians, and nurses. It also agreed to pay their salaries. The Hunan government agreed to provide a site for the construction of the building, contribute to the building costs, and meet the expenses of the day-to-day operation of the medical school. The agreement stated that a joint board of managers would operate the school, with each side appointing ten members. This board was to govern the school at the highest level.

In 1980, after a thirty-year interruption, Yale University re-established ties with what is now called the Hunan Medical College. This new agreement again sends instructors from Yale to Hunan, but this time the emphasis is on English teachers, with only a few short-term medical scholars sent to teach or conduct research in Hunan. The draft agreement of 1980 proves far less specific than the original agreement of 1913 and emphasizes the need for the medical college to offer English classes as well as medical programs. It calls on Yale University to solicit funding from Siang-ya (Xiangya) graduates residing in the United States and guarantees that Yale faculty will be assisted in their desire to pursue research in the areas of history and social sciences. The difference in the two documents proves striking, as the earlier document is geared almost completely to the advancement of medical training in China, with little or no reciprocal benefit to those affiliated with Yale beyond involvement in the school. The new agreement emphasizes English learning for the Chinese and scholarly benefits to the Yale affiliates.

Since the draft agreement of 1980, Yale University and Hunan Medical College have signed revised agreements. The 1987 agreement differs from the 1980 document in its attention to detail. While continuing to provide English language teachers, it takes care to provide the Yale teachers with as meaningful and protective an experience as possible. It states that the Yale instructors should have "an experience of life in China today as broad as possible . . . inside and outside of the college." Yale agrees to cover the cost of airfare and to provide an annual stipend to the instructors. Hunan Medical College agrees to assign no more than ten to twelve hours of teaching duties to the instructors, "one hour of taping, and one to four hours of office consultation, for a total not to exceed fourteen hours per week for each instructor." This stipulation reflects a concern by Yale that the instructors sent since 1980 have spent an excessive number of hours on instructional duties outside the classroom, which they had not expected and which takes time away from pursuing their own interests in China.

While Yale University paved the way for joint programs between Western and Chinese concerns, other programs followed. One, the Nanjing University-Johns Hopkins University Center for Chinese and American Studies, was established through consecutive agreements signed in 1981 and 1984. The Nanjing-Johns Hopkins agreement of 1984 stipulates that students from China and the United States will attend this school on the campus of Nanjing University, with Chinese students studying under American professors and American students studying under Chinese instructors. As with the 1913 Yale agreement with Hunan province, Nanjing authorities agreed to contribute the land for construction of the Center, with Johns Hopkins providing the capital for the construction. The agreed sum was $1,000,000, with further contributions forthcoming in materials and supplies. As for administration, the 1981 document states that the presidents of each university will meet "regularly" to discuss management experiences and that each designates a co-director to operate the program.

Another program to follow in the Yale tradition is the Yellow River University, which was established through a 1984 agreement signed in Henan province. The Yellow River agreement shows an attempt by a group of independent overseas Chinese to establish a school of graduate study in China. Dr. John Chen of Temple University leads this effort, and his name appears frequently in the agreement as the person most responsible for starting the school. Following in the tradition of the Yale and Nanjing programs, Henan province agreed to donate land for the Yellow River University. It also agreed to provide maintenance for new buildings, including a library, classrooms, laboratories, dormitories, and a grocery. The Americans agreed to provide materials and books for these facilities. Administratively, the Yellow River program followed the pattern of the 1913 Yale agreement by establishing a joint board of directors with seven members appointed by each side.

In addition to agreements between universities and provincial authorities, formal agreements between the central Chinese government and foreign governments have been signed over the years. The 1956 agreement between the Soviet Union and China acknowledged the need to develop direct relations between institutions of higher learning in both countries and committed to the exchange of professors and other intellectuals. In 1978 and 1979, the United States government and the Chinese government signed agreements similar in intent to that signed by the Soviet Union and China in 1956. While these agreements established a wide range of potential programs, it was through these agreements that the Fulbright program entered China, with the commitment that American scholars enter Chinese institutions of higher learning as professors in their chosen fields.

Two final documents presented here provide insight into the environment the independently recruited foreign teacher finds in China. While those entering China through formal programs are covered through the agreements signed by officials representing the Chinese and Western parties, individuals entering China sign a personal contract with their college or university that provides the only agreed-upon conditions for their employment and daily life while in China. The two contracts that follow are examples. The first is the one I signed with Xinxiang Teachers' College in 1979. Because one other foreigner and I arrived as the first Westerners to teach at this school since it was founded in the early 1950s, officials were unfamiliar with Western practices and proved reluctant to give us a contract. They had no experience with contracts or with foreigners. After arriving in February of 1979, I finally received and signed my contract in June of that year.

The second contract presented here is from the same school and was written in 1987. By this time, the school had changed its name to Henan Teachers' University. A study of the two contracts shows the heightened attention to detail that the Chinese have developed over the years of this new era. When I signed my contract, my duties were spelled out only generally, and the document makes only minor mention of the need to follow the laws of the country. The second contract, that of John Leggett, clearly spells out who is to be taught, who will direct his teaching, and for how long a period the teacher is to remain in the classroom. It also shows greater concern for obedience to Chinese law and the need to pay attention to security regulations governing China. Of special concern is the need to keep "state secrets" from leaving China. The 1987 contract also spells out in much greater detail the daily living arrangements for the foreign teacher.

All of the documents included here are important to understanding how

China and the West view each other, as seen in their formal, legal agreements. By studying them alongside the perceptions of those involved in this exchange, we see the roles and motivations of each party in a more complete light.

COMPLETE TEXT OF THE AGREEMENT BETWEEN THE HUNAN GOVERNMENT AND THE YALE MISSION FORMING THE SIANGYA MED. EDUC. ASSOC. (1913)*

The provincial government of Hunan and the Yale Mission hereby form the Siang-ya Medical Educational Association for the cooperative conduct of an up-to-date hospital and a high grade medical school, and enter upon the contract contained in the following twelve clauses:-

Section I

The Siang-ya Medical Educational Association is formed by the Hunan provincial government and the Yale Mission. Its name shall be "The Siang-ya Medical Educational Association." It shall be hereinafter spoken of as "This Educational Association."

Section II

The object of this educational association is to study and make known all the best methods of medical education and practice.

Section III

The methods by which this educational association is to reach its object are as follows:-

A. By erecting in Changsha a most modern and complete hospital for the treatment of disease and a number of branch dispensaries for the treatment of outpatients and emergency cases.

B. By establishing a medical school of high grade which shall prepare medical practitioners of high rank and obviate the necessity for sending students abroad for the study of medicine. The curriculum of this school shall be in all respects equal to the most modern schools abroad.

C. By establishing nursing schools for the training of young men and women in the art of nursing and by establishing as a special department a course in obstetrics available to graduate women nurses.

D. By establishing a department of Pharmacy for instruction in the art of preparing drugs.

E. By appointing special lecturers on Hygiene who shall instruct citizens and

---

*All documents presented in this appendix appear in their original format. For example, abbreviations, punctuation, and capitalizations reflect the original document. Only spelling and grammar have been corrected.

make them familiar with the principles of hygiene and by establishing in the medical school a department of Hygiene for the training of sanitarians.

F. By establishing a laboratory for the study of the causes of disease peculiar to China.

G. Since the physician has a very intimate relationship to the deep springs of human society, therefore teachers secured for this school, in addition to imparting a knowledge of the principles and practice of medicine to their students, must be men that place great emphasis on moral character. Perfect freedom will be allowed as regards the religious beliefs of every person.

Section IV

This educational association is created by the joint action of both parties. Their duties and responsibilities shall be divided as follows:-

A. The responsibilities undertaken by the Yale mission are under three heads:- The Yale Mission agrees-

1. To build a thoroughly complete hospital: to buy for the hospital a site measuring 140,000 sq. ft.: to provide the equipment and instruments required for the hospital at the outset.

2. To secure Western university graduates as teachers and physicians as well as graduate nurses of high rank.

3. To provide the salaries and expenses of these teachers, physicians and graduate nurses.

B. The responsibilities undertaken by the Hunan government are under three heads: -The Hunan government agrees-

1. To provide a site measuring 300,000 sq. ft. for the medical school buildings.

2. To provide $156,000 (mexican) for the medical school building and the students' dormitories: half the sum shall be spent at first, namely $78,000. Of this amount, $30,000 shall be paid to the association within the present year (1913), and the remaining $48,000 within two years.

3. To meet the expenses of a medical school of 200 students, of a school for nurses, of the departments of Hygiene and Pharmacy, and to meet the current expenses of the hospital (i.e., above receipts). These amounts shall be discussed by this educational association each year and a budget shall be prepared in regular order, but the total annual allowance shall not exceed $50,000 (Mexican).

Section V

The control of this association shall be vested in a Board of Managers numbering twenty, ten of which number shall be appointed by the Hunan government and ten by the Yale Mission. All important problems shall be handled by this Board.

After this Board of Managers comes into being, if any one of its members proves lacking in ability or to be hindering the progress of the association, he may, by vote of at least three-quarters of the members present at a meeting of the Board of Managers, be removed from office. The vacancy shall be filled by a further nomination from one party or the other: but his election shall be valid only after the approval of at least three-quarters of the members of the Board.

Section VI

The responsibilities and powers of the Board of Managers shall be as follows:
a) To vote on all co-operative issues
b) To vote on methods of progress for the association
c) To appoint or dismiss all employees of the association
d) To vote on all matters brought up by the hospital staff or the medical school faculty relative to the organization as a whole or to the progress of their particular department
e) To safeguard all moneys and properties belonging to the association
f) To manage and supervise all other matters in connection with this association

Section VII

The Board of Managers shall elect seven of its own number to serve as an Executive Committee, to carry out the votes of the Board and to manage and supervise all matters naturally falling within the scope of such an executive committee. Of the seven, one shall be elected chairman: two shall be secretaries—one Chinese and one American: two shall be treasurers—one Chinese and one American: the secretaries shall have charge of documents and records, and the treasurers shall be custodians of properties and moneys belonging to the association, shall order supplies and solicit subscriptions. The remaining two members of the Committee shall be physicians who shall have charge of purely professional matters. Members of the Executive Committee who do not receive salaries from either party to the contract may receive their expenses from this educational association.

Section VIII

Directly after the signing of this contract this educational association shall begin its activities: but during the two years before the hospital and medical school are completed and the regular work commenced, the special responsibilities and duties of both parties shall be as follows:-
A. The responsibilities assumed by the Yale Mission are under three heads
    1. The present hospital in Si Pai Lou shall be entrusted to the management of this educational association.
    2. The Yale Mission shall at once take steps to secure high grade physicians and men of the first grade as teachers who may begin the study of Chinese so as to be prepared for the opening of the regular medical school in the fourth year of the Republic.
    3. Beginning at the present time, The Yale Mission shall start a preparatory department for the Medical School, the course lasting two years: and an associated school for Nurses: The teachers for these shall be secured by the Yale Mission.
    The responsibilities assumed by the Hunan government are the payments of the annual allowances according to the budget entered on the records of this educational association and proportional to the number of students. Payments shall be made at four stated times during the year, namely, on the first of July, October, January and April. The allowances are for the current expenses of the Medical preparatory school, nurses' schools and hospital upkeep. If there be any surplus it is to be de-

posited in savings bank for the later purchase of supplies for the medical school proper.

Section IX

If after the lapse of time either party, the Hunan government or the Yale Mission, wishes to dissolve the co-operation, this may be brought about after the carrying out of certain preliminary conditions, namely:-

A. The present agreement must continue in force for ten years from the date of formation of the association.

B. Notice of the proposed dissolution must be given one year in advance.

C. All problems then arising must be settled by harmonious conference or referred to arbitrators.

D. All matters requiring arbitration shall be referred to a board of five men, of which number the Hunan government shall appoint two, the Yale Mission two, and the Board of Managers shall elect someone outside the association as a fifth.

E. The hospital shall revert to the Yale Mission: the Medical School to the Hunan government: but any other arrangement may be reached by mutual agreement.

F. If the Yale Mission wishes any ground in addition to the 140,000 sq. ft. purchased by it, such land may be purchased from the government at a price to be determined by the government at a price to be determined by the arbitrators.

Section X

If either the Yale Mission or the Hunan government wishes, outside the limits of this agreement, to conduct another hospital or medical school, or to undertake other medical activities, this is absolutely permissible, and cannot be prevented by limitations due to the existence of this association. The matter of co-operation in such work shall be determined by the Board of Managers.

Section XI

The educational association shall commence the erection of hospital and med. school during the autumn of the present year (1913), so as to prepare for their being opened in the fourth year of the Republic. At that time, since students will have graduated from the medical preparatory course, and since the Chinese study of the teachers will have advanced far enough to permit of their using Chinese in teaching, and since the number of nurses will then be adequate, the building operations and other obligations undertaken by both parties can then proceed simultaneously.

DRAFT AGREEMENT BETWEEN THE HUNAN MEDICAL COLLEGE AND THE YALE-CHINA ASSOCIATION, 10 NOVEMBER 1980

1. The ties between the Yale-China Association and the Hunan Medical College date from 1914, when the Association helped to found the Xiangya Medical College

in Changsha. After an interruption of these ties of nearly thirty years' duration, both sides have agreed to resume contacts and to strengthen cooperation. The Yale-China Association agrees to give active support to the development of medical education, research and treatment at Hunan Medical College.

2. The Yale-China Association has agreed to send two Yale "Bachelors" as English language teachers to Hunan Medical College each year. Each of these Bachelors will remain at the College for a period of two years. Hunan Medical College agrees to provide them with room and board. The Yale-China Association agrees to provide them with their traveling expenses and salaries. The terms of their employment will be stipulated in letters of appointment drawn up by the Yale-China Association, and by contracts drawn up by the Hunan Medical College. The Bachelor teaching program at Hunan Medical College is one of three such programs, the others being located in Wuhan and Hong Kong. These programs are under the direct supervision of the Yale-China Association representative, who is based in Hong Kong. In order to maximize the effectiveness of these programs, interchange of experience among participants in the three programs and contact with the Yale-China Association Representative are necessary. Hunan Medical College agrees to receive visits to the Changsha campus by the Representative and by participants in the Wuhan and Hong Kong programs. Such visits will be at no cost to Hunan Medical College.

3. The Yale-China Association, upon the concurrence of the medical committee of its Board of Trustees, agrees to provide funds for up to four Yale-China Association Medical Exchange Fellowships annually. Up to two fellowships in the amount of $10,000 each will be awarded annually to research scholars from Hunan Medical College. These fellowships are to be used to cover the traveling and living and research expenses of the recipients during the year that they spend at Yale University School of Medicine. Their salaries will continue to be paid by the Hunan Medical College during their term as fellows. Two fellowships in the amount of $2,500 each will be awarded annually to scholars from Yale University School of Medicine and are to be used to cover the traveling expenses of the recipients during the period that they spend at Hunan Medical College conducting research and/or teaching. Their salaries will continue to be paid by Yale University School of Medicine during their term as fellows. Their room and board will be paid for by Hunan Medical College.

4. The Yale-China Association agrees to solicit contributions from graduates of Xiangya Medical College currently residing in the US. These funds are to be used exclusively for the procurement of equipment and research materials for Hunan Medical College. Hunan Medical College agrees to provide Yale-China Association with a prioritized list of the material needed by the College. Equipment and materials will be provided as funds are received by the Yale-China Association. Except under unusual circumstances, the Yale-China Association will cover the costs of shipping the material to Changsha.

5. The Yale-China Association agrees to explore the possibility of awarding a research fellowship to a member of the Foreign Languages Department of Hunan Medical School for English language study in the US.

6. The Yale-China Association extends an invitation to the Hunan Medical College to send a delegation from the College to visit New Haven in April 1981 in conjunction with the Association's 80th anniversary celebration. The Yale-China Asso-

ciation offers to pay for the travel costs and accommodations in the US of the leader of the delegation. The delegation is encouraged to spend two weeks in the US and to visit other medical institutions, in addition to spending time in New Haven and conducting meetings with their colleagues at the Yale University School of Medicine. The Yale-China Association proposes to ask Yale Bachelor Nancy Chapman to accompany the delegation on this trip as their escort-translator.

7. There is an active interest on the part of scholars in the Yale-China Association and at Yale University in historical research and in social scientific investigation of contemporary affairs in Hunan Province. The Hunan Medical School agrees to help facilitate this research by assisting interested scholars to make contact with relevant governmental and academic units in Hunan Province and by assisting in the procuring of materials and the gaining of access to archival collections. Hunan Medical College further agrees to receive one such scholar each year for a period of three to six months and to make available living and office space for the scholar. An appropriate sum, to be determined at the time by mutual agreement, shall be paid to the College for room and board during the period the Scholar is in residence in Hunan. The traveling expenses of these scholars will be separately funded by the Yale-China Association, or by other US funding agencies.

8. Points 2 and 4 of this agreement have already been approved by the appropriate authorities on each side and were implemented on 1 September 1980. The remaining points will be implemented, pending approval by the appropriate authorities on both sides, by 1 September 1981. This agreement will remain in effect for a trial period ending 30 August 1983, at which time it will be reviewed by both sides and renewed, modified or terminated as deemed appropriate by both sides.

AGREEMENT BETWEEN HUNAN MEDICAL COLLEGE AND THE YALE-CHINA ASSOCIATION CONCERNING THE PROGRAM IN ENGLISH LANGUAGE INSTRUCTION, 6 APRIL 1987

I. The ties between the Yale-China Association and the Hunan Medical College date from 1914, when the Association helped to found the Xiangya Medical School in Changsha. After an interruption of these relations of nearly thirty years' duration, both sides agreed in 1979 to resume contacts and to strengthen cooperation, with the understanding the activities would be non-political and non-religious, and that each party would not restrict the other from making agreements with third parties. The Yale-China Association is a non-governmental non-religious organization, the purposes of which include the enhancement of medical education, research and care, and English language instruction at institutions of higher education in China, and the fostering of understanding between the Chinese people and the people of the United States.

II. The purpose of the Yale-China Association programs of English language instruction is three-fold:

A. It is the purpose of the program to assist the Foreign Language Department at Hunan Medical College to enhance the level of English language instruction by providing the teaching services of native speakers of English who are educated in a variety of disciplines at Yale University and who possess at least a Bachelor's degree from that institution.

B. It is the purpose of the program to provide, through a variety of informal contacts outside of the classroom, the opportunity for students, faculty and staff members of the Hunan Medical College to become acquainted with Americans and, through them, to learn about contemporary American science and culture and the American people.

C. It is the purpose of the program to provide the American instructors with an experience of life in China today as broad as possible under current Chinese government regulations through travel, study and the pursuit of extra-curricular interests and activities inside and outside of the College. This experience will increase their understanding of China and its people so that, following their return to the United States, they will be able to help Americans to interpret and better understand contemporary China.

III. Toward the accomplishment of these purposes, the Yale-China Association agrees:

A. To select two candidates each year for a two-year appointment. Candidates will be selected from among the senior class, graduate students and recent graduates of Yale.

B. To prepare them for their work at Hunan Medical College through an orientation program.

C. To cover the cost of international airfare and an annual stipend for the instructors. These costs will be stipulated by the Association on an annual basis and formalized in a letter of appointment for each instructor drawn up by the Association. The current cost to the Association of these items is approximately US $9,000 per instructor per year.

IV. Toward the accomplishment of these purposes, Hunan Medical College agrees:

A. To assume responsibility for assignment of teaching duties to the instructors. These duties will include some combination of ten to twelve hours of classroom teaching, one hour of taping, and one to four hours of office consultation, for a total not to exceed fourteen hours per week for each instructor. In assigning classes to these instructors, first priority will be given to classes of physicians preparing to study in the United States; second priority will be given to classes of English stream medical students. Teaching schedules will be reviewed jointly by a representative of the Foreign Language Department and a representative of the Association staff annually in May. Each year they will receive nine to ten weeks of vacation as stipulated by Chinese government regulations. At the same time, considering their actual needs and assuming they have completed their teaching duties, they will receive an additional two to three weeks of vacation by arranging their work schedules so that they shall receive four weeks of winter vacation and nine weeks of summer vacation.

B. To provide the instructors with housing within the College free of charge. Their housing will not be used for any other purposes during the period of their service at the College; neither will the instructors indiscriminately use their rooms for foreign tourists. The College will provide a monthly stipend *in the amount of Y350* to cover the cost of food and incidental expenses. The College will also supply free medical care on the same basis as is provided to regular staff members of the College.

C. To provide the instructors with a travel stipend based on Chinese government regulations for foreign teachers who do not enjoy the privileges of foreign experts. The College will also assist them in arranging their travel.

D. To provide the instructors with up to six hours of Chinese language instruction per week. Language instruction will be arranged by the College's Foreign Language Department after considering the instructors' opinions and in cooperation with the Foreign Affairs Office. The cost of this instruction will be borne by the Association.

E. To arrange for the shipment of the instructors' personal effects to the United States at the termination of their period of service and to cover the cost of shipment to the port of exit from China.

V. The Yale-China Association and Hunan Medical College agree to maintain the program at its current level of four instructors. Within the period of this agreement, if either side considers it necessary to reduce the number of instructors, it will notify the other side at least nine months in advance.

VI. While they are teaching at Hunan Medical College, the instructors will respect Chinese laws and relevant social customs.

VII. Should an individual instructor choose, for personal reasons, to terminate his or her work at the College, he or she will submit a letter of resignation to the College and to the Association. This letter must be submitted sufficiently early to allow for one month to elapse between receipt of the letter by both institutions and the actual termination of employment.

VIII. The Chinese and English versions of this agreement are equally valid. The period of the agreement is for three years beginning 1 September 1987. It will take effect when approved by the relevant authorities on both sides.

For the Yale-China Association: John Bryan Starr
                                    Executive Director
For the Hunan Medical College   Xu You-heng
                                    President

AN AGREEMENT ON SCHOLARLY EXCHANGES BETWEEN NANJING UNIVERSITY OF THE PEOPLE'S REPUBLIC OF CHINA AND THE JOHNS HOPKINS UNIVERSITY OF THE UNITED STATES OF AMERICA, SEPTEMBER 28, 1981

A delegation led by President Steven Muller from the Johns Hopkins University (JHU) visited Nanjing University (NU) between September 21 and 28, 1981. President Kuang Yaming and other leaders of NU warmly received their American friends from the other side of the Pacific, and had full discussions on scholarly exchanges. Both sides are gratified by the success of this visit.

Both sides agree that, in order to further development in education, science, economy, and culture of the world, and strengthen the friendly relations between the Chinese and American peoples, NU and JHU should take concrete steps to establish the following collaboration according to the principles outlined in the memo signed by President Muller and President Kuang in June/July 1980.

I. Both sides agree that they should establish in Nanjing a permanent academic center to be called "The NU-JHU Center for Chinese and American Studies" (The Center) for the training of advanced professionals. The Center will be a corner-stone for long-term collaboration between NU and JHU to develop further activities of academic exchange according to common needs. The agreement for the establishment of the Center is in the Appendix "An Agreement for the Establishment of the NU-JHU Center for Chinese and American Studies".

II. In the meantime, NU and JHU will carry out exchanges of administrative leaders, faculty, scholars, graduate and undergraduate students according to mutual needs and opportunities. These exchanges will take the following forms:

1. Leaders of the two universities can meet regularly at either one of the universities to exchange management experience. These meetings, when necessary and possible, can be expanded by each side inviting several other universities to participate.

2. The exchange of faculty, scholars, graduate students and undergraduate students: Each university can select people, upon the agreement of the other side, to study or to do research work at the other university. In principle, the international travel expenses will be paid by the sending university or the individual involved. The receiving university will be responsible for the tuition, research expenses, room and board at the local level, and the medical expenses as required by the indigenous medical system. Each university will do its best to help in providing the information, equipment and space needed for research by the visitors.

3. Upon mutual agreement, distinguished professors and scholars of one university can be invited to the other university to pursue teaching, lecturing or research work. In principle, the inviting university will pay for the international travel for long-term visiting scholars, and provide faculty salary and privileges at the inviting university. However, expenses can also be voluntarily paid by the visiting scholars' home university.

4. NU will be glad to offer short elementary Chinese classes for JHU when needed.

III. In order to continuously develop the scholarly collaboration between NU and JHU, the two presidents shall appoint separate liaison for the task. Details shall be decided after discussions by both sides.

IV. The JHU delegation warmly invited NU to send a delegation to visit JHU next spring. NU happily accepted this invitation and decided to visit JHU in March/April 1982.

The above agreement is signed by representatives of NU and JHU on September

28, 1981 at NU. Its Chinese and American versions will be equally valid when signed. It shall be effective after the necessary ratification procedures are completed.

Nanjing University	The Johns Hopkins University
Kuang Yaming, President	Steven Muller, President
(signature)	(signature)
Zhang De, Vice-President	George Packard, Dean of SAIS
(signature)	(signature)
Zu Fuji, Vice-President	Chih-Yung Chien, Professor of Physics
(signature)	(signature)

AN AGREEMENT FOR THE ESTABLISHMENT OF THE NANJING UNIVERSITY-JOHNS HOPKINS UNIVERSITY CENTER FOR CHINESE AND AMERICAN STUDIES, SEPTEMBER 28, 1981

Nanjing University (NU) and the Johns Hopkins University (JHU) agree to collaborate to establish a permanent academic research center in "Nanjing University-Johns Hopkins University Center for Chinese and American Studies" (The Center). The Center will be located at and operated under the auspices of NU, with the partnership participation of JHU. The purpose of the Center is to train advanced professionals. The basic aspects of the Center are as follows:

1. Curriculum

The Center will offer two semesters of seminar courses in Chinese and American language, literature, history, economics, education, society, political science and international relations and law and other topics. Instructions in these subjects on the United States shall be offered to Chinese students in English, and on China to American students in English and Chinese. Chinese faculty will teach the American students and be available as academic advisors to the Chinese students; American faculty will teach the Chinese students and be available as academic advisors to the American students. Curriculum, text material, teaching plans, etc. will be decided by both sides jointly.

2. Students

The Center shall enroll approximately 100 students each year, composed of an approximately equal number of Chinese and Americans. To qualify for admission, students must have completed a degree at the MA level or have experience at an equivalent level, have a working knowledge of English if they are Chinese or Chinese if they are American, and be judged to have outstanding potential. Students will come not only from NU and JHU. NU will have responsibility for the quality of the Chinese students and JHU for that of the American students.

3. Faculty

There shall be a core full-time faculty of six to eight professors from each of the two countries, and each faculty member shall be prepared to conduct seminars at the graduate level. Members of the faculty will not necessarily come only from NU and JHU, but NU will have responsibility for the quality of the Chinese faculty and JHU will have responsibility for the quality of the American faculty. It is intended that faculty appointment shall be for limited duration and that faculty members will change after several years.

4. Administration

The Center shall operate under the supervision of NU, and its day-to-day operation shall be conducted by a Chinese and an American co-director. The co-directors shall be appointed separately by NU and JHU from the faculty members they appointed at the Center. Each co-director shall serve as chairman of the professors from his nation and as the supervisor responsible for the students from his nation. Operation and maintenance of the physical plant, equipment, dormitories, etc. shall be the responsibility of a senior member of NU staff designated by the presidents of NU and JHU. At least once a year the presidents of NU and JHU, or their respective designates, should meet to review the work of the Center.

5. Facilities and Funding

The Center should be housed in its own building or buildings which shall contain high quality instructional facilities such as a reading room and library, auditorium, language laboratory and seminar rooms, as well as faculty offices, social lounge, dining facility and administrative offices. Housing accommodation for about 150 people is also needed for the students, faculty members and visitors. The costs of building construction and purchase of equipment shall be shared equally between NU and JHU, with the details to be worked out. JHU recognizes that NU will require sovereignty over these facilities; and NU recognizes that JHU investment in these facilities will require fair and equitable protection; detailed arrangements to satisfy mutual requirements will be worked out.

Each university shall arrange funding and tuition according to its own procedures for the expenses of faculty and students from its own nation including the national co-director. Lodging and food services will be provided by NU and paid by the students.

6. Additional Purposes

Because the Center will currently represent a unique Chinese-American partnership in higher education and will make available a core faculty of high quality, it may become a place for briefings to official Chinese delegations planning to visit the United States, and official American delegations newly arrived in China, and it may also be a location for special Chinese-American meetings on selected topics, such as higher education. In addition, highly qualified students from China may be selected after completion of their year at the Center for more advanced work in the U.S., and Americans to continue more advanced work in China.

7. Next Steps

NU and JHU now commit themselves to every effort to bring the Center into being as rapidly as possible. Approvals as needed will be secured on each side as well as the necessary funds. The Presidents of NU and JHU will set up a task force to work out the details and other preparations. The co-directors should be appointed for the academic year 1982–1983 and be involved in planning and recruitment of faculty and students. Plans for the required facilities shall be made and implemented as soon as possible. The aim shall be to begin operation in the academic year 1983–1984, and no later than 1984–85.

Nanjing University	The Johns Hopkins University
Kuang Yaming, President	Steven Muller, President
Zhang De, Vice-President	George Packard, Dean of SAIS
Xu Fuji, Vice-President	Chih-Yung Chien, Professor of Physics

MEMORANDUM OF AGREEMENT BETWEEN THE JOHNS HOPKINS UNIVERSITY AND NANJING UNIVERSITY, MAY 25, 1984

At the invitation of President Steven Muller of The Johns Hopkins University, Mr. Ling Yu-xuan, Vice Chairman of the Administrative Council of Nanjing University and three staff visited The Johns Hopkins University from 20 to 27 May, 1984. President Muller and the other leaders of The Johns Hopkins University accorded their Chinese friends from the other side of the Pacific a warm reception, for which the delegation from Nanjing University expressed their heartfelt thanks. With a view to ensuring the smooth progress of the preparatory work of the Center for Chinese and American Studies jointly set up by Nanjing University and The Johns Hopkins University, the two sides held full discussions on the basis of previous agreements in a friendly atmosphere and reached the following agreement. All the matters below represent the full agreement and determination of both parties, although during their execution, they are understandably subject to changes in detail and specifics by mutual agreement.

I. Courses

The two sides decided that the Center will offer the following courses for the 1986–87 academic year:

The courses to be offered by American professors to Chinese students:

Category I: History and Society
  1. Modern American History

2. Culture and Society in America
3. Study of Some Problems in Contemporary American Society

Category II: Economics
  1. Business Management
  2. American Economic Structure
  3. World Economy

Category III: Politics and Government
  1. American Political System and Institutions

Category IV: International Relations and Politics
  1. International Law
  2. Contemporary Theory in International Relations
  3. U.S. Foreign Policy since World War II
  4. U.S. Foreign Policymaking
  5. U.S. Policy Towards China since 1945

The courses to be offered by Chinese professors to American students:

Category I: History
  1. A General Survey of Chinese History from 1840 to 1984

Category II: Economics
  1. Domestic Economy in China
  2. China's External Economy
  3. Chinese National Economy and Population

Category III: Politics and Government
  1. The Constitution of the People's Republic of China
  2. Chinese Government and Politics
  3. Chinese Criminal Law
  4. Mao Tse-tung Political Thought

Category IV: Foreign Policy
  1. Modern and Contemporary Chinese Diplomacy
  2. Foreign Aid
  3. International Communist Movement
  4. China's Policy towards Regions

Category V: Advanced Modern Chinese
Considering the need of some American students to improve their Chinese in preparation for their studies at the Center, Nanjing University is willing to conduct summer Chinese courses for them. The students shall pay for all the costs involved. The Center will organize visits in Nanjing and neighboring regions from time to time in accordance with the needs of the courses. In addition, the Center will invite leading officials from government departments concerned and famous scholars to give lectures at the Center.

The courses for the subsequent years will be decided upon through consultations between the two co-directors.

II. Students and Faculty

According to the agreement of September 28, 1981, the Center shall enroll approximately 100 students each year composed of approximately equal number of Chinese and Americans and there shall be a core full-time faculty of six to eight professors from each of the two countries. The Johns Hopkins University indicated that it might have difficulty recruiting this number of students and that it was not in a position to give at present the exact number of students it could recruit. Nanjing University made it clear that it will recruit 40 students and 6–8 professors. Nanjing University indicated that difficulty will arise if the number of American students and faculty members is too small. Both sides agreed that the goal for the first academic year (1986–87) shall be 40 students from each country and The Johns Hopkins University pledged that there shall not be less than 15 American students. Both sides also agreed that the goal for professors shall be 5–7 from each side and shall not be less than 5. Both sides shall make joint efforts to reach as soon as possible the goal stipulated in the above mentioned agreement. Both sides also agreed that Chinese and American students should be understood as citizens of their respective countries.

III. Credits

The teaching at the Center should be first-class and shall maintain a high standard. To this end, both universities will recruit the best possible faculty from their respective countries to teach at the Center. Nanjing University and The Johns Hopkins University will grant joint credit to the students at the Center. This will undoubtedly contribute to the exchange of scholars and other academic exchanges between China and the United States. Both sides agreed that specific technical problems concerning the joint credits will be dealt with by the two co-directors when they are appointed.

IV. Scholarships

In the spirit of the memorandum signed between Nanjing University and The Johns Hopkins University on December 18, 1983, and in order to attract Chinese and American students of the highest caliber to study at the Center and to satisfy their need for further studies and obtain their doctoral degrees, both sides reaffirmed that each side will select every year from among their 50 students about 5 top students upon their graduation (or 10 percent of the actual number of their students if it is less than 50) for further training. The Johns Hopkins University will help arrange admissions and financial aid for Chinese students' further studies in the United States. Nanjing University will do the same for American students in accordance with the scholarships provided by the Chinese government.

V. Library

Nanjing University and The Johns Hopkins University reached unanimity in their discussions on the importance of books and materials for the Center's library. They hold that by books and materials are meant books, reproductions, newspapers, journals, maps, charts, microfilms and reference books related to the courses intended for the Center and to the fields of study of the Center.

Nanjing University indicated that it will acquire over 10,000 books and 200 journals and newspapers by 1986 when the Center begins operations and that the University's main library will be open to the Center. The Johns Hopkins University will provide the same number of books and journals and newspapers and will begin shipping them this year. Both sides will provide the Center with an additional 2,000 books every year after it begins operations.

With a view to gradually making the Center library a regional center of information on Chinese and American studies and modernizing its management, Nanjing University is willing to make its computer DPS6/48 (Honeywell) available to the Center's library and The Johns Hopkins University is willing to provide the necessary peripheral equipment that matches the above-mentioned computer or an alternate equipment. The Johns Hopkins University will inform Nanjing University before the end of 1984 of the type and specifications of the equipment it will provide and will, if necessary, send an engineer to Nanjing University to discuss the technical details with the people concerned in the Computer Center of Nanjing University.

Besides, The Johns Hopkins University is willing to send a librarian to work in the Center's library at the initial stage of its operation. Nanjing University will provide him/her with free housing.

VI. Opening Expenditures

In order to make the necessary material preparations for the first enrollment of the Center, a sum of U.S. $300,000 will be required to make provision for its teaching facilities and living quarters. The expenditure for teaching facilities, which is estimated to amount to U.S. $240,000, shall be shared equally by Nanjing University and The Johns Hopkins University. The Johns Hopkins University's share of $210,000 will be paid in the form of equipment as a gift.

During the discussions, Nanjing University gave The Johns Hopkins University a list of the equipment proposed for import and The Johns Hopkins University shall inform Nanjing University before September 1985 the types and specifications of the items of equipment it is going to provide and shall make an effort to have them shipped to Shanghai before the end of 1985.

VII. Operating Costs

According to the memorandum signed by the two universities on December 18, 1983, the various maintenance expenditures after the opening of the Center will be shared by both sides. The estimates for the first year will be U.S. $440,000 (the breakdown was presented to The Johns Hopkins University during the discussions). In the first year, the American side will pay U.S. $150,000. The depreciation charge for the teaching and office space is not included. The salaries of the employees will be shared according to the figures agreed upon by the two sides; all the other expenses will be shared equally according to the actual expenditures.

The Center shall keep its own independent accounting and the Center's accountant shall report periodically to the co-directors on the use of the funds.

VIII. Physical Construction

Both sides reaffirmed that physical construction is the prerequisite and the key to the establishment of the Center. Nanjing University has made trememdous [sic] efforts to ensure that the groundbreaking shall take place on September 1, 1984. The 1 million U.S. dollars to be provided by The Johns Hopkins University for the construction of the Center will be paid in accordance with the memorandum signed by the two sides on December 18, 1983. The additional sum to be provided by The Johns Hopkins University as a gift will be used to buy aluminum-alloy steel windows and doors, copper pines, air-conditioners, lifts, a service car, etc. Nanjing University will provide The Johns Hopkins University with the specifications of the above-mentioned items before August, 1984 and the latter will undertake to have them shipped to Shanghai before the end of April, 1985. Both sides have decided that all the preparations shall proceed strictly according to the timetable thus agreed so that the first enrollment shall begin as planned on September 1, 1986.

Signed this 25th day of May, 1984 in Baltimore, Maryland, U.S.A.

THE JOHNS HOPKINS UNIVERSITYNANJING UNIVERSITY

Steven Muller   Ling Yu-xuan

MEMORANDUM (CREATING YELLOW RIVER UNIVERSITY, 1984)

In March, 1984, Dr. John C. Chen, the contact person of the U.S. Preparation Committee for Huanghe University, arrived in Zhengzhou, Henan Province, to meet with Yang Changji and Zheng Xianrong of Henan. They discussed the issues concerning the co-establishment of a multi-disciplinary university. The university will be named "Yellow River University," and the funds shall be contributed by Chinese Americans. During the meeting, Dr. John C. Chen was received by the governor of Henan Province, He Zhubang. Governor He expressed his appreciation for the enthusiasm displayed by Dr. Chen and others who were willing to help and contribute to the course of strengthening China. Governor He also expressed his support for the idea of the co-establishment of Yellow River University.

Following are the preliminary opinions regarding the establishment:

First of all, both parties realized that Yellow River is the cradle of Chinese culture; therefore it was only appropriate to establish Yellow River University in the city of Zhengzhou which is situated on the bank of Yellow River. The establishment of Yellow River University would greatly benefit the scientific and cultural development of Henan Province. The parties were hopeful that Yellow River University would become a unique, multi-disciplinary, and up-to-date higher education institute, including several colleges, a graduate school, and several training centers.

Second, in order to speed up the preparation, a Preparation Committee for Yellow River University would be organized both in America and in China. The parties agreed that Dr. John C. Chen would act as the contact person for the U.S. Preparation Committee, and the Undersecretary of the People's Government of Henan Province, Yang Changji, would be the contact person for the Henan Preparation Committee.

Third, both parties agreed that the Henan Preparation Committee would provide 100 acres of land, of which about 40,000 sq. metres for building construction. This would be the investment of the Henan party. The Henan party would also be responsible for building maintenance and handling of reports and registration regarding the co-establishment of the Yellow River University with the National Education Committee. The U.S. Preparation Committee would be responsible for raising funds that would be needed to construct all the new buildings (including the library, classroom buildings, labs, indoor physical education facilities, dormitories for teachers and students, a supermarket, a kindergarten, an elementary school, a middle school, etc.). The U.S. Preparation Committee would also provide all lab facilities, books and material for the library, etc.

Fourth, both parties recognized the immediate work for both Preparation Committees as follows:

1. Organizing a joint board of directors for Yellow River University immediately, each side recommending seven people, and the annual board meeting to be held in Zhengzhou, Henan and Philadelphia, United States alternately.
2. Discussing in detail the overall plan for Yellow River University, there will be two phases in completing the plan. In five years, the preliminary plan would be finished; in ten years, the overall plan will be completed. Finalizing the scale of the university, facilities for Department and University regulations, as well as the resources for educational funds, etc.
3. Discussing training programs starting from 1984, within three years, twenty people would be selected and sent to the U.S. for training. This would be the primary method for teacher training for the Yellow River University.
4. Trying to start computer, English, and machine maintenance training programs in September, 1984.
5. Trying to establish a graduate school in September, 1985.
6. Actively promoting the cooperation between Yellow River University and other higher educational institutes and encouraging joint departmental operation.
7. Discussing and determining various plans related to the preparation work taking place in the United States and Zhengzhou for 1984.

Fifth, both parties agreed to keep in touch in the process of the preparation, and meet again as soon as possible to discuss several immediate concerns in detail.

U.S. Preparation Committee for Yellow River University Contact Person	Henan Preparation Committee for Yellow River University Contact Person
John C. Chen	Yang Changji
April 1, 1984	April 1, 1984

AGREEMENT BETWEEN THE UNION OF SOVIET SOCIALIST
REPUBLICS AND THE PEOPLE'S REPUBLIC OF CHINA
CONCERNING CULTURAL COOPERATION, SIGNED AT
MOSCOW ON JULY 5, 1956, TYC 1956, V(1958), 152–154.

The government of the People's Republic of China and the government of the
Union of Soviet Socialist Republics

With a view to strengthening still further the close bonds of fraternal friendship
between the peoples of both countries, promoting a rapid development of cultural
construction in both countries, and maintaining the cause of world peace and
human progress,

Profoundly desiring to take all possible steps to strengthen and develop Sino-
Soviet cultural cooperation relations on the basis of the principles of respect for state
sovereignty, noninterference in internal affairs, equality of rights and mutual
benefit,

Have decided to conclude the present Agreement and for this purpose have
appointed as their plenipotentiaries:

The Government of the People's Republic of China:
   Chien Tsun-jui, Deputy Chief of the Second Department of the State Council and
      Deputy Minister of Culture of the People's Republic of China,
The Government of the Union of Soviet Socialist Republics:
   Nikolai Aleksandrovich Mikhailov, Minister of Culture of the Union of Soviet
      Socialist Republics,
Who having exchanged their full powers, found in good and due form, have
agreed as follows:

Article 1. The Contracting Parties shall strengthen and develop cooperation
between the two countries in the spheres of science, technology, education, literature, art, public health, physical culture, journalism, publishing, broadcasting, and
television, and in other cultural spheres.

Article 2. The Contracting Parties have decided:

1. To strengthen direct relations between the scientific research institutions of the
two countries, to exchange the results of scientific research and to provide for
exchanges of visits of scientists and their participating in scientific conferences and
joint scientific research work;

2. To promote and develop direct relations between higher educational institutions and the exchange of pedagogical experience, teaching materials, and publications;

3. To dispatch professors, writers and artists, literary and art organizations, and
workers in the fields of education, public health, journalism, publishing, broadcasting, television, and the cinema to visit and inspect each other's country, to participate in conferences, to give academic lectures and to conduct art performances;

4. To exchange students, graduate students, and teachers who wish to improve
their qualifications;

5. To exchange cultural materials and to assist and to sponsor presentation of
plays and the performance of musical compositions of the other country;

6. To assist and to sponsor exhibitions introducing the economic and cultural achievements of the other country;

7. To assist each other in the translation and publication of the famous political, scientific, literary, and artistic works of the other country;

8. To promote the cooperation between libraries, museums, and publishing, and other social and cultural enterprises of the two countries;

9. To strengthen direct relations and cooperation between the physical culture and sports organizations of the two countries, to exchange visits of athletes and sports teams, and to exchange experience in the sphere of physical culture and sports;

10. To promote cooperation between the journalistic organs of the two countries, and to exchange visits of and furnish assistance to correspondents;

11. To assist the showing in their respective territories of feature, documentary, and science education films produced by the other country.

Article 3. With a view to implementing this agreement, the Contracting Parties shall each year, through diplomatic channels, send representatives jointly to draw up, by October at the latest, the plan executing this agreement the following year.

Article 4. Expenses connected with the implementation of this agreement shall be determined in detail on a basis of equality and mutual benefit during the preparation of the annual plans for cultural cooperation.

Article 5. The present agreement is concluded for a period of five years. If neither of the Contracting Parties gives notice, six months before the expiry of the said period, that it wishes to terminate the agreement, the latter shall automatically be prolonged for a further period of five years and similarly for further periods thereafter.

Article 6. This agreement shall be ratified by the governments of the Contracting Parties and shall enter into force on the date of the exchange of the instruments of ratification. The instruments of ratification shall be exchanged at Peking.

DONE at Moscow on 5 July 1956 in duplicate; in the Chinese and Russian languages, both texts being equally authentic.

For the Government of the   For the Government of the
People's Republic of China: Union of Soviet Socialist
Chien Tsun-jui   Republics:
                                     N. Mikhailov

AGREEMENT BETWEEN THE GOVERNMENT OF THE UNITED STATES OF AMERICA AND THE GOVERNMENT OF THE PEOPLE'S REPUBLIC OF CHINA ON COOPERATION IN SCIENCE AND TECHNOLOGY, JANUARY 31, 1979

The Government of the United States of America and the Government of the People's Republic of China (hereinafter referred to as the Contracting Parties);

Acting in the spirit of the Joint Communique on the Establishment of Diplomatic Relations between the United States of America and the People's of China;

Recognizing that cooperation in the fields of science and technology can promote the well-being and prosperity of both countries;

Affirming that such cooperation can strengthen friendly relations between both countries;

Wishing to establish closer and more regular cooperation between scientific and technical entities and personnel in both countries;

Have agreed as follows:

Article 1

1. The Contracting Parties shall develop cooperation under this Agreement on the basis of equality, reciprocity and mutual benefit.

2. The principal objective of this Agreement is to provide broad opportunities for cooperation in scientific and technological fields of mutual interest, thereby promoting the progress of science and technology for the benefit of both countries and of mankind.

Article 2

Cooperation under this Agreement may be undertaken in the fields of agriculture, energy, space health, environment, earth sciences, engineering, and such other areas of science and technology and their management as may be mutually agreed, as well as educational and scholarly exchange.

Article 3

Cooperation under this Agreement may include:

a. Exchange of scientists, scholars, specialists and students;

b. Exchange of scientific, scholarly, and technological information and documentation;

c. Joint planning and implementation of programs and projects;

d. Joint research, development and testing, and exchange of research results and experience between cooperating entities;

e. Organization of joint courses, conferences and symposia;

f. Other forms of scientific and technological cooperation as may be mutually agreed.

Article 4

Pursuant to the objective of this Agreement, the Contracting Parties shall encourage and facilitate, as appropriate, the development of contacts and cooperation between government agencies, universities of both countries, and the conclusion of accords between such bodies for the conduct of cooperative activities. Both sides will further promote, consistent with such cooperation and where appropriate, mutually beneficial bilateral economic activities.

Article 5
Specific accords implementing this Agreement may cover the subjects of cooperation, procedures to be followed, treatment of intellectual property, funding and other appropriate matters. With respect to funding, costs shall be borne as mutually agreed. All cooperative activities under this Agreement shall be subject to the availability of funds.

Article 6
Cooperative activities under this Agreement shall be subject to the laws and regulations in each country.

Article 7
Each Contracting Party shall, with respect to cooperative activities under this Agreement, use its best efforts to facilitate prompt entry into and exit from its territory of equipment and personnel of the other side, and also to provide access to relevant geographic areas, institutions, data, and materials.

Article 8
Scientific and technological information derived from cooperative activities under this Agreement may be made available, unless otherwise agreed in an implementing accord under Article 5, to the world scientific community through customary channels and in accordance with the normal procedures of the participating entities.

Article 9
Scientists, technical experts, and entities of third countries or international organizations may be invited, upon mutual consent of both sides, to participate in projects and programs being carried out under this Agreement.

Article 10
1. The Contracting Parties shall establish a US-PRC Joint Commission of Scientific and Technological Cooperation, which shall consist of United States and Chinese parts. Each Contracting Party shall designate a co-chairman and its members of the Commission. The Commission shall adopt procedures for its operation, and shall ordinarily meet once a year in the United States and the People's Republic of China alternately.

2. The Joint Commission shall plan and coordinate cooperation in science and technology, and monitor and facilitate such cooperation. The Commission shall also consider proposals for the further development of cooperative activities in specific areas and recommend measure and programs to both sides.

3. To carry out its functions, the Commission may when necessary create temporary or permanent joint subcommittees or working groups.

4. During the period between meetings of the Commission, additions or amendments may be made to already approved cooperative activities, as may be mutually agreed.

5. To assist the Joint Commission, each Contracting Party shall designate an

Executive Agent. The Executive Agent on the United States side shall be the Office of Science and Technology Policy; and on the side of the People's Republic of China, the state Scientific and Technological Commission. The Executive Agents shall collaborate closely to promote proper implementation of all activities and programs. The Executive Agent of each Contracting Party shall be responsible for coordinating the implementation of all activities and programs. The Executive Agent of each Contracting Party shall be responsible for coordinating the implementation of its side of such activities and programs.

Article 11

1. This Agreement shall enter into force upon signature and shall remain in force for five years. It may be modified or extended by mutual agreement of the Parties.

2. The termination of this Agreement shall not affect the validity or duration of any implementing accords made under it.

DONE at Washington this 31st day of January, 1979, in duplication in the English and Chinese languages, both equally authentic.

FOR THE GOVERNMENT OF THE FOR THE GOVERNMENT OF THE
UNITED STATES OF AMERICA: PEOPLE'S REPUBLIC OF CHINA:

Jimmy Carter   Deng Xiaoping

EXCHANGE OF LETTERS

January 31, 1979

His Excellency
Fang Yi
Minister in Charge
The State Scientific and Technological Commission
Beijing
Dear Mr. Minister:

With reference to the Agreement Between the United States of America and the People's Republic of China on Cooperation in Science and Technology, signed in Washington today, it is the understanding of the Government of the United States of America that existing understandings in the fields of education, agriculture and space will become a part of the formal specific accords to be concluded in those fields under Article 5 of the Agreement.

Attached as annexes to this letter are the Understanding on the Exchange of Students and Scholars reached in Washington in October 1978, the Understanding on Agricultural Exchange reached in Beijing in November 1978, and the Understanding on Cooperation in Space Technology reached in Washington in December 1978.

If the Government of the People's Republic of China confirms this understanding and the texts of the understandings annexed hereto, this letter and the letter of confirmation of the People's Republic of China will constitute an agreement relating these fields between our two governments.

Sincerely,
Frank Press
Director, Office of Science and Technology Policy

UNDERSTANDING OF THE EXCHANGE OF STUDENTS AND SCHOLARS BETWEEN THE UNITED STATES OF AMERICA AND THE PEOPLE'S REPUBLIC OF CHINA

An understanding on educational exchanges between the United States and China was reached in Washington, D.C. in October 1978 during discussions between the Chinese education delegation headed by Dr. Chou Pei-yuan, Acting Chairman of the PRC Science and Technology Association, and the U.S. education delegation headed by Dr. Richard C. Atkinson, Director of the National Science Foundation, as follows:

1. Both sides agreed they would pursue a program of educational exchange in accordance with and in implementation of the spirit of the Shanghai Communique;

2. There will be a two-way scientific and scholarly exchange which will provide mutual benefit to both countries;

3. The exchanges will include students, graduate students and visiting scholars for programs of research and study in each country;

4. The two sides exchanged lists of fields in which its students and scholars are interested and lists of institutions where they wish to work. Each side will use its best efforts to fulfill the requests of the other for study and research opportunities. Each side will expeditiously grant visas for such exchanges in accordance with its laws and regulations;

5. The sending side will pay the costs associated with its participants;

6. Both sides may take full advantage of any scholarships which may be offered;

7. Each side will be responsible for the implementation of the program in its territory, including responsibility for providing advice to the other side and relevant information and materials about the universities and research institutions concerned;

8. The two sides agreed that the students and scholars sent by both sides should observe the laws and regulations and respect the customs of the receiving country;

9. The Chinese side indicated it wishes to send a total of 500 to 700 students and scholars in the academic year 1978–1979. The United States side indicated it wishes to send 10 students in its national program in January 1979 and 50 students in its national program by September 1979 as well as such other numbers as the Chinese side is able to receive. Both sides agreed to use their best efforts to implement such programs;

10. To set each year the number of students and scholars to be exchanged and to discuss the progress of the program of exchanges, the two sides will meet when necessary. Consultations on important matters may also be by the governments of the two countries. In addition, both sides will encourage direct contacts between the universities, research institutions, and scholars of their respective countries;

11. Both sides believe that the discussions mark a good beginning and have opened up the prospect of broadened opportunities for exchanges between the two countries in the fields of science, technology and education as relations between them improve. Both sides also believe that such exchanges are conducive to the promotion of friendship and understanding between their two peoples.

January 31, 1979

His Excellency
Dr. Frank Press
Director, Office of Science and Technology Policy
Washington, D.C.
Dear Dr. Press:

With reference to your letter and annexes of this date, I confirm, on behalf of the Government of the People's Republic of China, that the Understanding on the Exchange of Students and Scholars reached in Washington in October 1978, and the Understanding on Cooperation in Space Technology reached in Washington in December 1978, constitute a part of the specific "Agreement Between the United States of America and the People's Republic of China on Cooperation in Science and Technology" concluded today in Washington, D.C.

Attached hereto are the Understanding on the Exchange of Students and Scholars Between the People's Republic of China and the United States of America, the Understanding on Agricultural Exchange Between the People's Republic of China and the United States of America, and the Understanding on Cooperation in Space Technology Between the People's Republic of China and the United States of America.

Accept, Excellency, the renewed assurances of my highest consideration.

Fang Yi
Chairman, The State Scientific
and Technological Commission
The People's Republic of China
January 31, 1979

PROTOCOL BETWEEN THE GOVERNMENT OF THE UNITED STATES OF AMERICA AND THE GOVERNMENT OF THE PEOPLE'S REPUBLIC OF CHINA FOR COOPERATION IN EDUCATIONAL EXCHANGES 1985

The Government of the United States of America and the Government of the People's Republic of China [represented by the United States Information Agency and the State Education Commission of China], hereinafter referred to as "the Parties," recognizing the role of education in furthering progress in both nations and in building understanding between the people of the two countries, subject to the "Agreement on Cooperation in Science and Technology between the Government of the United States of America and the Government of the People's Republic of China," and in accordance with the principles of the "Cultural Agreement between the Government of the United States of America and the Government of the People's Republic of China," have, with a view to promoting educational exchanges, agreed on activities of educational exchanges described in this agreement.

Article I – Guiding Principles

The Parties agree and affirm that the principal objective of this accord is to provide opportunities for cooperation and exchange in educational fields based on equality, reciprocity, and mutual benefit. Recognizing differences in the societies and systems of the two countries, both Parties will initiate educational exchange activities based on their own as well as mutual interests. The receiving side will facilitate and assist in implementing those educational exchange projects to every extent possible to assure that the requests of the sending side for study and research opportunities are met to the extent required in each case in accordance with each country's laws and regulations.

Both Parties will undertake measures to enhance educational exchange objectives. Scholarly data and information derived from activities under this accord may be made available to the world scholarly community through customary channels in accordance with the normal procedures the participating institutions and individuals would follow in their own countries.

Receiving institutions of each country will have final approval of students and scholars applying from the other country. Both Parties will, however, use their best efforts to assure the fulfillment of the principles of this accord.

The Parties further agree that the principles of this accord will be the basis of all official educational exchanges. While recognizing the independence of non-official arrangements, these principles should also be extended, to the degree applicable, to the full range of educational exchanges between the two countries.

The Parties will reach detailed agreement on specific programs through regular exchanges of letters or other instruments on at least an annual basis.

Article II – Official Exchanges of Individuals

The Parties agree on the following categories of official exchanges of individuals:

(A) *Research Scholars*
Each Party may select and sponsor scholars from its own country to engage in research in the other country. Each Party may select and sponsor scholars from the other country to engage in research in its own country. Scholars may be placed in association with educational research or other institutions relevant to the accomplishment of research objectives or may, with the approval of the host government, engage in independent research. Research fields will include the humanities, the social sciences, the natural sciences and the technological sciences.

(B) *Graduate Students*
Each Party may select and sponsor qualified graduates of institutions of higher learning or equivalent of its own country to pursue degree or non-degree graduate programs of study and research in the other country. Each party may select and sponsor qualified graduates of institutions of higher learning or equivalent from the other country to pursue degree or non-degree graduate programs of study and research in its own country. Fields of study will include the humanities, the social sciences, the natural sciences and the technological sciences.

(C) *Teachers and Lecturers*
The Parties agree to encourage and sponsor teachers, lecturers, professors and other qualified people of the institutions of higher learning of their respective countries to teach or to give a series of lectures in the other country. Fields of teaching and lecturing will include the humanities, the social sciences, the natural sciences and the technological sciences.

Article III – Official Delegations and Groups Projects

The Parties agree to exchange delegations and groups in various educational fields which may include participation in joint meetings such as conferences and symposia in the areas of mutual interest as agreed.

Article IV – Exchange of Materials

The Parties agree to encourage and facilitate the exchange of scholarly and other educational materials between educational and research institutions of both countries and individuals. Materials may include books, periodicals, monographs and audio-visual materials.

Article V – Non-official Exchange

The Parties agree to continue to encourage and promote direct educational exchanges and cooperation between educational organizations, universities, colleges, schools, research institutions and individuals of their respective countries. The assistance to these exchanges should be facilitated in accordance with each country's laws and regulations.

Article VI – Financial Provisions

(A) The Parties agree that the expenses for official delegations and groups under the auspices of Article III of this agreement will be as follows: The sending side shall bear the two-way international travel expenses of the delegation or group. The receiving side shall bear the expenses of board and lodging, transportation, and medical care or health and accident insurance when the delegation or group is in its territory; any exception to these provisions shall be determined by written agreement of the Parties.

(B) The Parties agree that the necessary expenses for the official exchange of individuals under the auspices of Article II of this agreement shall be based on the principle that the sending side pays the costs associated with its participants. Exceptions to this principle will be by agreement of the Parties.

(C) The Fulbright and university-to-university affiliation programs, and other designated programs shall share certain costs mutually agreed by the Parties and the participating institutions.

(D) The financial provisions for non-official exchanges shall be determined by the participating institutions, recognizing that public and private institutions of both countries have limited capacity to support educational exchange activities.

(E) The Parties agree that activities under this accord shall be carried out subject to the availability of funds.

Article VII – Executive Agents

(A) The Executive Agent of this agreement on the United States side shall be the United States Information Agency. The Executive Agent of this agreement on the People's Republic of China side shall be the State Education Commission of the People's Republic of China.

(B) Upon signature, this agreement will become a part of the official agreements concluded under Article 5 of the Agreement between the Government of the United States of America and the Government of the People's Republic of China on Cooperation in Science and Technology signed January 31, 1979, extended January 12, 1984.

(C) As agreed by the Executive Agents of the Parties, the representatives of agencies or organizations concerned in both countries will exchange visits for the working out of plans and programs of educational exchange and for discussing progress, problems and matters related to educational exchange projects. These meetings may be held in the United States of America or in the People's Republic of China as agreed.

(D) This agreement will supersede the "Understanding on the Exchange of Students between the United States of America and the People's Republic of China" reached in October 1978, and be the guiding document for educational exchange of the two countries.

This agreement shall enter into force upon signature and remain in force for a five-year period. It may be amended or extended by the written agreement of the two Parties; it may be terminated by either Party by giving six months written notice to the other Party of its intention to terminate.

Done at Washington, this 3rd day of July 1985 in duplicate in the English and Chinese languages, both equally authentic.

Document #8193A

CONTRACT (XINXIANG TEACHERS' COLLEGE)

Xinxiang Teachers' College (hereinafter referred to as the first party) has engaged Mr. Ed Porter (hereinafter referred to as the second party) as a teacher of English, the two parties having in a spirit of friendship entered into the present agreement.

1. The term of service is two years, that is, from February 3, 1979 to February 3, 1981.

2. During his term of service the second party will undertake work of the following character:

a. Training teachers of the Foreign Languages Department

b. Conducting English classes, correcting students' written work, and advising students on term-paper writing and

c. Compiling English teaching materials and undertaking other work connected with the language.

3. The second party will receive a monthly salary of 460 yuan (Chinese currency).

4. Details concerning working hours and concrete tasks will be settled by mutual consultation within the scope mentioned above. The second party undertakes to observe the school regulations and carry out all tasks on schedule and is to see that the results come up to a high standard. The first party welcomes any suggestions put forward by the second party in the course of his work and will take them into favorable consideration in so far as circumstances permit; on the other hand, the second party is to do his work in compliance with the decisions of the first party.

5. Full particulars regarding the treatment that will be accorded the second party are specified in the appended articles.

6. Neither party shall without sufficient cause or reason terminate the contract herein agreed upon before it expires. Should one party seriously violate the terms of the contract, then the other party, after due explanation, would have the right to serve advance notice of contract termination, in which case the present contract ceases to be effective two months after such notice is given.

7. The present contract comes into effect on the first day of the term of service herein stipulated. If either party wishes to renew the contract, the other party shall be notified at least two months before it expires, so that the matter may be settled through mutual consultation. If neither party asks for a renewal, or if one of the parties does not want to renew the contract when such a proposal is made, then the present contract ceases to be effective at its expiration.

8. In the course of its execution, should any questions arise which are not covered by this contract, they should be settled by mutual agreement.

9. The present contract is drawn up in Chinese and English, the two versions being equally valid.

Ed Porter
(For the First Party)

Zhang Chuanrong
(Second Party)

June 11 1979

ANNEX

1. The salary of the second party will be fixed in two steps: First, the two parties will agree upon the pay range after the consultation abroad, and then, after the second party has worked in China for two months, the first party will fix within the said range the amount of a regular salary commensurate with his (her) professional proficiency. His (her) salary starts from his (her) day of arrival in China.

2. After the second party has accepted the offer made under this contract, he (she) will receive a settlement equivalent to one month's salary. If both husband and wife are engaged to work in China, only one of them will receive the settlement, that is, either the husband or the wife, who has the higher pay.

3. Provided that the second party's term of service exceeds one year, he (she) may bring his (her) family to China. (The word family refers throughout to the second party's wife or husband and children under 18.) For their journey to China and back when the contract expires, the traveling expenses (i.e., passage, luggage, transportation, hotel and food expenses) of the second party and his (her) family will be paid by the first party, in accordance with relevant regulations. (Passage: "soft berth" in a sleeper, second-class cabin on a steamer, or ordinary seat on a scheduled passenger plane; luggage: 80 kg. by train for each person and a maximum of 240 kg. for a family of three or more; 24 kg. by air for each person and a maximum of 72 kg. for a family of three or more.)

The route to be taken by the second party and his (her) family both in coming to China and when leaving the country, along with their means of travel, will be specified by the first party. Should the second party prefer a different route or means of travel, he (she) will pay any additional expenses thus incurred.

4. In case of need the second party may apply to the first party for foreign exchange (a) to a total amount not exceeding thirty percent of his (her) salary if his (her) family is in China, and (b) to a total amount not exceeding fifty percent of his (her) salary if his (her) family are not in China. In the latter case, the settlement mentioned above may also be paid in foreign exchange.

5. The second party and his (her) family will, according to regulations, be provided free of charge with furnished quarters with heating and lighting. They will also be provided with restaurant service and enjoy free medical service under the health scheme of China. In addition, the second party will enjoy free transport in going to and from work.

6. The second party whose contract is for more than one year will have a month's vacation in China every year. Both the time and place for the vacation are to be fixed by the first party. (For teacher the vacation is fixed by the school calendar.) The transport fares and accommodation bills, both for the second party and for his (her) family, will be paid by the first party, while all other expenses will be borne by the second party.

If the second party's family are not with him (her) in China, and if his (her) term of service extends over two years or more, he (she) may go on home leave during the vacation after each full year's service. If his (her) family are also in China, the second party, after working for two years under this contract, may spend the vacation in his (her) own country, provided he (she) will continue to work in China for at least another year. In all such cases, the vacation shall not exceed one and a half months, including the time spent on the journey home and back to China. The first party, who specifies the means of transport as well as the route of travel, will pay the passage of the second party alone. All other expenses will be borne by the second party.

During the vacation the second party will receive his (her) regular salary. Should the requirements of his (her) assignment prevent him (her) from taking his (her) vacation, he (she) will later have a number of days off corresponding to the actual working days he (she) has put in during that period or alternatively, receive an extra pay on the basis of his (her) monthly salary as a recompense.

7. In case of illness or on account of private business requiring absence from work, the second party may ask for leave, which will be duly considered by the first part. Sick leaves are to be certified by the doctor. The second party will receive full pay on sick leave. Should the second party find it necessary to go back home on private business, the leave granted will not affect his (her) pay if it does not exceed one month; if it exceeds one month, his (her) pay will be stopped as from the second month of absence. In such cases all traveling expenses will be borne by the second party.

8. On the expiry of the present contract, the second party, prior to his (her) departure from China, will receive a termination allowance the equivalent of one month's salary if he (she) has worked in China for two years; the equivalent of semi-month's salary if he (she) has worked for one year but the second party will receive no termination allowance if he (she) has worked for less than one year.

CONTRACT (HENAN TEACHERS' UNIVERSITY)

Party A (Henan Teachers' University) wishes to engage the services of Party B (Mr. John Leggett) as an English teacher. The two parties, in a spirit of friendly co-operation, agree to sign and comply with this contract.

1. The period of service is fixed for one calendar year(s), commencing on September 1 of 1987 and ending on July 5 of 1988.
2. The duties of Party B are as follows:
   Six working days a week, 14–16 class hours a week.
   The assignments:
   a. Teaching English reading and writing of the third grade, 12 periods a week.
   b. Undertaking other work connected with the language.
3. Requirements for Party B to observe:
   (1) Observing the laws, decrees and relevant regulations of the Chinese government and Party A's work regulations.
   (2) Cooperating actively, working hard to complete on time the assignments stipulated by this contract.
   (3) Accepting the guidelines and arrangements of Party A's teaching organization and teaching according to the teaching outline. Party B may not accept any other work during the duration of this contract without the prior approval of Party A.
   (4) Making suggestions to improve teaching work and submitting a brief summary of the work at the end of each term.
   (5) Undertaking responsibility for keeping China's secrets and following abiding by the security regulations of the PRC.
4. Party A shall pay Party B a monthly salary of one thousand yuan renminbi. Party B shall also be provided with benefits concerning living conditions according to Regulations Concerning the Living Conditions of Foreign Experts Working in Cultural and Educational Establishments attached to this contract.
5. The two parties should abide by this contract. Neither party shall terminate or change this contract without cause prior to the agreed date of expiration. If Party A wishes to terminate the contract, at least 30 days notice must be given, with reasons attached. Party B's salary shall be paid according to the regulations within the time limit of this contract, and include in addition the cost of the economy air ticket(s) and the cost of the luggage for a limited amount according to regulations incurred by Party B and family (refers to the spouse and his/her children who are less than twelve years old approved to come to China simultaneously to live for a long period of time) and shall be paid by Party A.

If Party B wishes to terminate the contract, he/she must hand in a written application 30 days in advance and give reasons. Party A shall cease to pay Party B his/her salary and cease to provide Party B and family with relevant benefits concerning living conditions from the date of its consent to Party B's application. All traveling expenses for Party B's return journey shall be borne by Party B. Party A reserves the right to ask Party B to compensate for the loss caused by its terminating this contract. In the event of either party wishing to terminate this contract the contract shall continue to operate until such time as both parties have agreed that it shall be terminated, except that this clause shall not apply in the circumstance specified in clause 6 below.

6. Under the circumstances listed below Party A reserves the right to terminate this contract.

   (1) When Party B violates one of the regulations stipulated under clause 2 or clause 3, and after having been notified of the violation, continues to do so, Party A reserves the right to terminate this contract, and in these circumstances Party B shall leave the P.R.C. within 30 days of the termination of the contract. The cost of the economy air ticket(s) and the cost of transporting luggage (including that of his/her family) shall be borne by Party B.

   (2) If, because of bad health, Party B has been absent from work for 60 days in succession with a doctor's certificate and is still not able to work, Party A shall arrange for Party B to return to his/her [home country] within 30 days having due regard for Party B's health. The cost of the economy air ticket(s) and the cost of transporting luggage of Party B (and family) shall be paid by Party A.

7. This contract is effective from the date of commencement of service and shall be terminated upon the expiration of the stipulated period of service. It may be extended on 90 days' notice by either party prior to the date of expiration if both parties consent. In such circumstances an extension contract shall be signed.

   After the expiration date of the contract, any further expense incurred by Party B shall be borne by Party B.

8. This contract is written in Chinese and in English, both texts being equally authentic.

Signed on the 1st day of September, 1987.

Party A	Party B
Zhang Binxin	John Leggett

ATTACHED DOCUMENT

Regulations Concerning the Living Conditions of Foreign Experts Working in Cultural and Educational Establishments

1. Salary

   (1) Party A shall fix Party B's salary according to his/her work and professional abilities, with consideration of his/her record of education and experience.

   (2) The regular monthly salary shall be paid from the date of commencement of service to the expiration of the stipulated period of service. If the period of time is less than a full month, the daily salary shall be paid. It is 1/30 of the monthly salary.

   (3) The salary shall be paid by Renminbi. Party B's monthly salary shall be

exchanged for foreign currency under the following conditions: If Party B has not brought his/her spouse or children to China, he/she may apply [to] Party A for a sum not exceeding seventy (70) percent of his/her monthly salary; if Party B has brought his/her dependents (the spouse and his/her children who are less than 12 years old approved to come to China simultaneously to live for a long period of time), he/she may apply for a sum not exceeding fifty (50) percent of his/her monthly salary; if Party B's spouse is also a foreign expert working in China and Party B has not brought his/her children to China, Party B may apply for a sum not exceeding seventy percent of his/her monthly salary. Party B may exchange his/her foreign currency allowance every month or all at once before leaving China.

2. Traveling Expenses
    (1) If the period of service in China is one (1) calendar year or more, Party B may bring his/her spouse and children under 12 approved to come to China simultaneously to live for a long period of time. Party A shall purchase the economy air tickets for Party B and family from the airport of Party B's usual residence or temporary residence at the time of application on coming to the place of work in China, and on return home on expiration of the period of service, and shall not pay the airport service fee. As long as there's CAAC airline, Party A will only provide the ticket of CAAC.

    The dependents of Party B come to China for a visit or travel for a short time, the expenses shall be borne by Party B.

    (2) Party A shall pay the cost of the luggage by air incurred by Party B and family on coming to China and on their return on expiration of the period of service not exceeding twenty-four (24) kilogrammes per person (or seventy-two [72] kilogrammes for a family of more than three). Expenses for packing and delivering luggage between residence and airport in Party B's home country shall be borne by Party B. If Party B wants to have his/her luggage transported all the way by Sea Party A shall pay the cost of the luggage by sea (including the cost from the working place to the seaport) not exceeding one (1) cubic metre per person (or two cubic metres for a family of more than two). Expenses for packing and transporting from Party B's residence to the seaport shall be paid by Party B.

    Party B's expenses for transporting luggage for coming to China shall be reaimbursed [sic] on handing in the tickets up to the stipulated amount.

3. When Party B works in China, Party A shall pay for Party B as follows:
    (1) Housing (with furniture, bed linen, toilet and bath, TV set, refrigerator and heating and temperature-lowering equipment);
    (2) Providing Party B with subsidized medical service in accordance with China's medical system, but expenses incurred in registering, making a house call, fitting false teeth, cleaning teeth, cosmetic surgery, buying spectacles, board expenses in hospital and non-medical tonics shall be borne by Party B.

4. Holidays
    (1) In addition to China's legal holidays Party B is entitled to one (1) month's vacation in China every year. The vacation time of teachers working in colleges and universities shall correspond with the summer or winter vaca-

tions. If Party B has worked for one (1) calendar year, he/she shall be given an additional eight-hundred (800) yuan renminbi vacation allowance. If Party B has worked for less than one (1) year but more than half a year (½ year), he/she is entitled a two (2) week vacation and shall be given half (½) of the stipulated allowance, 400 yuan Renminbi.

The vacation allowance shall not be exchanged for foreign currency.

Party B shall receive his/her salary as usual during vacation.

(2) If Party B comes to China alone and is on a contract of two (2) years, he/she may spend the vacation visiting his/her home country once at the end of each year's work. Party A shall purchase the economy air tickets both ways. As long as there's CAAC Party A will only provide the CAAC tickets. During the period of vacation, Party B shall receive that month's salary as usual, all of which can be exchanged for foreign currency, but shall not receive that year's vacation allowance.

If Party B abandons the vacation visiting his/her home country, Party A shall pay renminbi corresponding with the price of a one-way air ticket, but shall not pay the vacation allowance that year. If the amount is less than eight-hundred yuan (800), Party A shall supply the eight-hundred yuan (800).

5. Sick leave and leave for personal reasons

(1) If Party B is absent from work with a doctor's certificate because of sickness for a period not exceeding sixty (60) days, he/she shall receive his/her salary as usual. If the absence exceeds sixty (60) days and Party A does not perform the right regulated by Article 6, Section 2 of the Contract, that means that when Party A does not terminate the contract, Party B shall receive seventy (70) percent of his/her salary until he/she resumes work or the contract expires.

(2) If Party B asks for leave for personal reasons, he/she should reguest [sic] for Party A's agreement and a deduction in salary shall be made for each day.

6. Termination pay

Termination pay shall be granted Party B on the following scale when Party B finishes the task regulated by the Contract and leaves China at the end of the period of service: half a month's (½ month's) salary for service of one (1) full calendar year. No termination pay shall be granted Party B if he/she works less than one (1) calendar year.

Termination pay may be exchanged for foreign currency.

Questions and Answers Regarding the Work of Foreign Experts

INTRODUCTION

In 1986, a national meeting was held in China to discuss the policies and tasks facing Chinese officials who interact with foreign experts in China. At that meeting, the National Meeting on Work with Foreign Cultural and Educational Experts, Chinese officials considered procedures to deal with hundreds of questions raised by the presence of foreigners in China's schools and institutions. Following that meeting, a document presenting 219 questions and answers appeared. This document, presented in the following pages, remains an internal document not meant for foreign eyes. It outlines the policies that Chinese officials should follow when dealing with foreign experts. While aspects of the information presented can be found in public materials, much of what is contained here is considered secret by the Chinese government. I was able to obtain this document during the heady days of the democracy movement in China, in the spring of 1989, when a friend brought it out through Hong Kong on his way to the United States. To my knowledge, this is the first time this information has been made public.

The document is especially important when placed side by side with the comments of those foreigners and Chinese who contributed to the preceding pages. How do their views correspond to the official government view as seen through the document? How closely do the Chinese interacting with the foreign teachers follow the letter and intent of this document, and how closely do the foreigners conform to the type of behavior the Chinese government wishes them to exhibit? A brief look at some key sections of the document begins to answer these questions.

Chapter one, section eight shows concern for recruiting high-quality foreign experts into the country. This corresponds to the concern voiced in earlier comments by several Chinese and foreigners who lament the poor quality of so many foreign experts. As stated in this section, "It is better to suffer a lack of personnel than to hire indiscriminately; one must not regard candidates as more 'appetizing' merely because one is 'hungry' for foreign experts."

One other place where the perception of the Chinese and foreigners corresponds to the official policy seen in this document concerns the concept of friendship. As foreigners commented, the lack of meaningful friendships with Chinese, as understood in a Western sense, proves difficult for many foreigners to accept. In chapter six, question 119 asks, "What must one pay attention to in making friends with a foreign expert?" The response, in part, reads, "The purpose of befriending a foreign expert is to promote understanding, deepen friendship, ensure cooperative relations, and stimulate the expert's enthusiasm." We see here that the primary reason to befriend foreigners is to ensure good work from them. It is essential to understand the word "friendship" and how it is used. This word, as it appears in Chinese documents and in official language, refers to a general concept of mutual appreciation and respect. It is seen more in terms of friendship between peoples rather than between individual people. The difference is difficult for many foreigners to comprehend, but, as seen in previous pages, it is one that must be dealt with daily. Question 119 further cautions Chinese involved in "friendship" relationships by stating:

As long as the bounds determined by law, regulations, discipline, and socialist morality are not violated and rules of secrecy are not infringed, then everyone's active promotion of and participation in various friendly activities with foreign experts should be encouraged. When one participates in such activities, one must take care to preserve the distinction between internal and external and to avoid revealing state secrets.

In question 120, the relationship built on "friendship" is spelled out clearly when the document states:

emphasis must be placed on encouraging personnel with direct working relationships with experts to take the initiative to actively work at developing friendly relationships with them, in order to promote mutual understanding and friendship, thus benefiting the cooperative working relationship and enabling [people on our side] to learn even more from foreign experts.

As can be seen from these statements, the Chinese government invites foreigners so its citizens can learn as much from them as possible while keeping "secret" information about the country away from them. Most foreign teachers in China discover these Chinese concerns soon after they arrive. Most Chinese never question it. In this instance, the official document and the present reality converge.

The perception appears to diverge from the official policy over the question of foreigners engaged in administrative responsibilities. Chinese and foreigners voicing opinion on this issue state clearly that the foreign teacher in China has no role to play as an administrator. The reasons fall into two categories. Either foreign teachers are not knowledgeable enough about China and/or the leadership style of the Communist party to make a meaningful contribution, or the party leadership would never allow a foreigner to reach such a position in the first place. Chapter four, question 59, however, argues clearly that if a foreigner is deemed talented enough, he or she may be employed in a leadership capacity "with decision making authority, for example as department heads, heads of research institutes, editors-in-chief or executive editors of publishing houses, heads of training centers, etc." They should, the document continues, have authority "commensurate with that of Chinese cadres of the same level." This position, although the official policy on the issue, remains an unlikely scenario in the minds of most Chinese and foreigners in China's institutions of higher learning. In reality, they say, this will not happen. In this case, the official view seems more open than the perception of those engaged in the day-to-day activities of this cross-cultural interaction. Based on my experience in China and my conversations with Chinese and foreigners in China, I conclude that those at the grass roots know that if such a policy ever became practice, the leadership would in fact stifle foreign input from the beginning, thus making the policy a meaningless one.

This document covers every conceivable area of life, from marriage between Chinese and foreigners to the treatment of proselytizing missionaries entering the country under the guise of teachers. It covers contracts, salaries, and vacation periods. It explains how to deal with foreign teachers seeking to engage in quantitative research (they may not) and how to handle foreigners promoting bourgeois political ideology and sexual freedom. It also describes how best to propagandize foreigners while they live in China so that they will present China in a favorable light when they return to their native countries.

Aspects of this document do not deal directly with issues raised in the earlier part of this book. However, studying the document as a whole after viewing the perceptions of both Chinese and foreigners allows us to grasp a deeper understanding of what the Chinese desire out of this relationship, how the official policies correspond to Chinese and foreign perceptions, and, perhaps of most importance, how they view the role of the foreigners populating their institutions.

Questions and Answers Regarding the
Work of Foreign Experts

(Internal Document Including 13 Sections and 219 Articles)

Table of Contents

EXPLANATION OF KEY TERMS (Author's notes)

The following terms, which will be encountered in the text, may require some explanation:

1. *"Work unit." The basic unit of Chinese society, excepting perhaps the family. The following is a useful definition: Everyone is a member of a work unit or residential unit—in many cases the two are the same. An individual's work unit—danwei— defines one's social status; sets the level of income, health care, and old-age pension; provides (in cities) ration coupons for scarce basic commodities; may regulate the purchase of durable consumer goods; authorizes marriage; and even attempts to regulate the conception of children. One's unit often also provides a family-like social support.(Goldstein, 1984, p. 151)*

2. *"Foreign Expert" vs. "Foreign Worker." These are essentially two grades of foreign employees of Chinese organizations, the former being the higher. Experts are hired according to a quota of positions allowed to the individual work unit by the State Foreign Experts' Bureau, a central government organization directly under the powerful State Council, and are paid via a central government plan. Foreign workers are hired and paid by the individual work unit (or rather, by its supervisory government organ).*

3. *"Directly administered municipality." These are provincial-level municipal districts under the direct administration of the central government, much like the District of Columbia in the United States. At present, there are three: Shanghai, Tianjin, and Beijing.*

4. *"[Autonomous] Region." These are nominally autonomous provincial-level regions in which ethnic minorities constitute a significant proportion of the popula-*

tion. At present, there are five: the Guangxi Zhuang A.R., Inner Mongolia, the Ningxia Hui A.R., Tibet or Xizang, and the Xinjiang Uighur A.R.

5. *"Areas open to travel" vs. "areas not open to travel." In fact, in this document, both of these terms indicate areas to which foreigners may travel; in the latter case, however, they must obtain a permit first. In addition to the areas indicated by these terms, there are of course areas to which foreigners are categorically forbidden to go.*

6. *"The Four Modernizations." A guiding target in the development plan of the current leadership. China's achievements are supposed to reach "advanced world levels" by the year 2000 in the following four areas: industry, agriculture, national defense, and science and technology.*

CHAPTER ONE: HIRING

(1) Q: What principles are to be followed by the Chinese side in hiring foreign cultural and educational experts?

A: The policies and tasks set forth at the 1986 National Meeting on Work with Foreign Cultural and Educational Experts were as follows: Actively and methodically recruit foreign cultural and educational experts, seek to stimulate their enthusiasm, allow them fully to display their talents, earnestly learn from their expertise, and take the greatest possible advantage of their presence, thereby strengthening friendship between the Chinese and other peoples and contributing to the construction of China's socialist modernization. The principle whereby foreign cultural and educational experts are to be hired is, then, "active and methodical recruitment."

In order to put this principle into effective practice, we must pay particular attention to the following three points:

1. We must reject outmoded ways of thinking and heighten our awareness. Hiring foreign experts to come to China to help us with our work is an important part of our larger project of importing foreign know-how. In accordance with the spirit of the *Decision of the Central Committee of the CCP and the State Council on Importing Foreign Know-How to Aid in the Construction of the Four Modernizations* (Party Central Document No. 30, 8/24/83), the importation of foreign talent and the hiring of foreign experts must be seen as an important strategic policy for accelerating the construction of the Four Modernizations, as well as an important component part of the policy of opening to the outside world. This perspective reveals the hiring of foreign experts to be a long-term task of considerable significance, and prompts us to create conditions favorable to its execution. The channels [through which experts may be recruited] must be widened, and only the best candidates hired. We may consider as candidates for the placement of foreign experts all academic disciplines in which China ostensibly lacks the expertise demanded by the Four Modernizations.

2. We must seek truth from facts, and take stock of our ability as we proceed. The hiring of foreign cultural and educational experts must accord with the needs of the construction and development of China's cultural/educational, scientific/technological, and economic fields, as well as with [the strictures imposed by] the country's financial strength. Distinctions must be drawn between the essential and the non-essential, the urgent and the less pressing. We must seek truth from facts, and take stock of our ability as we proceed.

3. We must successfully identify and address essentials, guarantee the fulfillment of urgent needs, design an overall plan, and make arrangements in a unified and reasonable fashion. Each work unit employing foreign experts must closely relate its own needs to the development of the overall plan; while keeping the large plan in mind, special emphasis may be placed on the particular needs of the unit. However, redundant employment and disorganized deployment must be scrupulously avoided.

When post-secondary institutions plan to hire foreign experts, they should emphasize the development of key disciplines and new areas of study, as well as those in which there is a lack of qualified personnel, with a view to training a corps of educators to take up the task of teaching these subjects in the future.

(2) Q: What administrative processes are involved in the hiring of foreign cultural and educational experts?

A: Generally stated, there are five steps to the process:

1. A plan for hiring is written up [by the hiring unit], which must then be submitted via the chain of command—through ministries, commissions, and organs directly under the State Council; provincial, regional, and directly administered municipal organs, etc., as appropriate—to the State Foreign Experts' Bureau [hereafter "FEB"] for collection and examination, and finally to the State Council for approval.

2. Channels for recruitment must be opened, and candidates evaluated and selected in accordance with the approved hiring plan.

3. Terms of hire, including the type of work and the amount of compensation, must be discussed with the chosen candidate(s), and the two parties must sign an employment contract.

4. Application must be made to the relevant government organs for a visa for the foreign expert, and a notice of hire must be sent to the requisite departments.

5. All necessary preparations must be made for the arrival of the expert, and a plane ticket for his trip to China must be purchased. Finally, the expert must be greeted upon arrival.

(3) Q: How does one write up and submit the plan for hiring? To what points must particular attention be paid?

A: The first step a work unit must take in hiring foreign cultural and educational experts is application to the higher authorities (ministries, commissions, and educational departments and bureaus directly under the State Council; provincial, regional, and directly administered municipal educational commissions, bureaux of post-secondary education, departments of education). After the application documents have been collected and reviewed by these departments, they will be submitted to the FEB for an overall evaluation and then to the State Council for approval, which is then conveyed back down the chain of command. Beginning in the Seventh Five-Year Plan, the process will be modified so that a single hiring plan is submitted for each five-year period, so that the plan may be coordinated with the five-year plan for national economic and social development. Each five-year plan for the hiring of foreign experts will be divided into individual years for implementation, and may be modified during the process to respond to new developments and meet changing needs. Modifications may be made yearly, but must be submitted to the FEB via the chain of command for review and approval before October of the preceding year.

The plan for hiring should include the following information: areas of expertise, nationalities, and numbers of foreign experts needed; purposes for which they will be needed; date by which they need to arrive in China; length of employment; name of the unit into which they will be hired; reasons why their hire is necessary; etc. The plan should use "man-years" as a unit of calculation; in other words, not only should the number of experts to be hired be taken into account, but also the length of time for which each will be hired. Educational institutions should regard each academic year as a year of employment.

While developing its plan for hiring, each unit must fill out and submit to the higher authorities an Application for Permission to Hire Foreign Experts, clearly stating the purpose of hiring experts, the qualifications that will be required of employees, and the tasks the experts will be expected to carry out. A copy of the application must be filed with the FEB as a basis for comparison with the finished plan.

Standardized formats for both the hiring plan and the Application for Permission have been developed by the FEB. For the former, please see the appendix to FEB Document No. 40, 1986; for the latter, the appendix to FEB Document No. 87, 1987.

(4) Q: Is there a limit to the period for which a foreign cultural/educational expert may be hired?

A: In the past, the period of employment of foreign cultural/educational experts was usually greater than one year, and regulations for their remuneration were made on this basis. However, with the expansion of contacts between China and the outside world, the areas of expertise in which experts have been hired have changed. The number of experts hired for purposes other than work with language has increased, and it is difficult to hire these other types of experts for periods even as long as a year. Moreover, from our point of view, it is not even always necessary. In order to respond to this change, a decision was made at the National Conference on Work with Foreign Cultural and Educational Experts at the end of 1986 to loosen the strictures on the period of employment of foreign experts, so that each unit may follow the dictates of necessity in determining the length of each individual expert's period of employment. In this fashion, the resources that might normally be required to hire a long-term expert may be spread among several short-term experts.

One thing, however, must be made clear: Although the resources originally reserved for the hire of long-term experts may now be used for the hire of short-term experts, such use must be strictly separated from the funding of scholars who come for ordinary visits or exchanges. All foreigners to be included in a hiring plan as short-term experts must engage in educational work or scientific research work; in other words, they must teach at least one or two classes or cooperate in actual research work.

(5) Q: Please explain the sources of funding for the hire of foreign cultural and educational experts.

A: Monies for the hire of foreign cultural and educational experts by units and educational institutions under the ministries, commissions, and organs directly under the State Council are disbursed by the Ministry of Finance according to the quota in the plan approved by the State Council.

Monies for the hire of foreign cultural and educational experts by units and educational institutions belonging to provincial, regional, or directly administered municipal government agencies are disbursed by the local provincial Department of Finance or lower-level Bureau of Finance, again according to the quota in the plan approved by the State Council.

Experts at ordinary post-secondary institutions set up in accordance with procedures of examination and approval established by the State may be funded through the institution's supervisory ministry or commission, or through the local government offices in charge of education.

Responsibility for funding experts at other institutions, such as research institutes, administrative cadre schools, etc., will be assumed by the relevant higher authorities. Plans for hiring filed by local government offices in charge of education must be cosigned by the Ministries of Finance and Foreign Exchange Control and the State Planning Commission, whereupon they must be submitted to the local government for review before being submitted for approval to the State Council.

Media units (i.e., news and publishing organizations), which are enterprises rather than academic institutions, are to meet the cost of hiring experts from a budget entry devoted to same.

(6) Q: How does one prepare and submit a budget for the cost of hiring a foreign cultural/educational expert?

A: The costs involved in hiring a foreign cultural/educational expert include: salary, bonus for the fulfillment of the contract, travel costs (international, domestic, cargo shipping costs), accommodation costs (these are included only when the expert is going to stay at a guesthouse; if he lives in quarters owned by the work unit, only maintenance and utility costs are included), transportation to and from work, medical costs, vacation bonuses, and miscellaneous expenses (such as banquets, bonuses for friendship activities, entertainment and propaganda, souvenirs, gifts, etc.).

(7) Q: At present, what are the primary channels through which foreign experts are hired?

A: The two primary sources at present are recommendation by an organization or evaluation on an individual basis. Recommendations by organizations may be divided into three general types: recommendation through governmental channels, exchange of personnel between schools, or recommendation by other organizations. Individual candidates may be selected from among those who have applied at Chinese embassies and consulates in other countries requesting to work in China, those who have been found by Chinese going abroad who were requested to keep an eye open for talent, those attracted by advertisements placed in the foreign media, those invited by delegations sent abroad expressly for this purpose, those already in China who have written or visited the unit to seek employment, those introduced by friendship associations or individuals, etc.

(8) Q: How does one ensure quality in the employees one hires? In other words, how do we "hold the pass" against unqualified candidates?

A: The following three procedures must be followed during the evaluation and selection process in order to ensure quality in hired foreign personnel:

1. Carefully examine candidates' application materials. The materials supplied by the candidate must include a curriculum vitae, letter(s) of recommendation, and a certificate of health for the candidate and all family members who will be coming to China. In addition, such materials as diplomas, verification of present position, evidence of publications, etc., may be requested of the candidate. Since these materials are the basis upon which candidates will be accepted or rejected, they must be examined and analyzed with great care.

2. Strengthen communication with candidates, and try if possible to arrange interviews. The purpose of exchanging letters with candidates is not only to become better acquainted with them, but also so that the unit and candidate may apprise each other of their current situations, discuss terms of employment, set forth requests or conditions, and all in all lay the groundwork for the successful candidate's arrival and work in China. If there are any parties from the Chinese side abroad who can arrange an interview with candidates, get to know them directly, and even test their abilities, that is even better.

3. Strictly maintain hiring standards—in other words, "hold the pass." It is better to suffer a lack of personnel than to hire indiscriminately; one must not regard candidates as more "appetizing" merely because one is "hungry" for foreign experts. Regardless of the channel whereby a candidate has been introduced, the hiring unit must make its own examination according to standards; introductions made by others must not be lightly accepted. A number of academic institutions have set up academic or administrative committees to carry out the work of selection.

(9) Q: By whom is the *Notice of Hire of a Foreign Cultural/Educational Expert* issued? To what government organs should copies be sent?

A: Once the hiring unit has selected a candidate and has settled the terms of hire with him, and before the expert has arrived in China, the unit must apply to the higher authorities (educational commissions/bureaux of higher education at the provincial, regional, or directly administered municipal level; provincial Departments of Education; or the bureaux of foreign affairs or of education under the various ministries, commissions, and directly administered organs under the State Council) for the issue of a *Notice of Hire of a Foreign Cultural/Educational Expert*. Notices of hire for those experts who have been recommended via exclusive channels under the supervision of the FEB or the State Educational Commission will be issued by the Office of Foreign Affairs of one of these organs. Notices of hire for experts of media and publishing units will be issued by the offices supervising experts' affairs for those units.

Copies of the *Notice of Hire* should be sent to the unit where the expert will be working as well as to the Office of Foreign Affairs; the educational commission (or department or bureau of education); and the Bureaux/Departments of Public Security, Finance, Foreign Exchange Control, Customs, Public Health, and Taxation of the province, region, or directly administered municipality wherein the unit is situated. A copy should also be sent to the FEB.

(10) Q: If a particular unit has a special need, is it possible for that unit to arrange for the hire of foreign cultural/educational experts outside the plan for hiring?

A: Yes, it is possible, but a report must be filed with the FEB, and all funding must be provided by the individual unit.

(11) Q: What points must be observed in corresponding with candidates to discuss the terms of employment?

A: Reply must be decided upon and made as soon as possible to requests and conditions proposed by the candidate after he communicates them; they must not be set aside or ignored. Don't be embarrassed or restrained by considerations of face in responding to questions or discussing conditions proposed by the candidate. Be frank. Be objective, honest, and comprehensive in describing the situation at the unit. When responding to questions, be precise; do not take a stand on or make promises regarding affairs that have not been decided or over which you have no control. As for conditions that have been agreed to, provide guarantees of their fulfillment.

CHAPTER TWO: THE CONTRACT

(12) Q: Why is it necessary to sign a contract with a candidate who is being hired as a foreign expert?

A: A contract is an agreement between parties doing business regarding the definition, alteration, or termination of their mutual rights and obligations.

The chief functions of a contract are as follows: 1) to guarantee the orderly progress of cooperation between the parties; 2) to bind the two parties, so that neither shirks its responsibilities; 3) to protect the rights of both parties against incursion. A contract signed by both parties is legally binding as the basis for cooperation in their mutual venture; both parties must strictly abide by its articles, fulfilling their respective responsibilities and discharging their duties. Should disagreements arise, they must be resolved according to the stipulations of the contract. Therefore, any unit wishing to employ a foreign expert must sign a contract with him.

(13) Q: What basic items should the contract include?

A: A contract for the hire of a foreign expert should usually include the following items:
1. Responsibilities and obligations of the employee;
2. Responsibilities and obligations of the employer;
3. Terms of remuneration and accommodation of the employee;
4. Provisions for arbitration and recourse to law.

(14) Q: Should a preliminary agreement be initialed before the final contract is signed?

A: Usually this is not necessary. After the candidate and the unit get to know about each other and come to an agreement, a responsible person from the employing unit should, after signing, send an official copy of the contract to the candidate, who should then sign and return it. After this, the employer may initiate visa and travel procedures for the expert's arrival. Once the contract has been signed, the employer may assume managerial power over the expert according to its provisions. In the past, many units first initialed an agreement and brought the expert to China for a trial period before signing the actual contract. Although this method had its advantages, it also tended to give rise to problems, such as when the experts, having arrived in China, began to dicker over the terms of remuneration, amount of work, work times, etc., comparing them to those offered by other units and shopping around for the best deal. Some delayed signing interminably, and some even refused to sign outright. From the expert's point of view, not having signed a final agreement can leave him with a feeling of insecurity or suspicion that his job is not guaranteed, that the employer feels no obligation toward him and may even at any time ask him to look for work elsewhere, putting him in a very difficult position. Once the pros and cons have been weighed, it appears best not to initial a preliminary agreement.

(15) Q: When is the best time to sign the contract?

A: If the party to be hired is outside China, then the final contract should be signed before he comes to China. If he is in China, the final contract should be signed before he begins work.

(16) Q: What should be the administrative rank of the person who signs the contract for the Chinese side?

A: Under the usual circumstances, it is sufficient to have the contract for the hire of a foreign cultural/educational expert or a foreign worker signed by an officially responsible person from the governing office of work unit, such as a departmental or section head or the head of the foreign affairs department. It is not necessary to have the person with the highest official responsibility in the unit sign the contract.

(17) Q: What if one party to the contract wishes to alter its terms?

A: When one party wishes to amend the contract, both parties must arrive at complete agreement about the change, and must attest alterations, additions, or deletions in writing. Until the parties have reached agreement about such changes, however, the terms of the original contract will remain in force until the expiration of its term.

(18) Q: What if one party to the contract wishes to terminate the contract before its term is up?

A: Again in this case, the party that wishes to terminate the contract early must obtain the agreement of the other party. Until such agreement is obtained, the terms of the original contract must be upheld.

When the employee proposes early termination of the contract, starting on the day the employer agrees to such termination, the employer will cease to provide for all the employee's expenses, and the employee will be responsible for his own transportation home. The employer may also require the employee to make compensation for losses incurred due to his termination of the contract.

If, due to inability to arrange for work for the employee, the employer proposes early termination of the contract, the employer must pay all wages and bonuses stipulated in the contract (including vacation bonuses and the bonus for completion of the contract), and must also assume the cost of the employee and his family's return home, as well as cargo shipping costs.

(19) Q: Under what circumstances may the employer annul the contract?

A: In general, the employer must not lightly undertake the step of annulling the contract, but in the following situations such action may be taken:

1. The employee commits a serious breach of the laws or decrees of the Chinese government, or of the rules of the workplace;

2. The employee proves not to measure up to his professed qualifications, and is unequal to the tasks outlined in the contract;

3. There is dereliction of duty or malfeasance on the employee's part, precluding fulfillment of the tasks set forth in the contract;

4. The employee, without the agreement of the employer, enters into other employment unrelated to the employer, and does not desist even after being criticized;

5. The employee is unable to recover from illness in a short period of time, in which case the employer should arrange for his return home as soon as possible.

(20) Q: What if one party proposes extension of the term of the contract?

A: Such a proposal must be made at least ninety days before the expiration of the current contract. After negotiating the question, if both parties agree to the extension, a new official contract may be signed.

(21) Q: What if the employee refuses to sign a contract after arriving in China?

A: If, for whatever reason, the employee has not signed a contract before arriving in China, and, having arrived, refuses to sign without legitimate reason, the employer may first work at persuading him to sign. If repeated attempts prove unsuccessful, the employer may inform the employee that refusal to sign a contract will result in implementation of the following measures:

1. Throughout the originally agreed-upon term of employment, the employer will pay only the originally agreed-upon wage, and will not increase it; moreover, the employee will enjoy none of the special privileges usually accorded to foreign experts.

2. The employee will receive neither a vacation bonus nor a bonus for the completion of the contract;

3. At the end of the term of employment, the employer-employee relationship will be terminated; no proposal to extend the term of employment will be entertained.

(22) Q: What if the foreign expert violates the terms of the contract by beginning work at another unit?

A: A foreign expert who comes to China to work must strictly observe the terms of his contract; he must not terminate the contract without authorization and take up employment elsewhere. If the employer encounters such a situation, it must be immediately reported to the higher authorities, and the other employer must be notified of the necessity to take appropriate steps to terminate the unauthorized employment. In serious cases, wherein the employee seriously affects the work of the original unit by his actions and refuses to desist, application may be made to the organs of public security to shorten the term of his residence permit.

CHAPTER THREE: WAGES AND COMPENSATION

(23) Q: What is the chief basis for determining the salary of a foreign cultural/educational expert?

A: Primary considerations in determining the foreign cultural/educational expert's wage include the length of his tenure in the field, the academic degrees he has earned, and his professional title. A moderate salary should be fixed with reference to these qualifications. After the expert has worked two months in China, a salary adjustment may be considered on the basis of his demonstrated level of competence, working ability, attitude towards work, and productivity. Experts whose contracts are extended are usually given a pay raise.

(24) Q: What are the current pay standards for foreign cultural/educational experts?

A: In 1976, the FEB, along with the Ministry of Finance and the State Bureau of Foreign Exchange Control, established the following standards for the monthly salaries of foreign cultural/educational experts, which were then approved by the State Council:

Level One: 2,000–3,500 yuan Renminbi;
Level Two: 1,400–2,000 yuan Renminbi;
Level Three: 900–1,400 yuan Renminbi.

(For details, please see *Table of Standards for the Salaries of Foreign Cultural/Educational Experts.*)

(25) Q: What is the proportion of convertible currency in the salaries of foreign cultural/educational experts?

A: The proportion of convertible currency in the monthly salaries of experts who are unmarried at the time of their arrival in China is 70 percent; of those who bring family members with them when they come, 50 percent; of childless married couples who are both foreign experts, 70 percent.

(26) Q: When may the employee convert the allowable portion of his salary into foreign currency?

A: The employee may make the exchange monthly or may choose to make a single exchange transaction at the end of his contract. In both of these cases, the exchange shall be at the bank rate current at the time of the exchange. Since the rate is subject to fluctuation, in order to avoid trouble it is best to effect the exchange monthly.

(27) Q: How are the international airfares for the expert and his family handled?

A: 1) Foreign cultural/educational experts who are hired for a period of more than one year, as well as their spouses and children under twelve years of age who will live with them throughout their period of employment, will be provided with round-trip economy-class air tickets [to and from their city of residence in their home country] by the shortest possible route.

2) Foreign experts who are hired for half a year, or a single semester, are generally provided only with a one-way international air ticket.

3) Those who sign a special agreement with a given government organ or unit in China will be provided for according to the terms of the agreement.

(28) Q: Who provides for food, lodging, and other expenses incurred by the employee en route to China?

A: In every case, such expenses are the responsibility of the employee.

(29) Q: What if the employee asks to return home via Hong Kong or Moscow?

A: In principle, the employer provides only a single economy-class return air ticket by the shortest route. The employer may agree to the employee's proposal to stop in Hong Kong, Moscow, or elsewhere on his way home as long as the cost does not exceed that of the economy-class return air ticket by the shortest route, in which case the employer will purchase a ticket on a Civil Aviation Administration of China [hereafter "CAAC"] air route for the employee. If the employee wishes to buy his air ticket himself, the employer may adopt the solution now practiced at a number of units and provide the employee with 80 percent of the cost of the shortest-route economy ticket on CAAC in nonconvertible Renminbi funds and allow the employee to take care of his own ticket.

(30) Q: How much of the cost of the employee's cargo shipping does the employer assume?

A: The employer will assume the cost for 24 kilos of air cargo for the employee (or not more than 72 kilos for one family of three or more persons), at the regular air cargo rate.

If the employee works in a coastal city and proposes at the time his contract is up to change from air cargo to sea cargo, the employer will pay for one cubic meter of sea cargo (or not more than two cubic meters for a family of two or more persons), as well as the land transport charge from the place of work to the nearby harbor. The employee will assume all packing charges, as well as any transport charges from the port of destination to the city from which he was hired (or his city of permanent residence). If the employee works in an inland city and asks for his cargo to be sent by sea rather than air, the employer may provide the employee with the currency equivalent of the cost of 24 kilos of air cargo (at the regular rate) and leave the arrangements to the employee.

The air cargo charges incurred by the employee on his way to China to assume his post may be reimbursed, within the limits outlined above, upon his presentation of receipts.

(31) Q: Who assumes the cost for insuring sea cargo at the time the employee leaves China?

A: Usually the employer provides only the cost of shipping. If the cargo must be insured according to regulations, however, then the employer must assume the cost of insurance. If insurance is optional and the employee wishes to insure his cargo, then he shall assume the cost of insurance.

(32) Q: What free services are provided to foreign cultural/educational experts during their stay in China?

A: According to the present practice, the employer provides the foreign cultural/educational expert with free housing, medical benefits, and transportation to and from work.

(33) Q: What sort of lodgings should the employer provide?

A: The employer should provide the employee with lodgings equipped with furniture and with heating and cooling apparatuses, and with toilet and bathing facilities attached. Moreover, the employer should provide a television, a refrigerator, and a washing machine. If possible, every room should have a telephone. Quarters for long-term experts should have a kitchen with stove, but the employee should provide his own cooking utensils and pay for cooking fuel.

(34) Q: What are the regulations concerning the bonus for completion of contract?

A: According to the *Notification on the Implementation of New Rules Governing Contracts and Compensation of Foreign Cultural and Educational Experts* (FEB Document No. 100, 1984), issued by the FEB, the Ministry of Finance, and the State Bureau of Foreign Exchange Control, employers must issue a bonus equal to half a month's salary to employees who work for one year (or academic year) and who fulfill all the terms of their contract. Employees who do not work a full year (or academic year) will not receive the bonus. The entire contract fulfillment bonus will be issued in convertible currency.

The amount of the contract fulfillment bonus should be calculated according to the salary paid the expert in the final month of his contract. If the employee extends his contract, the employer should promptly issue the bonus for the fulfillment of the first contract at that time rather than waiting until the employee has worked a number of years. In this manner, unnecessary trouble may be avoided.

(35) Q: What are the current standards for the salary of foreign workers?

A: In 1976, the FEB, along with the Ministry of Finance and the State Bureau of Foreign Exchange Control, established the following standard for the monthly salaries of foreign workers:

400–800 yuan Renminbi

The salaries of foreign workers whose professional titles, academic degrees, and professional skill are relatively advanced may be fixed according to the standards established for foreign experts; however, they may not enjoy the various other privileges accorded foreign experts.

(36) Q: Are the salaries of foreign workers issued in convertible currency?

A: Because the employment of foreign workers is not an item in the national planning budget, funds for their hire are provided independently by the government organs or units employing them. Because of this, the government has made no regulations concerning the payment of foreign workers in convertible currency.

(37) Q: Do foreign workers receive a contract fulfillment bonus?

A: At present, there are no government documents providing for the payment of such bonuses to foreign workers.

(38) Q: Under what circumstances may a return air ticket be provided to a foreign worker?

A: A return air ticket may usually be provided to those foreign workers who display a good attitude towards their work, who have a high level of skill, and who, in response to the needs of their work unit, extend their contract an additional year or two. For those foreign workers who have displayed a good attitude towards their work and have made significant contributions, but who have real difficulties paying for a ticket home upon fulfillment of their contract, the employing unit may provide a ticket or an appropriate amount of assistance, according to the dictates of the situation. The text of a contract to be signed with a foreign worker, however, should usually contain no provision for a return air ticket; it is better for the work unit to wait until the worker has fulfilled his contract before deciding whether or not to provide one, as this provides more leeway in decision making.

(39) Q: What are "foreign experts invited for a short term"?

A: The following are termed "foreign experts invited for a short term": those whose invitations to China for a period of less than half a year (or a single semester) for purposes of lecturing, directing scientific research, teaching special short-term classes, engaging in non-commercial technological exchange, collaborating on scientific research, or providing consultant services have been approved by the provincial, regional, and directly administered municipal organs, or ministries, commissions, and organs directly under the State Council; and also those whose period of employment is included in the foreign cultural/educational experts' hiring plan approved by the State Council, and whose employment has been approved through the FEB.

(40) Q: How are the salary and living arrangements of foreign experts invited for a short term arranged?

A: According to the provisions of FEB Document No. 146 (1987), *Rules Governing the Salaries and Living Arrangements of Foreign Experts Invited for a Short Term,* drawn up by the FEB, the State Commission on Science and Technology, the State Education Commission, the Ministry of Finance, and the State Bureau of Foreign Exchange Control, the expenses of short-term foreign experts shall be provided for at the rate of from 40 to 75 yuan Renminbi daily; such expenses shall include meals, laundry, and miscellaneous expenses.

The funds provided for the daily expenses of short-term foreign experts are non-convertible. In order to resolve the problem of Foreign Exchange Certificates [hereafter "FEC"] being required of them when they dine, lodge, or use transportation outside the unit or when traveling, the unit which has invited them may apply for a Certificate of Exemption from Payment in FEC [hereafter "white card"] on their behalf.

In special situations, where the short-term expert may need to exchange some of his expense funds for foreign currency, the employing unit may provide part of his funds in FEC from its own reserves; this must not, however, exceed 50 percent of his total funds. Units which also employ regular foreign cultural/educational experts may choose the solution of diverting to the short-term expert some of the quota of convertible currency allocated to them under the hiring plan.

Funds for the lodging, work-related transportation (transportation for other purposes shall be his own responsibility), emergency medical treatment, and work-related post and telecommunication fees (private ones shall be his responsibility) of the short-term expert shall be paid by the inviting unit in Renminbi, as authorized by the *Notification of Authorization for the Hire of a Foreign Expert Invited for a Short Term.*

(41) Q: Is an international air ticket provided for the short-term expert by the inviting unit?

A: In principle, the short-term expert provides his own international travel expenses. However, in special situations, after approval from the higher authorities, a one-way or round-trip economy-class ticket by the shortest route may be provided.

(42) Q: What regulations are there concerning the provision of funds for taking short-term experts on sightseeing trips?

A: As stipulated in the *Rules Governing the Salaries and Living Arrangements of Foreign Experts Invited for a Short Term,* short-term experts may be taken on paid excursions around the area where they are working, but funds are not usually provided for their travel to other parts of China. As for those for whom it is necessary to arrange such travel, their expenses must be strictly managed and kept within the range of 400 to 900 yuan Renminbi.

(43) Q: What provision is made for the expenses of short-term experts' family members?

A: In principle, no funds for the expenses of members of the short-term foreign expert's family are to be provided, except for lodging. In special cases, assistance may be provided by the inviting unit.

(44) Q: What is the standard amount stipulated for the purchase by the inviting unit of mementos or gifts for the short-term foreign expert?

A: The inviting unit may present the short-term expert with a gift, or a memento bearing the name of the unit, with a value of 40 to 60 yuan, depending on the time the expert spent at the unit and the degree of his contribution. In special situations where it is deemed necessary to spend more than this amount, the approval of the higher authorities must be obtained.

(45) Q: Do short-term experts enjoy the discount on domestic air and rail tickets [that other foreign experts do]?

A: No. According to the regulations of CAAC and the Ministry of Railways currently in force, foreign cultural/educational experts must show three pieces of identification—namely, their residence permit, employee identification, and white card—in order to obtain such discounts.

(46) Q: Can non-working members of a foreign expert's family obtain a white card?

A: According to the regulations of the State Bureau of Foreign Exchange Control, all experts, teachers, and technicians of foreign nationality whose hire is part of the [five-year] hiring plan and is approved by provincial, regional, directly administered municipal governments, or municipal governments included in the [five-year] plan, or by commissions and ministries under the State Council; all students of foreign nationality; and all high-level [overseas Chinese] experts who have returned to China (with approval of the proper authorities) to establish residence, whose wages or expenses are paid by the Chinese side in [nonconvertible] Renminbi, are to be issued a white card with a photo of the individual holder affixed. Therefore, non-working members of a foreign expert's family may not obtain a white card.

(47) Q: Where is the white card to be used?

A: According to the regulations of the State Bureau of Foreign Exchange Control, the white card is to be used as follows:

1. Its use is restricted to state- or collectively-run guesthouses; hotels and restaurants; Friendship Stores; foreign trade centers; and souvenir, antique, and curio shops, for the purchase of ordinary consumer goods, but not for such articles as color television sets, refrigerators, and other high-level goods, and

2. to the purchase of domestic air, rail, and ship tickets; the payment of excess luggage fees; and the hiring of taxis.

(48) Q: Where is the white card not accepted?

A: According to the regulations of the State Bureau of Foreign Exchange Control, the white card is not accepted in the following places and situations:

1. Guesthouses, hotels, restaurants, shops, and places of entertainment which are foreign enterprises or Chinese-foreign joint ventures or cooperatives, and

2. for the purchase of international air, rail, and ship tickets; the shipment of international packages; the payment of international telecommunications fees; the purchase of foreign goods being sold on consignment; and the purchase of imported goods from tax-free shops supervised by Customs.

(49) Q: How is the matter of provisions for members of the foreign expert's family to be handled, if they are hired to work?

A: If a member of the foreign expert's family begins work, an emendation of the original contract must be discussed.

If the family member is hired as a foreign expert, then the original work unit will relinquish all responsibility for his expenses.

If the family member is hired as a foreign worker, then the original work unit must still assume responsibility for his return airfare.

If the family member is hired to work at a foreign embassy or consulate, trade organization, or foreign or joint-venture enterprise, then the original work unit will relinquish all responsibility for his expenses.

(50) Q: May dining halls serving foreign experts turn a profit?

A: Dining halls established for foreign experts must serve foreign experts; they should not be run for the purpose of earning profits. In general, only a small management fee may be collected, so as to ensure that they do not operate at a loss.

(51) Q: Who should assume the cost of shipping reference books, materials, and educational instruments that the foreign expert brings to China when he assumes his post?

A: Shipping costs for reference books, materials, and educational instruments that the foreign expert needs for work and brings to China with the approval of his employer may, within reason, usually be reimbursed upon presentation of receipts. If such materials have been brought without the prior agreement of the work unit and the expert brings up the question of transportation costs, the question may be resolved through negotiation. If the expert plans not to take the materials back to his country, but rather to present them as a gift to the school or unit where he works, then the school or unit should assume the shipping costs.

(52) Q: What if the foreign expert purchases his own air ticket to China?

A: If, due to special circumstances, the foreign expert purchases his own air ticket to China, in principle he should be reimbursed in convertible currency, but if the expert agrees, he may also be reimbursed in [nonconvertible] Renminbi.

(53) Q: Are foreign experts paid in convertible currency for overtime?

A: No. In general, overtime pay is nonconvertible.

(54) Q: If the employee is sent on an official assignment to someplace else in China, how are his expenses handled?

A: In addition to providing for the employee's lodging and transportation expenses, the employer must provide a suitable amount for meals, as stipulated in the document *On the Provisional Regulations Governing Standards and Operational Procedures for Expenses of Accommodating Foreign Guests.*

CHAPTER FOUR: MANAGEMENT IN THE WORKPLACE

(55) Q: How can schools strengthen their management of foreign experts' teaching work?

A: Strengthening the management of foreign experts' teaching is an important aspect of educational institutions' work with foreign experts. Its purpose is to bring the expert's skills into full play, thus increasing the advantages derived from his hire. Therefore, respect for the expert's professional integrity is of primary importance, as is an open-minded willingness to emulate his strengths. Experts must be regarded as our co-workers; a cooperative working relationship must be cultivated with them, and a favorable work environment and working conditions created for them. We must seek to stimulate their enthusiasm and allow them fully to display their talents. At the same time, management of their teaching must be strengthened in accordance with the dictates of the applicable regulations and procedures established by the State Education Commission, the individual institution, and the contract signed by both parties. In undertaking the work of management, principles must be upheld, but care must also be taken as regards style and methods: boldness in management is called for, but skill in management is equally important. Educational policies and goals as well as questions relating to the educational system, school rules, and basic curriculum must be approached according to our regulations; as for educational materials and methods, choice should be left to the expert, although these must be subject to review by our side. In matters of language and scholarship, the expert should be deferred to and emulated; if there are points of disagreement, they should be resolved through negotiation, after which the two parties may agree to disagree on certain matters. The foreign expert should be required to draft a lesson plan and should write a summary of his work at the end of each semester as well.

(56) Q: What are the primary purposes of hiring foreign cultural/educational experts?

A: In general, the employ of foreign experts should serve the following ends:

1. Training of a cadre of middle-aged and young teachers;

2. Strengthening the construction of new and important academic disciplines, or those which are lacking in China, and establishing new curricula;

3. Teaching graduate students and higher-level students;

4. Setting up new laboratories, writing and revising educational materials, etc.;

5. Cooperating in the establishment of new classes or training centers, the pursuit of research, the guidance of graduate students, etc.

(57) Q: How should the foreign expert's teaching schedule be arranged?

A: The legally established work week in China is six days per week, eight hours per day. In order to accommodate the customs of foreign experts, their teaching hours may be scheduled from Monday through Friday, or at the latest Saturday morning. Class hours per week should generally not drop below twelve, but this number may be adjusted with a view to the difficulty of the academic discipline or particular class being taught. Foreign language practice classes may be scheduled at the rate of around sixteen hours per week, whereas lecture-type classes in language theory, literature, etc., should be scheduled for fewer hours per week. In addition to teaching, the foreign expert may be required to compose or edit teaching materials, record tapes, entertain queries, etc.

(58) Q: What sort of introduction to the school should the foreign expert be given upon his arrival?

A: Upon his arrival, the foreign expert should be briefed by the Dean's Office, the Foreign Affairs Office, and his own department respectively on our educational policies, educational reform, educational goals, the educational system, the larger educational plan, classroom facilities, educational materials, the general situation of teachers and students at the school, and school rules. They should discuss with him the proposed curriculum, scheduling, and workload, and should introduce him to his colleagues and take him on a tour to see the campus, the educational facilities, library, etc., in order to familiarize him as quickly as possible with the general situation, so that he may readily begin work.

(59) Q: May foreign experts assume official positions with decision-making authority?

A: Foreign experts of real talent, scholarship, and management ability may be employed in various leadership capacities with decision-making authority, for example as department heads, heads of research institutes, editors-in-chief or executive editors of publishing houses, heads of training centers, etc. Foreign experts employed in such positions must be given real duties, responsibilities, and authority; in principle, their authority should be commensurate with that of Chinese cadres of the same level.

(60) Q: May foreign experts be nominated as candidates for the title of Advanced Worker in their unit?

A: According to the FEB document *On the Implementation of the Trial Method for Giving Awards to Foreign Cultural, Educational, and Economic Experts,* all foreign experts working in China at the invitation of or in the employ of official educational institutions, news media and publishing organizations, or cultural, artistic, public health, sports, industrial, or mining enterprises, who display a friendly attitude towards China and a positive attitude towards their work, and who have made clear contributions, may be given rewards both on the spiritual level, in the form of praise and encouragement, and on the material level, in the form of bonuses and awards. The unit where the expert works may, as it deems fit, award citations, prizes, bonuses, and pay increases, or may name the expert an Advanced Worker or Model Teacher, just as some of his Chinese colleagues may have been named. Famous scholars who have made clear contributions may, upon the approval of the higher authorities, including the provincial, regional, or directly administered municipal government, be given an honorary title, with accompanying certificate.

(61) Q: Are the libraries of the hiring units open to foreign experts? Are foreign experts allowed to borrow and read internal books and periodicals, and foreign works that have been photocopied and published in China [in contravention of international copyright conventions]?

A: According to the *Trial-Basis Regulations Concerning Work with Foreign Cultural and Educational Experts,* the expert's professional colleagues at his unit should inform him of all government policies, plans, and developments that have to do with their common professional work; invite him to attend all meetings and activities that have to do with the work; and provide him with all professional material available. It is allowed for the foreign expert to borrow and read internal periodicals and books that have to do with his professional work at his unit, and to use foreign reference works that have been photocopied and published in China. However, none of these may be reproduced or carried out of the country. Therefore, the work unit's library may be opened to the foreign expert; however, state and technological secrets must be safeguarded. (Other classificatory restrictions may be relaxed as appropriate.)

(62) Q: May foreign experts organize or take part in lecture series or academic discussion meetings?

A: According to the *Trial-Basis Regulations Concerning Work with Foreign Cultural and Educational Experts*, the regulatory organs of each profession, along with the hiring units, should make efforts to organize exchanges among foreign experts and between foreign experts and personnel at the corresponding level of their profession, with a view to encouraging Chinese-foreign mutual academic exploration. Experts whose attainments are considerable should be organized to give lectures and attend academic conferences in their field. Experts' scholarly articles may also be published in the appropriate Chinese journals. Therefore, after obtaining the approval of his hiring unit, the expert is free to organize lectures or academic discussions, and the unit may provide him the necessary help.

(63) Q: How should a foreign expert's independent acceptance of another unit's invitation to lecture or participate in academic exchange be dealt with?

A: The contract stipulates that the foreign expert must not assume other employment without the agreement of the hiring unit. However, in order to bring the expert's special talents and usefulness into full play and to accord with the principle of "while one unit hires, many units benefit," as long as such activities do not interfere with the employee's regular work, permission may be granted for him to accept such invitations outside of work time or on holidays. The inviting unit should directly contact the responsible people at the expert's unit to discuss the matter and seek their agreement and cooperation. If the foreign expert wishes to teach part-time in addition to his regular duties, he must obtain the prior approval of his unit.

(64) Q: May educational films, video cassettes, and feature films supplied by the expert be shown?

A: According to the FEB document, *Revised Opinions on Socializing with Foreign Experts and Other Questions,* among the video cassettes or movies supplied to the Chinese side by the expert, all documentaries, travelogues, and feature films which benefit professional or educational work may, after being previewed and approved by leaders in the administrative or departmental office or at a corresponding level, be shown to the appropriate people; however, they must not be lent out or shown publicly. Materials with reactionary or obscene content must be refused.

(65) Q: May books, materials, experimental apparatuses, etc., presented by the expert to the unit or to an individual be accepted?

A: According to the FEB document, *Revised Opinions on Socializing with Foreign Experts and Other Questions,* and the State Education Commission document, *Measures for the Management of Foreign Teachers in China,* the school may accept such presents and prepare commensurate gifts in return. As long as the books and materials in question do not contravene our country's present foreign policy or harm our country's interests, they may be presented to the appropriate people for reference or disposed of as the recipient sees fit—after review and approval by unit leaders. All materials with politically reactionary or obscene content must be refused or destroyed; when necessary, the viewpoint of our side should be explained to the expert so as to avoid similar problems later on.

(66) Q: What if a foreign expert independently reschedules or switches classes or has someone else substitute teach?

A: According to the State Education Commission document, *Some Additional Opinions on Strengthening the Management of Foreign Teachers' Work,* the foreign teacher must strictly abide by the terms of the contract. He must not independently reschedule or switch classes according to his own whims, and he certainly must not use class time to go traveling or sightseeing. In order to guarantee the quality of education, it is usually not permitted for foreign teachers to find teaching substitutes on their own. If special circumstances do in fact exist necessitating the finding of a substitute, the approval of the departmental head or the dean must first be obtained.

(67) Q: Are foreign teachers permitted to attend meetings called by their countries' embassies or consulates during class hours?

A: According to the State Education Commission document, *Some Additional Opinions on Strengthening the Management of Foreign Teachers' Work,* if notice of such a meeting has not been received by the school from the embassy or consulate, then time off will not be granted. Foreign teachers attending such meetings after obtaining the approval of their superiors will be responsible for all expenses connected with attending.

(68) Q: How should the organization of teacher-student round-table discussions or

the distribution of survey forms by foreign embassies or consulates through teachers of that nationality be regarded?

A: According to the *Trial-Basis Regulations Concerning Work with Foreign Cultural and Educational Experts,* if a foreign teacher wishes to bring any foreign diplomatic personnel, reporters, or tourists to the work unit, or organize a discussion between them and Chinese employees or students, he must first obtain the approval of the Chinese side. Foreign experts must not distribute propaganda or social survey outlines or forms at their workplace or residence.

(69) Q: Are the requests of foreign experts to organize film exhibitions, conferences, or reading rooms at their work units to be granted?

A: According to the *Trial-Basis Regulations Concerning Work with Foreign Cultural and Educational Experts,* requests by experts to organize film exhibitions, conferences, or reading rooms open to the public at their work units should be tactfully refused.

(70) Q: If a foreign expert uses the classroom as an arena for the conducting of social surveys, how should the situation be dealt with?

A: According to the FEB document, *Revised Opinions on Socializing with Foreign Experts and Other Questions,* the conducting of social surveys by foreign experts must be dealt with on a case-by-case basis. Foreign experts wishing to gather information about such topics as the general social situation, family situations, personal histories, ideals, hobbies, income, etc., may be given such information in accordance with the situation. Their desire to gain a partial picture of China's general situation or to find out about people's individual histories must not be regarded as inimical to our side. However, experts may not distribute survey outlines or forms to students or other teachers. If the expert is found to be engaged in intelligence-gathering activities, the matter should be reported to the appropriate authorities at once.

(71) Q: What if a foreign expert refuses to teach or translate a given text because it contravenes his political opinions?

A: The formal refusal by an expert to teach, record, or translate politically oriented lessons or texts because of political differences must be dealt with effectively according to the dictates of the situation. In principle, we should agree to disagree on political questions and make our viewpoint clear without forcing it on anyone or getting involved in quibbling. At the same time, it should be explained to the expert that he is not being asked to accept the opinions contained in the material in question; rather, as a foreign teacher, he is being asked to approach the material from a linguistic standpoint. If he is still unwilling, he should not be forced; a teacher or translator from the Chinese side may substitute. Open attacks in the classroom on our country's social system or leadership are not to be allowed; our attitude on this point must be strictly emphasized. If the expert has a differing opinion on certain international matters or on some of our country's policies, these should be tolerated; they must not be permitted to affect his work or his cooperation with his colleagues.

(72) Q: What if the foreign expert uses the classroom as a forum to advocate decadent bourgeois ideology?

A: The majority of foreign experts hail from capitalist countries, and their ideological consciousness and life-style are very different from our own; therefore, elements of bourgeois consciousness will almost certainly appear in their lectures. Such problems must be dealt with using extreme care, in accordance with the dictates of the situation. However, teachers who purposefully advocate such patently unacceptable aspects of decadent bourgeois ideology as sexual liberation must be severely criticized or warned. Foreign experts who distribute obscene materials to students or other teachers should be advised to desist immediately. Experts who pay no attention to repeated criticisms and remonstrations may be dismissed, while efforts are made to strengthen the education of students and teachers [i.e., contain the "damage"].

(73) Q: How may a distinction be drawn between missionary activity and the explication of topics of a religious nature?

A: Foreign experts are not permitted to engage in proselytism in the classroom, but they may introduce general religious knowledge. How is one to draw the distinction between these activities? If the foreign expert is a believer or a member of the clergy, openly distributes the Bible or religious propaganda, lectures systematically on the Bible, organizes religious activities for the students, and attempts to win converts, he may be regarded as engaging in proselytism. If, due to curricular demands, the expert explains religious allusions found in literature or introduces general knowledge about religion, it should not be regarded as proselytism.

(74) Q: How should foreign experts who go on strike be dealt with?

A: First of all, the reason for the foreign expert's action should be ascertained, and "medicine" appropriate to the "illness" be prescribed. If the expert's refusal to work is due to problems originating on the Chinese side, e.g., if the expert's quarters are poorly heated in winter, impeding his normal life and work, and the problem is not solved after numerous requests on his part, or there is no hot water for bathing, or some apparatus is broken and has not been repaired after repeated notifications, then we must take stock of our own work and take steps to improve the situation as quickly as possible, while at the same time carrying out ideological work [i.e., attempting to calm the expert down]. As for those experts who strike at the slightest provocation or who use any pretense to strike, they should first be severely criticized and counseled to desist. It should be pointed out to them that such actions harm the cooperative relationship between the two parties. Experts who strike or kick up a fuss without any reason at all should be both severely criticized and advised that their actions are unfriendly. When necessary, the employer may dock the expert's pay or dismiss him.

(75) Q: What about experts who are unable to work for extended periods because of illness?

A: According to the *Rules Governing Contracts and Compensation of Foreign Cultural and Educational Experts,* foreign experts and foreign teachers must have a medical certificate from a doctor in order to be granted medical leave. After an expert has been out of work for sixty days due to illness and is still unable to resume normal work, the employer may, in accordance with the employee's physical condition, arrange for his return to his own country within thirty days. The employer shall provide the employee and his family with air tickets and shall assume air freight costs. During the first sixty days of medical leave, the expert will still receive his full salary. Starting from the sixty-first day until the day he resumes normal work or returns home or his contract expires, he shall be paid 70 percent of his full salary.

Experts who are unable to regain their health and resume normal working hours within a short period should be sent back to their own country at the earliest opportunity.

(76) Q: How should one deal with experts who ask for time off because of private matters or who absent themselves from work without permission?

A: According to the *Rules Governing Contracts and Compensation of Foreign Cultural and Educational Experts,* foreign experts and foreign teachers who ask for time off for private matters shall have their salary docked one day's pay for each such day they take off, provided they have first obtained permission from their employer. Employees who absent themselves from work without permission shall, in addition to being docked as above, be subject to severe criticism or, after repeated incidents, dismissal.

CHAPTER FIVE: MANAGEMENT OF SOCIAL ASPECTS

(77) Q: What are the basic principles of the *Entry and Exit Law?*

A: The *Law Governing Foreigners' Entry To and Exit From the People's Republic of China* [hereafter "EEL"], passed by the Thirteenth Conference of the Standing Committee of the Sixth National People's Congress on November 22, 1985, took effect on February 1, 1986. The basic principles of the EEL are as follows: to protect the sovereignty, security, and social order of the state; to accord with our country's policy of opening to the outside world; to benefit the expansion of exchange between China and the outside world; to promote the construction of China's socialist modernization; and to protect the lawful rights of foreigners.

(78) Q: What are the regulations governing foreigners' entry to, transit through, and residence in China?

A: According to the EEL, entry to, transit through, and residence in China by foreigners may be undertaken only with the permission of the relevant organs of the Chinese Government. Nationals of countries whose governments have signed agreements with China mutually waiving visa requirements and who follow the dictates of those agreements, as well as foreigners in transit whose stay does not exceed twenty-four hours and who do not leave the airport, are exempt from the visa requirement.

(79) Q: How does one apply for an entry visa?

A: Application for visas is made to Chinese diplomatic representative organs, consular organs, or other Chinese missions abroad which have been authorized by the Foreign Ministry. Those foreigners who, due to real emergencies or other valid reasons, are unable to obtain a visa at the above-mentioned missions may proceed directly to an authorized visa-issuing office of the Ministry of Public Security at their point of entry to China, where they may apply for a visa upon presentation of their passport and a letter or telegram from their hiring unit.

(80) Q: Which points of entry to China have visa-issuing offices authorized by the Ministry of Public Security?

A: Beijing, Shanghai, Tianjin, Dalian, Fuzhou, Xiamen, Xi'an, Guilin, Hangzhou, Kunming, Guangzhou (at Baiyun Airport), Shenzhen (at Luo Hu [i.e., Lo Wu] and Shekou), and Zhuhai (at Gongbei [i.e., the Porta do Barro]).

(81) Q: What documents are required in applying for a visa?

A: One must provide the following: a valid passport or document acceptable in place of a passport; a completed visa application form, accompanied by a recent half-length full-face photo (without hat) of the applicant; documentation certifying the applicant's purpose in visiting China or a letter or telegram of invitation from the hiring unit; and, for those planning to reside in China a year or more, an official certificate of health from a medical facility certified by the government of the applicant's country of origin, which certificate has been issued in the previous six months.

(82) Q: What are the various types of regular visas?

A: After application for a visa has been made by a foreigner, the organ issuing the visa will, after examination of the presented materials, issue to the applicant a visa appropriate to the reasons for his visit as stated in his application, provided the applicant meets the requisite conditions. For ease of management, regular Chinese visas are divided into the following seven categories, each represented by a different initial according to the Pinyin romanization of its name:

D visa: for those establishing permanent residence in China;

Z visa: for those coming to China to take up employment or engage in business enterprise, or their family members;

X visa: for those coming to China for a period of six months or longer for study or internship;

F visa: for those coming to China on short-term official visits; investigative tours; lecture tours; business trips; or scientific, technological, or cultural exchanges;

L visa: for those touring China, visiting relatives, or attending to other private matters;

G visa: for those in transit;

C visa: for those entering China on active duty as flight, train, or ship officers, crew, attendants, or freight workers, and their accompanying family members.

(83) Q: Who may not enter China?

A: 1. Those who have been deported by the Chinese Government, and whose effective period of deportation has not yet expired;

2. Those who come to engage in terroristic, violent, or subversive acts;

3. Those who come to engage in smuggling, prostitution, or traffic in illicit drugs;

4. The mentally ill, or those who have communicable diseases which may endanger the public health;

5. Those who cannot guarantee they will have funds sufficient to cover their expenses while in China;

6. Those considered likely to engage in other activities detrimental to China's security or interests.

(84) Q: How does one apply for a residence permit?

A: Foreign experts and their family members who are holders of Z visas must report within ten days of their arrival in China to the Public Security Bureau of their city or county of residence in order to apply for Foreigner's Residence Permits or Foreigner's Temporary Residence Permits. The period of validity of the above-named documents is the period for which the foreigner is to be allowed to remain in China. Foreigners who are going to remain in China for one year or longer should apply for the Foreigner's Residence Permit; those who are staying for a shorter period, for the Foreigner's Temporary Residence Permit. The latter must always be accompanied by a passport [when presented for identification purposes]. Foreign scholars and their family members with F or L visas may remain in China for the period shown on their visas; they need not apply for residence permits.

Application for a residence permit involves the answering of relevant questions, as well as carrying out the following procedures: filling out the application form and, in the case of those applying for a Foreigner's Residence Permit, submitting a certificate of health and a recent ⅔ decimeter half-length full-face photo (without hat).

(85) Q: What if changes need to be made in the information inscribed in the Foreigner's Residence Permit?

A: The Foreigner's Residence Permit contains the foreigner's full name, nationality, occupation or status, work unit, residential address, passport number, etc. If any of these items needs to be altered, the holder should proceed within ten days to the local Public Security Bureau to register the change. It is not permitted for the holder or other persons to alter the content of the permit or to let the ten-day period pass without applying for the necessary changes to be made.

(86) Q: How does one apply for extension of a visa or the Foreigner's Residence Permit?

A: If the holder needs to remain in China beyond the expiration date of his visa or residence permit, he must apply for an extension at the local Public Security Bureau, filling out the appropriate application form and submitting a valid passport along with his current visa or residence permit and a letter from his employer.

(87) Q: What if a foreigner wishes to travel to areas not open to travel?

A: Foreigners with a valid visa or residence permit may travel to areas open to foreigners. Those wishing to travel to areas that are not open must apply for a travel permit at their local Public Security Bureau two days before they set out; only when they have received the permit may they set out.

(88) Q: What are the standard application fees for visas and residence permits?

A: Foreigners applying for the various kinds of visas and permits or their extension or alteration must pay the stipulated fees.

Visa fees are as follows (unit of currency: Renminbi): single visa, 20 yuan; two visas, 30 yuan; more than two visas in any one-year period, 50 yuan; more than two visas in any period longer than one year, 80 yuan.

Fees for residence permits are as follows: Foreigner's Residence Permit, 20 yuan; Foreigner's Temporary Residence Permit, 10 yuan; travel permit, 2 yuan; extension of Foreigner's Residence Permit, 10 yuan; extension of Foreigner's Temporary Residence Permit, 10 yuan.

(89) Q: May foreigners establish permanent residence in China upon expiration of their residence permits?

A: Foreign experts or scholars holding temporary employment in China who request the right of permanent residence in China for themselves and their family members upon expiration of their period of residence or stay in China are generally refused.

(90) Q: What sort of foreigners can receive the right of permanent residence in China?

A: Those who have invested very large amounts of money, thus making an important contribution to economic construction in their place of residence; those who have taken part in China's revolution and construction for many years, and who have made significant contributions; well-known figures who have lived in China many years, and other foreign experts and scholars who have made special contributions: all these may apply to the Public Security Bureau of their place of residence for status as permanent residents.

(91) Q: What sorts of privileges accompany the status of permanent resident?

A: Permanent residents need not extend their residence permits or submit their personal documents to the Public Security Bureau at fixed intervals; they may apply for a single five-year unlimited entry-exit visa (which, however, may not have a period of validity longer than that of their passport); their visa fees are waived; and their spouses and children also have the right of residence in China.

(92) Q: If a foreign expert moves from his original city or county of residence in China, what administrative formalities does he need to complete?

A: If at the end of his period of employment the foreign expert wishes to move to another place to take up new employment, he must register the move at the Public Security Bureau of his original place of residence, submitting the relevant documents. Within ten days of his arrival at his new place of residence, he must register his arrival with the Public Security Bureau of his new place of residence.

(93) Q: What must a foreigner do when he has overnight guests?

A: He must report the guests' presence within twenty-four hours to the service desk of his guesthouse, hotel, or hostel, or to the local Public Security Bureau. He may continue to host the guests only if he obtains permission. If the guests' temporary stay exceeds three months, then those of their number who are Chinese citizens over sixteen years of age must apply to the local Public Security Bureau for a Permit of Temporary Lodging. When applying, the guests' residence permits [if applicable], passports, or other valid proof of identity must be presented; in areas not open to travel, their travel permits [if applicable] must be presented as well. To fill out the Temporary Lodging Registration Form, a fountain or ballpoint pen must be used, the characters must be neat and clearly written, and the items must be correctly and completely filled out.

(94) Q: What must foreign experts do when they stay in the homes of Chinese citizens?

A: Foreign experts, scholars, and their family members staying in the homes of Chinese citizens must complete the following formalities: If the residence is in a town or city, the host or guests must take the guests' passports and other documents along with the host's household registration book and report to the local Public Security Bureau, where they shall fill out the Temporary Lodging Registration Form. If the residence is in the countryside, the arrival of the guests must be reported within seventy-two hours to the local police station or household registration office.

(95) Q: What if a foreign expert loses his residence permit?

A: Foreign experts, scholars, and their family members of sixteen or more years of age must carry their passport or residence permit with them at all times in case of inspection by an officer of the Foreign Affairs Section of the People's Police. If a foreigner's residence documents are lost or damaged, he must report the incident immediately to the local office of the Public Security Bureau in charge of entry to and exit from China, and apply for replacement or exchange. Those who lose their Foreigner's Residence Permit must put a notice in the local government newspaper invalidating the original permit.

(96) Q: What are the steps that must be taken by foreign experts applying for a Certificate of Loss?

A: Foreign experts, scholars, and their family members who lose property, passport, or the Chinese Customs Baggage Declaration Form [hereafter "BDF"] must immediately inform the unit hosting them and proceed to an office of public security to report the loss. The report must include a detailed description of the incident (time; place; features, number, and value of the lost articles) so as to assist public security personnel in their search. If the articles do not turn up, the public security office may provide, as appropriate, a Certificate of Loss of Property, a Certificate of Loss of Passport, or a Certificate of Loss of BDF. If, after reporting the loss, the foreigner finds the lost objects himself, he must immediately report the find to a public security office and return the Certificates of Loss to the issuing office. After obtaining a new passport, the foreigner must proceed immediately a public security office to apply for the alteration of the passport number on his residence documents.

(97) Q: What if property is stolen from a foreign expert's residence?

A: If it is discovered that property has been stolen from a foreign expert's residence, the incident must be reported immediately to the security office of the expert's guesthouse, hotel, or hostel or to an office of public security. The scene should be left undisturbed in order to aid the Public Security Bureau in its investigation and search for clues and evidence.

(98) Q: What if a foreign expert is bodily attacked?

A: If a foreigner is beaten, taken liberties with, or insulted [i.e., suffers rape or attempted rape] by criminal elements, an attempt should be made to seize the criminals and hand them over to public security organs or to record their names, occupation/status, or physical characteristics. The incident must be reported immediately to the Public Security Bureau.

(99) Q: What sort of penalty will be suffered by foreign experts who remain past the expiration date of their residence documents?

A: Foreign experts, scholars, and their children who overstay their permitted period of residence in China will be warned and/or fined an amount not less than 100 yuan and not greater than 500 yuan.

(100) Q: What sort of penalty will be suffered by foreign experts who disregard the lodging registration requirement?

A: Foreign experts or scholars who have foreign guests overnight without going through the requisite registration procedures will be warned and/or fined an amount not less than 10 yuan and not greater than 50 yuan.

(101) Q: What if a foreigner expresses disagreement with penalties imposed on him by the organs of public security?

A: If a foreigner disagrees with detainment, fine, or other penalties meted out to him by the organs of public security, he may, within fifteen days of his receipt of notification of the penalty, appeal to the next higher level of the public security system, either directly or via the organ that imposed the penalty. He may also file suit at the local Intermediate People's Court.

(102) Q: What practices must be followed in the translation/transliteration of foreign experts' names?

A: For the sake of consistency in the translation and use of the full name of the foreign expert, and to avoid mistakes occasioned by the use of multiple translations/transliterations of the same name with characters that have similar readings, the first time the foreign expert applies for his residence documents he should find a suitable name in the dictionary or according to his own wishes. Thereafter, when applying for any sort of documentation, he should follow the usage inscribed on his residence documents. If the translation/transliteration is found to be inaccurate or inappropriate, application for alteration should be made immediately. It is permitted neither to change the name on one's documents oneself nor to use a name inconsistent with the one inscribed thereon, including the name in Chinese characters.

(103) Q: What are the points to be observed by the foreign expert when he is leaving China?

A: Foreign experts or scholars and their family members are exempted from the necessity to obtain exit visas when they leave China upon completion of their contract. They need only present their valid passports and the documents that have authorized their residence in China, which latter must be surrendered to border officials when they leave China. If they wish to leave China for travel or vacation but plan to return after their trip, they must proceed to their local municipal or county Public Security Bureau to apply for a visa for re-entry to China. When they leave China, they must present their residence documents to border officials for inspection.

(104) Q: Who may not leave China, and under what circumstances may the same be allowed to leave?

A: The following may not leave China:

1. Those who have been indicted in criminal proceedings, or who have been designated criminal suspects by the organs of public security, the People's Procuratorate, or the People's Courts;

2. Those to whom notice has been issued by the People's Courts that they may not leave China pending settlement of civil cases;

3. Those with regard to whom it has been established by the relevant government organs that there is a need to investigate unresolved violations of Chinese law.

When the relevant processes have been carried through, resulting in the resolution of the above situations restricting egress from China, the relevant government organs will issue notice that the person in question may leave China. He may do so only when such notice has been issued.

(105) Q: What sorts of behavior are regarded as disruption of the monetary system?

A: According to the relevant sections of the *Provisional Regulations for the Management of Foreign Exchange in the People's Republic of China* and the *Provisional Measures for the Management of FEC [Foreign Exchange Currency] by the Bank of China,* the buying and selling of foreign currency or FEC privately, in the guise of another activity, or at rates higher than those fixed by the State Bureau of Foreign Exchange Control, and the counterfeiting of foreign currency or FEC, are all regarded as disruption of the monetary system.

(106) Q: What should foreign experts know about using bicycles?

A: If a foreign expert buys a new bicycle, in order to ride it legally he must take the receipt, along with certification from his work unit, to the traffic regulation branch of the local Public Security Bureau to register it and obtain a license plate. If he buys a used bicycle from its owner, he must register the change of ownership. Riding a bicycle for which the above procedures have not been completed is a violation of traffic regulations.

(107) Q: What should foreign experts know when they fill out various official application forms, e.g., for visas or other documents?

A: When filling out applications, one must use a fountain or ballpoint pen filled with high-quality blue or black ink. If simplified Chinese characters are used, they must be the official standard forms issued by the government. One's writing must be clear and neat, one must not alter information, and one must complete all items. One's full name should be written in the original language as well as in Chinese; all other items should be completed in Chinese. Application forms must bear the signature of the applicant or the official chop of his accommodating unit.

(108) Q: What if a foreigner loses his passport claim check?

A: Foreigners must present a passport claim check in order to pick up their passports and documents. This check must be well guarded in order to preclude the possibility of other people picking up the documents with a found or stolen check. If the check is lost, the applicant or his accommodating unit must provide certification of identity.

(109) Q: How are notarizations involving foreign nationals undertaken?

A: Application for such notarization must be made in person orally or in writing at a notary office, while certification of identity is presented. If the party requiring notarization is abroad or due to special circumstances cannot come to the notary office in person, he may request relatives or friends to apply on his behalf; these representatives of the applicant must present personal identification and a letter of application from the applicant. Notarizations of the following may not be undertaken through such representatives: commissions/consignments, wills/testaments, and adoptions, all of which require the personal signature and/or seal (chop) of the applicant.

(110) Q: What administrative procedures must be undertaken by foreign experts wishing to transport rifles or shotguns into or out of China?

A: In order to bring a rifle or shotgun into China, one must first obtain approval from the relevant government organs and the Bureau or Provincial Department of Public Security in the expert's province, autonomous region, or directly administered municipality of destination. When entering China, the gun must be declared and inspected at the border Customs station, which will then issue a transport certificate. Upon arrival at his destination in China, the expert must exchange the transport permit for a Gun Bearer's Certificate at the local organs of public security.

In order to take a rifle or shotgun out of China, the expert must exchange the Gun Bearer's Certificate for a transport permit at the original issuing organ. Upon exit from China, the bearer must declare the weapon at Customs and surrender the transport permit.

All those who bring guns or ammunition into China without prior authorization must declare them at Customs, where they will be placed under seal temporarily, to be returned to the bearer upon his exit from China or shipped from the border station to a point outside China.

(111) Q: May foreigners buy rifles or shotguns in China?

A: Yes, they may, but they must obtain approval and certification from their accommodating unit or from the foreign affairs organs of the province, autonomous region, or directly administered municipality where they are residents. Then they must apply for a gun purchase permit at the Public Security Bureau of the county or city where they are going to purchase the gun. After receiving approval, they may proceed to a designated shop and, upon presentation of their purchase permit, purchase a rifle or shotgun.

(112) Q: What are the regulations concerning foreigners who wish to seek livelihood in China?

A: Section 19 of the EEL states that foreigners who have not received residence documents and foreigners who have come to China for study may not be employed in China without the approval of the relevant departments of the Chinese Government.

(113) Q: Under what circumstances may the period of validity of a foreigner's residency documents or visa be shortened or his residency revoked?

A: These actions may be taken against foreigners who have acted in violation of laws or regulations and who would therefore not be appropriate to allow to remain in China, but whose offenses are not serious enough to warrant deportation. The foreigner must leave China before the new (revised) expiration date of his residency documents or visa.

(114) Q: What penalties will be imposed on foreigners who seek employment independently?
A: Section 44 of the *Detailed Rules on the Implementation of the EEL* stipulates that foreigners who are employed or do business without the approval of the Bureau of Labor and Personnel of the P.R.C. must both terminate such employment or business and pay a fine of not less than 200 yuan and not more than 1,000 yuan. Serious offenders will be deported.

(115) Q: What penalties will be imposed on those responsible for causing foreigners to violate laws or regulations?
A: The *Detailed Rules on the Implementation of the EEL* stipulate that all fines, detentions, and punishments specified for foreigners are also applicable to those who aid foreigners to enter or leave China illegally, cause foreigners to overstay their visa or residence documents, hire foreigners who are seeking employment illegally, or facilitate the travel of foreigners without special travel permits to areas not open to foreigners.

CHAPTER SIX:
EXTERNAL PROPAGANDA AND FRIENDLY RELATIONS

(116) Q: Why must propaganda work directed at foreign experts be strengthened?
A: Foreign experts who come to work in China are a propaganda audience delivered to our doorstep and are themselves important disseminators of external propaganda. The vast majority of them wish to understand China; many of them write books or articles for the foreign news media, deliver lectures, or put on exhibitions when they return to their own countries, describing China in enthusiastic terms. However, there are also some experts who, influenced by distorted propaganda in their own countries, lack a well-rounded and correct understanding, and who therefore express suspicion or misunderstanding of our government's policies or our political system. We must make an effort to present positive propaganda to this group.
The purpose of doing a good job of propagandizing foreign experts is to help them arrive at a correct understanding of China, while strengthening mutual understanding and friendship, stimulating foreign experts' enthusiasm, and allowing them fully to display their talents and to serve China's Four Modernizations.

(117) Q: How may we do a good job of propagandizing foreign experts?
A: In order to accomplish this task, one must follow the following principles: supplying information only when the recipient is willing and not forcing anybody; seeking truth from facts and examining the negative along with the positive; supplying information appropriate to the recipient, so as to achieve a palpable effect; and preserving the distinction between internal and external, i.e., not giving out key state or technological secrets, and not discussing not-yet-publicized internal matters of our side (the Party, government personnel, or plans or programs still under delib-

eration). It is not permitted to casually express views which diverge from the policies of the Central Committee of the Chinese Communist Party.

In presenting information to the foreign expert, place an emphasis on explaining the policies of the Central Committee of our Party, and the truth about, and our attitude towards, important events in China and abroad. This will help the foreign expert arrive at a correct understanding of China while strengthening the influence of our country abroad. Present to the foreign expert information on government policies, regulations, and plans relating to his work; this will benefit your cooperation and completion of your common tasks. Introduce our country's legal and political systems and our customs to the expert; this will facilitate the expert's compliance with them and thus help to ensure his friendly coexistence with us.

(118) Q: What are the forms of propaganda appropriate to employ with foreign experts?

A: There are many employable forms, the most important being lectures, discussions, visits [to factories, people's homes, etc.], tours, performances, sports events, celebrations and festivals, gift subscriptions or individual issues of foreign-language periodicals, Chinese language lessons, etc.

Propaganda aimed at foreign experts must be appropriate to the person, place, and time; usually this means striking a balance between speech and silence, activity and rest, and listening and watching. The best results are gained from allowing foreigners to see things for themselves, i.e., to use reality as your propaganda. During discussions, allow someone from our side first to introduce the essential points, and then allow the expert to ask questions. This press-conference style of discussion is the most appealing.

(119) Q: What must one pay attention to in making friends with a foreign expert?

A: The purpose of befriending a foreign expert is to promote understanding, deepen friendship, ensure cooperative relations, and stimulate the expert's enthusiasm; therefore, one must be honest in one's dealings with the expert. As long as the bounds determined by law, regulations, discipline, and socialist morality are not violated and rules of secrecy are not infringed, then everyone's active promotion of and participation in various friendly activities with foreign experts should be encouraged. When one participates in such activities, one must take care to preserve the distinction between internal and external and to avoid revealing state secrets. The informal adoption [a traditional custom] of foreigners is not encouraged, and it is not permitted to take advantage of one's connection to a foreigner to gain benefits, to exchange foreign currency, or to engage in any activity denigrating to one's own or the country's moral integrity. Education of personnel on our side concerning the upholding of the Four Cardinal Principles and foreign-affairs discipline must be strengthened.

(120) Q: What principles must be upheld in friendly relations with foreigners?

A: The principles of "two trusts and two free reins" must be upheld; i.e., trust the vast majority of foreign experts and the vast majority of Chinese personnel, and give free rein to those wishing to befriend foreign experts and those wishing to provide foreigners with information about China.

In normal daily relations between people on our side and foreign experts, such as conversation, mutual visits, invitations, and excursions, it is not necessary to ask for instructions [from unit leaders] in each instance and report back after; neither is it necessary to send a chaperone along when someone goes out with a foreigner. However, in such relations it *is* necessary to observe foreign-affairs discipline and to ask for instructions or report back in case something of importance occurs or there is a problem.

The procedures to be followed by Chinese comrades visiting the foreign expert should be simplified to the greatest degree possible. Personnel from the expert's own unit may be exempted from registration on presentation of their employee identification or school badge. However, people from the outside must still be required to register, and it must be explained to the expert that these procedures are meant to ensure the security of the persons and property of all foreign experts and are not aimed at restricting their activities.

Both breadth and depth should be sought in relationships. As long as no laws are broken or private advantage sought, anyone may associate freely with foreign experts. At the same time, organizational leadership must be strengthened: emphasis must be placed on encouraging personnel with direct working relationships with experts to take the initiative to actively work at developing friendly relationships with them, in order to promote mutual understanding and friendship, thus benefiting the cooperative working relationship and enabling [people on our side] to learn even more from foreign experts.

In organizing friendship activities with foreign experts, the principles of thrift and conservation must be observed. Extravagance, waste, ostentation, big displays, and especially insincerity and false friendship, must be avoided. Emphasis should be on the spiritual rather than the material.

(121) Q: What if foreign experts express the desire to visit military installations or jails, or to view courtroom proceedings?

A: Such excursions may be organized for foreign experts, but first negotiations in which the purpose of the visit is explained must be carried out with the relevant units in order to obtain their support and cooperation. Visits or viewings of this nature should be stringently scheduled.

(122) Q: What if a foreign expert propagates the notion of "two Chinas" or "one China, one Taiwan"?

A: First of all, the motive behind such speech must be ascertained. Those propagating such notions on purpose should be refuted and criticized; if after repeated warnings they refuse to desist, administrative measures leading to dismissal may be taken. Those who voice such notions out of ignorance should be corrected, and our standpoint should be explained to them; usually no strong measures should be taken against them.

(123) Q: What if a foreign expert wishes to set up an exhibition at his work unit?

A: We do not encourage foreign experts to organize exhibitions. If the expert strongly insists, the content of the exhibition must first be thoroughly examined, and permission refused if the material contains anything opposing our government policy or political system, denigrating or insulting our country's image, or constituting an affront to our morals or customs. If, on the other hand, the material proves to be helpful to the carrying forward of the unit's work and the deepening of friendship and understanding between Chinese and the people of other lands, then arrangements may be made for the exhibition to be held and the necessary help provided.

(124) Q: What if a foreign expert hangs pictures of nudes in his own quarters?
A: If the pictures are hung in the foreign expert's bedroom, no interference should be made; if they are hung in an office or public space through which Chinese teachers and students often pass, then the customs of our country's people should be explained to the expert, and he should be advised to take the pictures down.

(125) Q: May outstanding results obtained by the foreign expert in his work be publicly reported?
A: Before publicly reporting or commending exemplary work or results of a foreign expert, one must first seek his permission. If he refuses, then the results must absolutely not be publicized; if he grants permission, or if he has already left China, then a draft of the article or report commending him must be sent to the FEB for examination and approval before it may be publicized. This is to avoid disclosing secrets or posing a threat to the expert's personal safety.

(126) Q: What if the hiring unit has important information, valuable experience, or knotty problems regarding work with foreign experts?
A: The editorial offices of the *Journal on Work with Foreign Experts* may be contacted directly by phone or mail (Telephone: Beijing 894053). If knotty problems are encountered, a letter may be written directly to the editorial board, who will ask comrades at the appropriate government organs to suggest solutions.

CHAPTER SEVEN: VACATION AND TRAVEL

(127) Q: How much vacation time is granted to foreign cultural/educational experts and foreign workers who have worked in China one year? How large is the vacation bonus they receive?
A: According to the *Rules Governing the Salaries and Living Arrangements of Foreign Experts,* for each year of work, an expert will enjoy one month's vacation; for those who work for longer than half a year but less than a full year, the vacation period is two weeks. Those working in schools will have vacation during the summer and winter vacation periods of their school. Usually foreign teachers and foreign workers are entitled to the same amount of vacation time as foreign experts. During vacation, the employee continues to receive his regular pay.
When the foreign cultural/educational expert has completed a year's work, he is given a vacation bonus of 800 yuan Renminbi by his employer; those who work for longer than half a year but less than a full year receive 400 yuan. Usually foreign teachers and foreign workers receive 600 yuan after a year; those who work for longer than half a year but less than a full year receive 300 yuan. The vacation bonus may not be converted into foreign currency and is payable only upon completion of one-half year's (or one semester's) work.

(128) Q: May foreign cultural/educational experts who have worked for a full year return to their own country for vacation?

A: According to the *Rules Governing the Salaries and Living Arrangements of Foreign Experts,* if the foreign expert was single when he arrived in China and his period of employment is two years, he may return home for a single visit to see his relatives once he has worked a full year. The employer shall provide a round-trip economy-class air ticket by the shortest route for this purpose. If CAAC serves the route in question, then the tickets must be bought from CAAC. If the expert chooses this option, he shall forego his vacation bonus for that year; however, he shall be paid his salary for the month of his vacation, and that month's salary may all be converted into foreign currency.

If the foreign expert foregoes the option of visiting home, the employer shall give him Renminbi equivalent to the value of a one-way air ticket to his home, or shall give him that year's vacation bonus of 800 yuan Renminbi, whichever is greater.

Regulations do not provide for experts who bring family members with them to China to return home for vacation. However, if they work in China for two full years and extend their contract beyond that, they may return home for one visit, with the employer providing air tickets. They shall be paid for the month of their vacation, and their salary during the month they return home may all be converted into foreign currency.

(129) Q: What holidays are granted to foreign cultural/educational experts during their period of employment in China?

A: 1. Foreign experts receive the same time off for all the legal Chinese holidays (New Year's [January 1st], the Spring Festival or Lunar New Year, Women's Day [March 8th], Labor Day [May 1st], and National Day [October 1st]) that their co-workers receive.

2. Foreign experts, coming from various countries, have different religious beliefs and folk customs; for instance, Europeans and Americans celebrate Christmas, and citizens of the USA place emphasis on Thanksgiving Day and Easter; Moslems celebrate the Feast of Sacrifice (Corban); people from Southeast Asia, the Water-Splashing Festival. Foreign cultural/educational experts wishing to celebrate the major feasts of their own country may be granted vacation as follows: Christmas, two days; Corban, three days; the Water-Splashing Festival, Thanksgiving, and Easter, three days each.

3. Foreign experts wishing to celebrate their country's national day may be given one day's vacation.

The above stipulations regarding the granting of holidays to foreign experts apply in principle also to most foreign workers and foreign teachers.

(130) Q: What privileges does our country accord foreign cultural/educational experts at present? What documents entitle them to these privileges?

A: According to the provisions of the *Report Submitted by the FEB, the Bureau of Finance, and the Bureau of Commerce [to the State Council] Requesting Clarification of Privileges to be Accorded to Foreign Cultural/Educational Experts Working in China,* subsequently approved for circulation by the State Council, meals should be provided to the foreign expert at a price reflecting a gross profit of 15 percent on the cost of the foodstuffs used to make them, rooms and air tickets provided at 30 percent off the current basic rate charged most foreign guests, and rail tickets provided at the same price charged Chinese citizens.

When foreign experts travel in China, they may secure the above privileges by using their white card, employee identification, and Foreigner's Residence Permit.

(131) Q: How shall the expenses of Chinese staff accompanying foreign experts on self-paid tours organized by the work unit be arranged for?

A: FEB Document No. 60 (1984) stipulates that transportation and lodging expenses of the accompanying Chinese interpreters should be assumed collectively by the experts; for meals, a supplement may be provided according to the regulations of the Bureau of Finance concerning provision for the expenses of employees sent on assignment. This supplement may subsequently be reported by the employer to the higher authorities for reimbursement. Work and travel costs of the group leader shall be assumed by the organizing unit.

(132) Q: Who of the foreign expert's relatives may apply for permission to come to China to visit him? What procedures must be undertaken?

A: According to FEB Document No. 129 (1982), *Regulations Concerning Visits to China by Foreign Cultural/Educational Experts' Relatives,* the spouses, children, parents, and parents- or children-in-law of foreign cultural/educational experts employed for a period of one year or longer may receive permission to come to China to visit the expert. Permission for visits by other relatives should usually be tactfully refused.

Ideally, visits by relatives should be organized during the expert's vacation time, and the expert should submit a written application to the unit two months in advance. The application should include the relatives' full names in the original language, as well as their sexes, ages, nationalities, occupations, addresses in the original language, their relation to the expert, the length of time they will be in China, the location where they will apply for their visa, the point at which they will enter China, and their passport numbers. If the expert's unit approves his application, it may prepare a document to be submitted for approval by the appropriate supervisory bureau, commission, or organ directly beneath the State Council, or the foreign affairs office of the relevant provincial, regional, or directly administered municipal People's Government. A notice should also be sent to the appropriate Chinese diplomatic mission abroad to provide visas, and a copy of this be sent to the local organ of public security. Once the diplomatic mission has received the notice, it will prepare visas for the visiting relatives. If a special situation arises requiring the dispatch of an urgent telegram overseas, the expert shall assume the cost.

(133) Q: Can relatives of a foreign expert receive privileges when they visit him and travel in China?

A: According to the FEB's *Regulations Concerning Visits to China by Foreign Cultural/Educational Experts' Relatives,* all expenses of foreign experts' visiting relatives must be self-paid. In principle, none of the dining, lodging, or transport (plane and train) discounts accorded the foreign expert shall be extended to them. However, if they participate in group travel organized by the expert's unit, they may be given appropriate special treatment.

(134) Q: What documents must the foreign expert carry when he travels? What procedures must be undertaken in advance?

A: When the foreign expert travels in China, he must carry a valid visa [if appropriate], his passport, his residence permit, his employee identification, and his white card.

Those proceeding to areas open to foreigners need not apply for travel permits; however, those headed for municipalities or counties not open to foreigners must apply for a travel permit two days before their departure at the Public Security Bureau of their place of residence; only after receiving the permit may they proceed to the areas indicated thereon.

(135) Q: What are the points for attention for foreign experts taking photographs while traveling or touring?

A: According to the *Regulations Concerning Photography by Foreigners in China,* foreigners are forbidden to photograph any place or unit designated a restricted military area. While photos may be taken of the exteriors of protected cultural sites and museums, all portions designated by the relevant government organs as off-limits for photography must be pointed out in advance to the touring experts, and signs with the words "Please—No Photos" in Chinese and foreign script should be posted. In other situations, the following principle should be followed: If foreigners are not permitted to photograph a given location, they should not be taken to visit it, and if they are allowed to visit it, they should be allowed to photograph it.

(136) Q: May foreign experts take moving pictures in China?

A: According to the FEB document, *Revised Opinions on Socializing with Foreign Experts and Other Questions,* requests by foreign experts to make scenic or everyday-type non-commercial films of the places of their work and residence and of tourist sites may be granted. Those wishing to make feature films must undertake the procedures prescribed in the relevant state regulations. The filming of restricted military areas and of protected cultural sites and museums should be dealt with as outlined in the *Regulations Concerning Photography by Foreigners in China* referred to above.

CHAPTER EIGHT: CUSTOMS REGULATIONS

(137) Q: What are the customs regulations concerning luggage and articles brought into China by foreign cultural/educational experts?

A: 1. The second copy of the Chinese Customs' Baggage Declaration Form [hereafter "BDF"] filled out by the expert at his port of entry into China and stamped by the Customs must be retained by the expert for inspection on future occasions when the expert brings articles into China.

2. Baggage and articles carried by foreign cultural/educational experts reporting for work in China, as well as items shipped separately, are in principle handled by Customs according to the same regulations governing those brought in by ordinary travelers, although appropriate allowances are made. In normal situations, accompanied baggage will not be inspected if the BDF is clearly filled out. Experts entering for the first time who bring more than the duty-free limit of certain valuable or key items, such as cameras, may be granted exemption of duty, as long as the items are for personal use.

3. Foreign cultural/educational experts reporting for work in China who have

shipped unaccompanied baggage must report at their port of entry the number of items in the shipment and the port of destination, and must within ten days of their entry into China take with them to the Customs office at their place of residence or the port of destination of the shipment the second copy of their BDF, as well as two identical copies of an itemized list of the articles in the shipment, to be matched against the items that come in. Shipments arrived and inspected within six months of the expert's first entry may be included in the duty-free allowance granted at the time of that entry; however, the prescribed duty will be imposed on all shipments for which there has been no itemized list provided, on shipped articles which exceed the duty-free allowance, and on those which arrive after the cutoff date. If the recipient does not wish to pay duty, the articles in question must be shipped back out of China.

(138) Q: What are the special allowances granted foreign cultural/educational experts on items for personal use which they bring into China?

A: 1. Experts who mail out or receive by mail a reasonable amount of goods for personal use whose value does not exceed 200 yuan Renminbi are exempted from the requirement to obtain an import/export permit; instead they may use an itemized list provided to the Customs by the FEB or a certificate from the expert's work unit. Such goods will be subject to inspection and duty according to regulations, although in the case of imports, the first 100 yuan of value shall be duty-free.

Articles which do not fit the designation "items for personal use" or whose value exceeds the allowable limit shall, in the case of exports, not be approved for mailing, and in the case of imports shall be returned by post to the sender within a prescribed time limit.

2. Duty on valuable or dutiable items received in shipments or mailings by a foreign expert shall be determined by Customs according to the BDF from the expert's first entry, as long as the expert's BDF has been marked as such by the Customs officials at his original port of entry.

(139) Q: What are the regulations concerning articles brought into China by foreign experts returning from visits home, vacations overseas, or trips to Hong Kong?

A: Baggage and articles brought back by foreign experts from short trips abroad (including Hong Kong and Macao) made during their period of employment in China are handled by Customs according to the regulations governing short-term visitors; i.e., only articles needed for the trip are exempted from duty. Experts wishing to carry on a short trip consumer durables that have already been granted duty exemptions by Customs must, if they wish to bring the articles in question back into China duty-free upon their return, have a note made on their BDF by Customs at the time of their exit. Upon their return, exemption from duty on the articles will be granted upon presentation of the BDF and inspection of the articles. Those failing to report such consumer durables to Customs at the time of their exit will be assessed duty according to regulations when they bring the articles back in.

(140) Q: What are the customs regulations concerning the transfer of ownership or the sale of articles for personal use which were previously cleared for import by Customs?

A: The transfer of ownership (including the sale) by the expert of articles for personal use which were previously cleared for import by Customs must be cleared by the local Customs office in advance, and duty paid on those articles which were exempted from duty at the time of import. Experts wishing to sell such articles may only do so at the local designated foreign goods purchasing organization; they may not privately transfer ownership in China to any unit or individual, or the matter will be regarded and dealt with by Customs as smuggling or infraction of regulations.

(141) Q: What are the customs regulations regarding precious metals (gold, silver, and platinum) and articles made from them?

A: Precious metals and articles made from them brought in by a foreign expert shall be cleared for export at the expert's time of departure according to the declaration originally indicated on the BDF. Articles of gold, silver, or platinum purchased in China shall be cleared for export upon presentation of the "Special Bill of Delivery" issued by the selling unit.

(142) Q: What are the customs regulations concerning Chinese cultural relics, etc.?

A: Foreign experts who in China purchase Chinese cultural relics, or paintings or character scrolls by deceased famous modern artists, will be able to have such articles cleared for export by Customs only if the articles carry a seal of appraisal from the government organs in charge of cultural relics and a special bill of sale issued to foreigners buying cultural relics, or a certificate of export issued by the government organs in charge of cultural relics.

(143) Q: What are the customs regulations concerning the import or purchase of automobiles for personal use?

A: Foreign experts, engineers, or technicians who come to China to work for one year or longer and who have obtained a Foreigner's Residence Permit are permitted to import, duty-free, one automobile for personal use; however, according to the regulations of Chinese Customs and the Bureau of Transportation, they must pay a surcharge. Those purchasing the duty-free automobiles of departing foreign diplomatic personnel must obtain the approval of Customs before undertaking [transfer-of-ownership] procedures.

(144) Q: May books, educational equipment, etc., used in the foreign expert's work be imported duty-free?

A: Foreign experts who, in order to meet the demands of their work, bring in a reasonable amount of such articles for personal use when they enter China will not be assessed duty on them.

(145) Q: What items are prohibited for import to China?

A: The following items may not be imported to China:

1. Weapons, ammunition, or explosives of any kind;
2. Counterfeit currency and counterfeit financial instruments;
3. Any printed matter, film negatives, photographs, records, films, sound recordings, video tapes, video discs, computer storage media, or other objects [containing material] harmful to our country's politics, economy, culture, or morals;
4. Any deadly poison;

5. Opium, morphine, heroin, marijuana, and other addictive narcotics and psychoactive drugs;

6. Any animal, plant, or plant or animal product containing dangerous disease-causing microorganisms, insect pests, or other harmful organisms;

7. Foods, medicines, and other articles harmful to health or liable to spread disease [due to their] origin in a region beset by epidemic disease;

8. Renminbi (except for that treated in accordance with currency accords; FEC shall be handled in accordance with the relevant regulations).

(146) Q: What items are prohibited for export from China?

A: The following items may not be exported from China:

1. All articles included under the above prohibitions on imports;

2. Manuscripts, printed matter, film negatives, photographs, records, films, sound recordings, video tapes, video discs, computer storage media, or other objects [containing material] pertaining to state secrets;

3. Valuable cultural relics or cultural relics prohibited for export;

4. Endangered or valuable animals and plants (including specimens) and their seeds and reproductive material.

(147) Q: May the foreign expert be informed of relevant customs regulations?

A: Yes. We ask that every unit concerned take care to present and explain the regulations to foreign experts, and to assist Customs in strictly implementing them and carrying them out.

CHAPTER NINE: TAXATION

(148) Q: What is the minimum taxable individual income of foreigners working in China?

A: Article Five of the *PRC Individual Income Tax Law* stipulates: "That portion of monthly wages and salaries that remains after 800 yuan per month for expenses has been deducted shall be taxable." In other words, the minimum taxable monthly income is 801 yuan.

(149) Q: Are foreign cultural/educational experts and foreign workers required to pay individual income tax?

A: Document No. 73 (1986) of the General Office of the State Council, *Notification of the Report Concerning the Adjustment of Salary Standards for Foreign Experts and Foreign Workers,* originally issued by the FEB and other government organs, stipulates: "After the adjustment in the salaries of foreign cultural/educational experts has been implemented, they shall pay taxes in accordance with the relevant provisions of the *PRC Individual Income Tax Law.* . . . Foreign workers whose salary exceeds the minimum taxable income must pay taxes according to regulations." In other words, foreign cultural/educational experts and foreign workers whose salaries exceed the minimum taxable income must pay taxes according to regulations.

(150) Q: What portions of the income of foreign cultural/educational experts and foreign workers may be legally taxed? What portions are not taxable?

A: All income representing monthly wages and salaries or earnings belonging within the category of wages and salaries paid to foreign cultural/educational experts and foreign workers for their engagement in educational, teaching or research activities in China is taxable. The third article of Document No. 275 (1986) of the Taxation Bureau of the Ministry of Finance, marked "Foreign Affairs," stipulates: "The vacation bonuses and bonuses for the completion of contracts of foreign cultural/educational experts and foreign workers are temporarily exempted from taxation."

(151) Q: What are the taxation rates and method of calculation of individual income tax?

A: The rate of taxation for all income from 801 yuan to 1,500 yuan is 5 percent; for income from 1,501 yuan to 3,000 yuan, 10 percent; for income from 3,000 yuan to 6,000 yuan, 20 percent. At present, no foreign workers have salaries in excess of these amounts.

Tax is calculated at graduated rates: for instance, if an expert's monthly income were 1,600 yuan, the 5 percent tax on the portion from 801 yuan to 1,500 yuan would be 35 yuan, and the 10 percent tax on the portion from 1,501 yuan to 1,600 yuan would be 10 yuan, making a monthly total of 45 yuan. However, since according to State Council Document No. 72 (1987), *Provisional Rules Governing the Collection of Individual Income Tax on the Wages and Salaries of Foreigners Working in China,* taxes owed by foreign cultural/educational experts and foreign workers are collected at only 50 percent of the calculated rate, this expert's actual monthly tax would be 22.50 yuan.

(152) Q: At present, which countries have signed agreements with the Chinese government to prevent double taxation (taxation agreements)? When will they be put into effect?

A: At present, there are nineteen countries that have signed taxation agreements with the Chinese government. The countries, and the dates their agreements with the Chinese government go into effect, are as follows:

January 1, 1985: Japan, United Kingdom, Federal Republic of Germany;

January 1, 1986: France, Denmark, Singapore;

January 1, 1987: United States, Malaysia, Norway, Canada, Sweden, New Zealand, Thailand;

January 1, 1988: Belgium, Finland, German Democratic Republic, Czechoslovakia;

Date of implementation not yet determined: Italy, Netherlands.

(153) Q: When did the taxation of the individual income of foreign cultural/educational experts and foreign workers in China begin? How is their tax calculated?

A: Taxation of the individual income of all foreign cultural/educational experts and foreign workers began at the time of issue of Document No. 73 (1986) of the General Office of the State Council, i.e., September 1, 1986. No tax is to be assessed on income prior to this date, regardless of the time the expert in question entered China or the length of his stay. Teachers and scientific researchers from countries which have signed taxation agreements with the Chinese government are temporarily exempted from paying individual income tax for a period of three years. Teachers and scientific researchers from Sweden and Denmark are to be accorded a special exemption of three years beginning from the date of their entry to China; taxation of their income shall begin in the fourth year. Those who entered China before the date of implementation of the relevant treaty, or who have been working in China many years already, shall be exempted from taxation for three years, beginning with the date of implementation of the treaty. Teachers and scientific researchers from Japan, the United Kingdom, and France whose accumulated or continuous period of work in China totals not more than three years shall be exempted from payment of individual income tax.

(154) Q: What are the various methods of payment of tax by foreign experts?
    A: There are two basic methods: The first is independent reporting and payment by the foreign expert, and the second is withholding and payment by the expert's unit. At present, the vast majority, i.e., those paid wages or salaries by their Chinese employing unit, use the latter method, with the unit withholding monthly the amount of tax required by law from the expert's wages or salary and submitting it to government taxation organs before the seventh of the following month. The taxable portion of income other than wages and salaries of foreign cultural/educational experts and foreign workers should also be withheld and paid [to the Bureau of Taxation] by the paying unit, or, alternatively, it may be independently reported and paid by the foreign expert.

(155) Q: Is the convertible portion of the foreign expert's salary taxable?
    A: The salaries of foreign experts, and of some foreign workers, contain a portion of convertible currency. According to regulations, taxes on the Renminbi portion and the convertible portion of such salaries must be calculated separately; however, in view of the fact that the foreign currency income of foreign cultural/educational experts and foreign workers is extremely limited, in order to display [our] solicitude towards them, tax on their income shall be calculated according to the total amount of income [without regard to its convertibility], and shall be payable entirely in Renminbi.

CHAPTER TEN: HEALTH CARE

(156) Q: What is the longest period of employment for which a foreign expert planning to come to China to work may be hired without being required to submit a certificate of health?
    A: The fifth article of *Some Rules on the Management of AIDS Testing,* a document jointly issued by the Foreign Ministry, the Ministries of Public Health and Public Security, the State Education Commission, the State Bureau of Tourism, CAAC, and the FEB, and approved by the State Council, stipulates: "Foreigners coming to China to establish permanent residence or residence of one year (or academic year) or longer must, at the time of their application for a visa, submit a certificate showing the results of a serologic test for AIDS [The original text specifies a "serologic test for AIDS," not a test for the Human Immunodeficiency Virus (HIV), which is probably what is meant] issued within six months of the date of application for the visa by a public or government-accredited hospital of their country of origin. Said certificate must be verified by the Chinese embassy or consulate."
    Excluding those who work in news media or publishing units and whose contracts are for one year, most foreign experts and foreign workers in China work in

post-secondary educational institutions, and their contracts are signed for a single academic year. However, since after completion of their contract most of these will remain in China to travel, and hence their residency documents are usually valid for a full year, all foreign experts, foreign workers, and their family members coming to China are required to submit a certificate of health including certification of the serologic test for AIDS.

(157) Q: What are the specific procedures involved in obtaining the health certificate?

A: The hiring unit shall first proceed to the local government public health and quarantine office to obtain [several] copies of the standard Ministry of Public Health form, *Record of Foreigner's Physical Examination* [hereafter "FPE"], and the booklet, *What You Should Know About Public Health and Quarantine Regulations When Entering China,* and shall mail these to the foreign expert or foreign worker before he comes to China. Alternatively, the unit may advise the employee to obtain these documents at a Chinese embassy or consulate. No matter which of these methods is used, the hiring unit must remind the employee of his responsibility to have the health evaluation done and the FPE filled in by the hospital in duplicate. One completed copy is to be sent to the hiring unit, the other presented for verification at the Chinese embassy or consulate where the employee applies for his visa and also carried with him when he enters China. After the expert arrives in China, the hiring unit must take his FPE to the local government office of public health and quarantine, where it will be verified and a *Certificate of Verification of the FPE* will be issued. The organs of public security will require presentation of the *Certificate of Verification of the FPE* before they issue residency documents.

(158) Q: What if the foreign expert fails to have the serologic test for AIDS performed before coming to China, due to lack of opportunity in his own country?

A: The document *Some Rules on the Management of AIDS Testing* states: "Foreigners who due to limitations in their home country have not had the serologic test for AIDS performed there must proceed within twenty days of their entry to China to a designated medical organization and undergo testing there."

(159) Q: Who will assume the cost of the foreigner's physical exam?

A: All expenses for the physical exam (including all items on the FPE), whether performed in the expert's home country or, due to limitations in his home country, at a medical organization in China after his arrival, shall be borne by the expert. If the expert, due to conditions created by our side, is rendered unable to provide an FPE according to regulations, then expenses for his examination in China shall be borne by the employer.

(160) Q: What illnesses or medical conditions shall preclude a foreigner's entry into China?

A: According to the provisions of the *Detailed Rules on the Implementation of the EEL,* foreigners with mental illness, Hansen's disease, AIDS, venereal disease, active tuberculosis, or other contagious or infectious diseases may not enter the People's Republic of China.

(161) Q: What if it is discovered after an expert comes to China that he has a serious chronic illness which will compromise his ability to maintain normal work?

A: If the employer discovers that this is the case, it must terminate the contract immediately and undertake procedures to send the expert home as soon as possible. If the illness is a preexisting condition that the expert concealed from the unit before coming to China, then he shall be responsible for his own return travel expenses; if the chronic illness appeared only after the expert came to China, then the unit shall provide him an international air ticket, and the sooner [the employer] can send him off, the better.

(162) Q: What if the foreign expert requests inoculation against disease?

A: If the foreign expert requests an inoculation that is available at the local medical facilities, permission may be given for inoculation and the stipulated fee collected. If the foreign expert requests to be inoculated with blood products he has brought himself, permission must be politely refused and explanation duly provided.

(163) Q: What medical expenses are not covered by foreign experts' medical benefits?

A: [Even with medical benefits,] expenses for the following must be borne by the expert himself: registration, house calls, dental fillings/bridges, teeth cleaning, cosmetic surgery, eyeglasses, board while in hospital, and non-medicinal tonics.

(164) Q: If a foreign expert has a medical appointment at a non-designated hospital, can he be reimbursed for the cost?

A: Hospitals where they are to be treated are designated for most foreign experts in China by their employing unit. If personnel at the the designated hospital feel the expert should be transferred to another facility or a specializing hospital, then with the unit's agreement medical expenses at the non-designated hospital may be reimbursed according to regulations. However, if the expert proceeds on his own initiative to another hospital without the prior approval of the designated hospital or of his unit, then reimbursement of medical expenses incurred there is usually refused.

(165) Q: May the expert be reimbursed for the cost of medicines purchased in Hong Kong or other places?

A: No, he may not.

(166) Q: Should the employing unit provide a car to take the foreign expert to medical appointments?

A: Except in the case of those designated "senior experts," the employing unit usually does not provide a car for this purpose. If the expert is suddenly taken seriously ill and needs to be taken to the emergency room, then the unit shall provide a car free of charge or shall reimburse taxi expenses.

(167) Q: What are the special problems to look out for when a critically ill expert is transferred to another hospital for treatment?

A: When it is determined that a critically ill expert needs to be transferred to another hospital for treatment, the employing unit and the original hospital must first contact and obtain permission from the hospital to which the expert is to be transferred. A qualified person from the original hospital must accompany the expert during the transfer, and the employing unit must send someone who understands the expert's language. The results of all pertinent diagnostic tests, as well as the patient's medical history, should be sent over, and the receiving hospital should be notified of the patient's basic condition, so that the necessary preparations may be made.

(168) Q: What points must be observed if it is discovered that a foreign expert has died in China?

A: As soon as it it is discovered that a foreign expert has died, the employing unit must immediately notify the local Public Security Bureau and Office of Foreign Affairs [of the local government] and report to their supervisory organ and the FEB. Moreover, the embassy or consulate of the foreigner's native country, as well as his relatives back home, should be notified as quickly as possible. The contents of the notification should be simple and clear; for instance, if the cause of death is not clear, then relatives may be notified that the expert has died and that the cause of death is still under investigation. If the death was due to ordinary causes (such as advanced age or some illness), then the work of clearing up the expert's affairs shall be left to the employing unit. If the death was due to extraordinary causes (such as a sudden, unexpected incident), then the scene of death should be left untouched so that evidence may be collected by the organs of public security. In this case, the employing unit should actively cooperate [with the Public Security Bureau], and the body should be properly preserved (for instance, by embalming or refrigeration) before it is disposed of.

(169) Q: How should matters be arranged if an expert dies of ordinary causes?

A: When a foreign expert dies of ordinary causes in China, a death certificate must be issued by a hospital at the county level or above. If before his death the expert was in hospital for emergency or other treatment, then a certificate of diagnosis or a summary of the patient's medical history may be released to his relatives on their request.

Relatives who request permission to come to China to settle the affairs of foreign experts who die of illness must pay their own expenses; if they have difficulty coming up with the money, the employing unit may provide an appropriate amount of assistance.

(170) Q: How should matters be arranged if an expert dies of extraordinary causes?

A: A certificate of the cause of death will be issued by the organs of public security or of justice in the case of foreign experts whose death is due to traffic accidents, work accidents, unexpected injury, sudden incidents, or other extraordinary causes. Generally the Chinese side pays the round-trip transportation expenses of relatives of experts who die in this manner if they wish to come to China to settle affairs.

(171) Q: What if the relatives request that an autopsy be performed on the body of an expert who has died?

A: In the case of those dying of ordinary causes, or of extraordinary but obvious causes, it is usually not necessary to perform an autopsy. If the relatives of the deceased or the officials at the embassy or consulate of his home country request that an autopsy be performed, permission may be granted, but the request must be in written form and must be signed by a relative of the deceased or the appropriate official from his embassy. Autopsies determined necessary to determine the cause of death in extraordinary circumstances shall be handled, according to the relevant regulations, by the organs of public security and of justice.

(172) Q: What if the relatives of a deceased expert request to transport the body back home?

A: In general, the bodies of experts who die in China must be cremated or buried. (Excepting in the cases of those who die of AIDS, whose bodies must be cremated, the expert's religious beliefs and folk customs shall be respected.) Cremation may only be carried out after a written request signed by a relative of the deceased or the appropriate official from his embassy is submitted; ashes are to be carried or shipped back to the home country. If the deceased expert's relatives are opposed to cremation, arrangements may be made to ship the body to the home country; the employing unit should help make the necessary arrangements, but actual procedures and expenses must all be undertaken and borne by the foreign party.

(173) Q: What documents are required for the export of a body?

A: 1. In the case of ordinary death, a death certificate issued by a hospital;

2. In the case of extraordinary death, the certificate of the cause of death issued by the organs of public security or of justice;

3. A certificate of embalming from a hospital;

4. A permit for the export of human remains from the government organs of public health and quarantine.

(174) Q: In the event of a foreign expert's death, should his employing unit hold any sort of ceremony?

A: In order to meet the demands of foreign affairs work and of propriety, before the body is cremated or shipped home, a simple memorial service for the deceased may be held by the employing unit, at which wreaths should be contributed by the appropriate units. A few photographs may be taken at the memorial service to present to the relatives of the deceased. After cremation, the unit may present a container for the ashes of the deceased. If the foreign party requests that a religious service be held, a simple one may be arranged according to local conditions (depending upon whether there is a pastor, church, etc.).

(175) Q: Should compensation or a pension be issued [the relatives of the deceased] in the case of a foreign expert's death due to extraordinary causes?

A: If a foreign expert's death is due to a traffic accident, then the party responsible for the accident should provide economic compensation according to the regulations of the relevant government departments. If the expert's death is due to other causes, then the employing unit should judge for itself whether or not a pension should be issued the surviving relatives, and should obtain the approval of its supervisory organ.

(176) Q: What are the points for attention in disposing of a foreign expert's belongings in the event of his death?

A: A relative of the deceased or an official from his embassy, as well as a representative from the Chinese side, should be present when inventory is taken of the expert's possessions. If the deceased had no relatives and the embassy or consulate is unable to send an official, then a notary public may be asked to attend in their place. A notebook must be devoted to a detailed inventory of the belongings of the deceased, each item of which must be initialed by the parties present at the inventory. The recipient of the belongings must issue a receipt specifying the date, time, and place of transfer as well as the names of those present; this receipt must be notarized after being signed by all parties. If the deceased left a will, it should be photographed or photocopied and the original given to a relative of the deceased or an official from his embassy.

(177) Q: How are the belongings of a foreign expert who has died in China to be disposed of?

A: If the deceased left a will, then the belongings shall be disposed of according to its terms. If there is no will, then the expert's relatives must have full power of disposal. If the foreign expert's relatives back home do not come to China to settle his affairs, choosing instead to entrust matters to their embassy or consulate in China, then an official from said embassy or consulate must be asked to proceed to the place of residence of the deceased and decide how the belongings should be disposed of. If the expert had no relatives back home and left no will, then disposal of his belongings shall be decided by the local courts of law.

CHAPTER ELEVEN: MARRIAGE AND CHILDREN

(178) Q: What are the procedures that must be undertaken by foreigners who wish to get married in China?

A: If two foreigners wish to get married in China, then the parties to the marriage must apply to register the marriage at the Bureau of Civil Administration. After investigation of the matter by an official of this bureau has established that the male and female parties to the marriage meet the requirements of the *Marriage Law* of the PRC, permission to register will be granted and a marriage certificate issued.

(179) Q: What are the procedures that must be undertaken by a foreign expert wishing to marry a Chinese in China?

A: If a foreign expert or scholar and a Chinese citizen wish to get married in China, the male and female parties must first proceed to the designated marriage registry of the People's Government of the province, autonomous region, or directly administered municipality where the Chinese party is registered as a resident and there apply for marriage registration.

(180) Q: What documents are required of a foreign expert who wishes to marry a Chinese?

A: A foreign expert going to register his or her marriage with a Chinese must take along his valid passport, the residence documents or household registration book issued by the organs of public security, and certification of marital status and of health. Certification of marital status of the foreigner must be notarized by a notary in the foreigner's home country or provided by his embassy or consulate. Certification of marital status of the Chinese must be provided by the People's Government of the county (or level corresponding to county) where he or she is a registered resident or by his or her work unit.

(181) Q: Which groups of Chinese citizens may not marry foreigners?

A: Active military personnel, foreign service personnel, public security personnel, people with security clearances for confidential/classified information and others holding important secrets, and people currently undergoing reform through labor or serving sentence under law. With the exception of the above groups of people, any couple who are both willing to get married and who meet the requirements of the *Marriage Law* of the *PRC* will be given permission to register.

(182) Q: What status shall be accorded to a Chinese citizen who marries a foreign expert?

A: In principle, a Chinese who has married a foreign expert should be treated the same as the foreign spouses of other experts in all areas, including political considerations, protocol and etiquette, and privileges. Specific questions of how to treat such spouses should be resolved with a view to how the contract with the expert was originally signed and the current actual situation of the Chinese spouse. If the Chinese spouse of the expert has a job, his or her medical benefits shall continue to be covered by his or her work unit, and the expert's unit shall not assume responsibility for them. If the expert's spouse does not have a job or has left his or her job, the expert's employer shall extend medical benefits to the spouse.

(183) Q: Should the foreign expert's employing unit pay for the international travel expenses of the Chinese spouse of a foreign expert when the expert takes him or her back to the expert's country upon completion of the contract?

A: According to regulations laid down in FEB Document No. 190 (1985), there are two possible alternatives in this case: 1) When the foreign expert returns home upon completion of his or her contract, international air tickets shall be provided for his family members of Chinese citizenship who are accompanying him or her back. 2) The request of the foreign expert to maintain his or her status as a single expert as far as salary is concerned after marrying a Chinese may be accommodated if he or she agrees to assume all transportation expenses for his or her family members of Chinese citizenship when he or she returns to his or her home country upon completion of the contract. The options of being paid as a single expert and of receiving plane tickets for family members may not be exercised at the same time; one of the two options must be chosen at the time of the expert's marriage to the Chinese.

(184) Q: Once the foreign expert has left China after completing his or her contract, will the expert's work unit continue to provide for any expenses of a Chinese spouse who remains in China?

A: When the expert leaves China after his contract reaches term, this means that the contract has been completed. Since at this time the relationship between the original employer and employee is ended, the original employer will no longer assume responsibility for any expenses of the expert's spouse who remains in China.

(185) Q: How much honeymoon leave should be given to a foreign expert who marries a Chinese?

A: Honeymoon vacation should be granted according to the provisions of China's *Marriage Law;* usually, this means three days.

(186) Q: How is the nationality of children born in China to a foreign expert and his or her Chinese spouse to be determined?

A: According to China's *Nationality Law,* any child born in China to parents of whom one is a Chinese citizen is of Chinese nationality and must be registered at the offices of public security at the father or mother's place of registered residence.

(187) Q: How are residence documents for an expert's newborn child obtained?

A: When a child is born to a foreign expert or scholar whose spouse is also a foreigner, they must register at the Public Security Bureau of their place of residence, presenting a birth certificate and a passport bearing the newborn child's name. If the parents are in China only temporarily, the child's name may be added as "accompanying child" on the visa of either of the parents.

(188) Q: How much maternity leave is granted to female foreign experts who have children during their period of employment in China?

A: Usually fifty-six days' maternity leave is granted, during which time the usual salary continues to be paid.

(189) Q: May foreign affairs cadres involved in work with foreign experts engage in courtship and marriage with a foreign expert?

A: Anyone who meets the requirements of China's *Marriage Law* may receive permission to marry, but the Chinese party should not return to work involving foreign experts; rather, he or she should be reassigned.

(190) Q: May foreign affairs cadres informally adopt or swear brother- or sisterhood with a foreign expert?

A: Informal adoption and sworn brother- or sisterhood are old customs which should not be encouraged. Foreign affairs cadres represent the unit in its dealings with the outside, and practices on their part such as informal adoption not only reflect a less than serious attitude; in addition, such practices will greatly inconvenience their work with foreigners. We promote the active engagement of foreign affairs cadres in friendship activities with foreign experts; the purpose of these activities is to promote mutual understanding and friendship, to stimulate the experts' enthusiasm, and to allow the experts fully to display their talents.

(191) Q: May a student currently in school engage in courtship and marriage with a foreign expert?

A: According to the regulations of the State Education Commission concerning management of students' academic standing, students currently in school are not permitted to engage in courtship and marriage. If a Chinese student wishes to marry a foreign expert, the student must first withdraw from his or her studies.

(192) Q: How should the request of a foreign expert to adopt a Chinese child be handled?

A: The request of a foreign expert to adopt a Chinese child must be treated with great seriousness. Requests to adopt made by foreigners who are in China temporarily or whose period of work is short are usually not granted. As for foreign experts who have been working in China a long time, the first task is to ascertain their attitude towards China, their objectives in adopting the child, and their financial situation back in their own country. Once this has been done, matters should be handled according to the regulations of the relevant organs of the Chinese government concerning the adoption of Chinese infants by foreigners.

(193) Q: What sort of conditions must foreign experts meet, and what sort of documents must they provide, in order to adopt a Chinese child?

A: In order to adopt a Chinese child, the foreign expert and his or her spouse must appear in person at the local public notary office (or notary office of the judicial bureau) of the adoptee's place of registered residence bearing five types of documents (see below) in order to notarize the adoption. If due to special circumstances only one of the spouses is able to appear at one time, he or she must provide a notarized statement from the other spouse expressing agreement to the adoption.

The necessary documents are as follows:

1. An application requesting adoption of a Chinese child (including the purpose of adoption and guarantees that the child will not be abandoned or abused);

2. Certificates of health of the adopting parents;

3. Certification of employment and income (including the family situation, full names, ages, nationalities, address, and housing situation of both adopting parents);

4. Certification of marriage of the adopting parents;

5. Certificate from the relevant government department of the foreign expert's home country approving the adoption.

The party giving up the child for adoption must provide the following:

1. The infant's birth certificate;

2. Personally handwritten and signed statement of permission from the natural parents of the child;

3. Certificate from the local government of the child's place of residence.

(194) Q: How should the question of the nationality of a child adopted by a foreign expert be handled?

A: Article Four of China's *Nationality Law* states that when the child of Chinese citizens is adopted by citizens of a foreign country, it does not lose its Chinese nationality merely because of the adoptive relationship.

However, the foreign expert may apply on his adoptive child's behalf at the [local] county or municipal Public Security Bureau for a renunciation of Chinese citizenship.

(195) Q: What procedures must be undertaken by foreign experts filing for divorce in China?

A: In the event that efforts by mediators to effect a reconciliation fail, the procedures established by Chinese law may be followed.

The two parties must provide the following valid documentation: certificate of marriage, a document of assent to the divorce from the embassy or consulate of their home country, and a statement guaranteeing that questions of division of property and custody of offspring are settled. After [presenting these documents and] obtaining approval from the departments of the Chinese in charge [of such matters], the two parties may proceed to the Civil Affairs Bureau of their place of residence to apply for termination of their marriage agreement.

CHAPTER TWELVE: RELIGION

(196) Q: How should we implement China's government policies on religion in our work with foreign experts?

A: Our country's policy regarding religion provides for citizens' freedom of religious belief. Legitimate religious activities are protected by the state. All religious organizations in our country handle their affairs independently and freely, without the domination or control of any foreign element.

We do not interfere with the individual religious beliefs of any foreign expert who comes to China to work. Experts may participate in religious life at religious sites open to the public, but only in the capacity of ordinary believers; they are not permitted to propagate their religion in China, to proselytize, or to interfere with China's religious affairs.

(197) Q: What kinds of religious personnel may not be asked to come work in China?

A: Foreign clergy and missionaries are to be strictly limited. A few who are friendly to China, who possess particular knowledge and talent, and who are not in China to missionize may be hired with the permission of the higher authorities; in general, however, it is not appropriate to recruit religious personnel to come and work in China. As for professional missionaries who enter China in the guise of foreign experts, they must be notified that we are aware of their presence. We must explain to them our country's policies regarding religion and strengthen our management over them. Their contracts must not be extended.

(198) Q: What sorts of demands must we make of those foreign experts who are religious believers and of those who come from a [professionally] religious background?

A: We should explain our country's policies regarding religion to those foreign experts who are religious believers and those who are sent to China by organizations with religious backgrounds, demanding that they respect our country's constitution, laws, and regulations. They are permitted to participate in religious life at religious sites open to the public, but they may not engage in missionary activity or distribute Bibles or religious propaganda, nor may they proselytize or organize students to participate in religious activities.

(199) Q: What if it is discovered that a foreign expert is conducting missionary activities?

A: If it is discovered that a foreign expert is engaging in missionary activity such as the distribution of Bibles and other religious propaganda, proselytism, systematic propagation of religious dogma, etc., he must be sternly warned that these activities are in contravention of his work contract and ordered to cease. If the expert ignores the warnings and the situation worsens, the matter may be reported to the higher authorities—the appropriate departments under the Central Committee or the provincial, regional, or directly administered municipal governments— with whose permission the expert may be fired. As for those who are sent to China with special missions by international reactionary religious organizations, their presence should be reported to China's organs of public security so that the necessary actions may be taken.

(200) Q: May we establish relationships with foreign schools and bodies that are religious-affiliated or funded by religious organizations? May we accept their financial support?

A: In the past few years, many official, semi-official, and popular organizations and institutions of higher education abroad have, after receiving funds from religious organizations, sent experts, scholars, and teachers to China. Generally, the experts, scholars, and teachers who have come via these channels have done much to benefit our country by their teaching and their introduction of modern management techniques and scientific/technological knowledge. At the same time, we must also realize that foreign religious organizations will actively employ these channels to send people to China in the guise of "experts" and "teachers" to engage in missionary activity. We must be fully aware of this situation.

Generally, we may accept experts, financial support, and books and teaching materials from religious organizations as long as the contribution is unconditional, will not interfere with our use of funds, and will benefit the development of our educational and scientific endeavors. We may also establish exchange and cooperative relationships with these organizations and schools, but in order that control may be maintained over the situation and exchange of information facilitated, this may only be done after review and approval by the FEB and the State Education Commission.

(201) Q: May the Bible be used as teaching material?

A: Foreign experts may not use the Bible as teaching material in the classroom. However, if necessary, allusions to material from the Bible may be explained and some basic religious knowledge introduced. This should not be regarded as missionary activity.

(202) Q: Are Chinese personnel permitted to accept Bibles as gifts from foreign experts?

A: When a foreign expert offers a Bible as a gift to an individual, the individual may refuse with the explanation that he is not a religious believer. Alternatively, the Bible may be accepted and the matter reported to [the individual's work] organization. If it is discovered that a foreign expert is actively distributing a large number of Bibles, this must be regarded as missionary activity, criticized, and stopped. Efforts should be made to retrieve all Bibles.

(203) Q: May students invited or organized by an expert to visit a church be permitted to go?

A: Students invited or organized by a foreign expert to visit a church should politely refuse or advise the expert not to organize such trips. If a visit to a church is deemed necessary, it must be arranged by the school.

(204) Q: May interpreters asked by a foreign expert to accompany him to church services be allowed to go?

A: Foreign experts are free to visit temples and churches to sightsee, visit, or attend Mass or Djumah [Friday worship at the mosque]. The expert's request to be accompanied by a Chinese interpreter may be accommodated, but the interpreter must not take part in any ceremony.

(205) Q: What if a foreign expert requests that a venue for religious services be provided at his work unit?

A: Foreign experts may participate in religious life at church facilities that are open to the public or in their own living quarters. Public spaces may not be used for religious activities.

(206) Q: May the invitation [of Chinese co-workers] by a foreign expert to his church wedding be accepted?

A: A small number of the expert's colleagues and students may be allowed to attend an expert's church wedding as a matter of courtesy, but they must not participate in any religious ceremony. It is not appropriate for school authorities or department heads to attend church weddings; instead, they may offer their congratulations at the expert's quarters after the service.

(207) Q: After the death of a foreign expert, may the request of his relatives to hold a church funeral be granted?

A: This is a question of individual religious belief, with which we should not interfere. If the relatives require assistance, appropriate help may be provided.

CHAPTER THIRTEEN: OTHER QUESTIONS

(208) Q: What if a foreign expert requests to donate blood?

A: China does not publicly mobilize or issue calls to foreign experts to donate blood, but if they meet relevant age and health requirements, such a request may be granted. The same fee for supplemental nutrition that is provided to Chinese citizens who donate blood voluntarily, as established by the organs of public health, may be given to the donating expert. Those experts who refuse to accept the fee may be presented with an appropriate memento. Please note, however, that in making public the names of foreign experts who have donated blood, great care must be taken to avoid making experts who have not donated blood feel pressured to do so.

(209) Q: May the Chinese national flag be presented to foreign experts as a gift?

A: Experts who consistently display a friendly attitude towards China may be presented with a Chinese flag if they so request; however, it should not be a large flag—small flags are more appropriate. If the expert does not request a flag, do not present one unsolicited.

(210) Q: How should mementos presented by a foreign expert to our side be disposed of?

A: The sixth article of State Council Document No. 48 (1984) states that ordinary small gifts and mementos, such as ballpoint pens (including those with a digital watch display on the side), notebooks, lighters, handkerchiefs, scarves, children's toys, food products, and ordinary electronic watches and pocket calculators, may be retained by the receiving unit or distributed to its members.

(211) Q: May persons from the Chinese side take part in activities sponsored by foreign experts' embassies or consulates?

A: Celebrations, film festivals, or other friendship activities organized by an expert's embassy or consulate may be attended by persons from the Chinese side if an invitation has been issued by the embassy or consulate directly or via the expert. The expert's unit or the foreign affairs office of the local government should decide who is to attend, basing the selection on the nature of the activity. The number of attendees should be appropriately restricted. Other types of activities sponsored by embassies and consulates should usually not be attended.

(212) Q: May the employing unit provide a venue for foreign experts' celebration of Christmas?

A: Christmas is an important holiday in European and American countries. If foreign experts wish to organize a celebration or dance, the employing unit may provide a venue in accordance with the experts' request. In units with a relatively great number of experts, the Chinese side may actively assist in the organization of appropriate activities.

(213) Q: What are the points for attention in providing documents to foreign experts?

A: The following points must be observed by units issuing employee identification, white cards, residence documents, and medical cards to their foreign experts:

1) The beginning and ending date of validity (including year, month, and day) of each document must be clearly indicated thereon. The period of validity of the medical card should be identical with that of the expert's contract, and that of the white card, residence permit, and employee identification should match the expert's visa.

2) In principle, all documents issued to the expert by his unit should be returned to the unit before he leaves China. Some experts ask to keep their employee identification or school badge as a memento; the employing unit may decide whether this is appropriate. The medical card, however, must be returned to the unit.

3) When a foreign expert extends his contract, the employing unit must obtain new documents, or extend the validity of the existing ones, as soon as possible; otherwise, the expert may encounter problems when he presents invalid documents.

(214) Q: What are the specific procedures involved in applying for a Foreigner's Residence Permit?

A: A visa with validity of a year or longer should be applied for on behalf of experts whose period of employment will be one year (or academic year) or longer. Moreover, experts should be told to undergo the complete physical exam, including the AIDS test, before coming to China. When the experts arrive in China, their FPEs should be taken to the local government office of public health and quarantine to be exchanged for the *Certificate of Verification of the FPE,* which the Public Security Bureau requires before it can issue the (long-term) residence permit. Those who have not undergone the physical examination and who will be in China less than a year may obtain only a temporary residence permit.

(215) Q: What is the difference between a foreign expert's residence permit and a temporary residence permit?

A: According to *Detailed Rules on the Implementation of the EEL,* foreigners coming to China for one year or longer shall obtain a residence permit; those coming for less than one year shall obtain a temporary residence permit.

The (long-term) residence permit is deep green in color, and has a photo of the issuee attached; the (short-term) temporary residence permit is pale green and has no photo attached. Foreign experts holding the long-term permit enjoy exemptions from duty on certain regulated items when they bring them through Customs on their way into China; holders of the short-term permit do not enjoy this privilege. In addition, holders of the [long-term] residence permit enjoy discounts on plane and train tickets and hotel rooms. Therefore, units hiring experts for one academic year or longer should do their best to obtain the long-term permit for the experts.

(216) Q: May employee identification be issued to the spouses of foreign experts?

A: If the foreign expert's spouse does not work for the unit, he or she should not be issued employee identification; however, if any of the expert's family members are hired as foreign teachers, they should be issued employee identification.

(217) Q: How should an expert's request to donate money or goods to relief in a disaster area be treated?

A: The employing unit may accept and pass on such donations from experts who make them voluntarily, or the expert may be allowed to send the money or items personally by post. Government organs receiving such donations may express their thanks in a fashion appropriate to the situation.

(218) Q: What if the children of foreign experts ask to join the Young Pioneers or the Communist Youth League?

A: Experts' children who are studying in Chinese schools should not be discriminated against in this regard. If they request on their own initiative to join the Young Pioneers or the Communist Youth League, they may (if they meet the required conditions) carry out the same application procedures as apply to Chinese students.

(219) Q: Must Chinese people register as visitors when they enter a foreign expert's hostel?

A: Experts who live in hostels located at their employing unit will often receive visits in their quarters from their supervisors, colleagues, and students for various purposes, including socializing, discussing work, and tutoring. This activity is normal and should be supported and encouraged by all units. For this reason, all visitors who are supervisors, colleagues, or students of the expert in question and who are from the same unit need only show their employee identification, student identification, or school badge to be allowed in by the concierge; they need not be asked to register. As for visitors from society at large who are unrelated to the expert's work, the policy of requiring them to register must be strictly followed, in order to ensure the expert's personal safety.

References

Abe, H. (1987). Borrowing from Japan: China's first modern education system. In R. Hayhoe & M. Bastid (Eds.), *China's education and the industrialized world* (pp. 57–80). New York: M. E. Sharpe.

Agreement between Hunan Medical College and the Yale-China Association concerning the program in english language instruction. (1987). New Haven, CT: Yale University.

Agreement between the government of the United States of America and the government of the People's Republic of China on cooperation in science and technology. (1979). Washington, DC: U.S. Information Agency.

Agreement between the Union of Soviet Socialist Republics and the People's Republic of China concerning cultural cooperation, signed at Moscow on July 5, 1956. (1974). In J. Cohen & H. Chio (Eds.), *People's China and international law: a documentary study,* pp. 1174–1176. Princeton, NJ: Princeton University Press.

Agreement for the establishment of the NU-JHU Center for Chinese and American studies. (1981). Unpublished. Nanjing.

Agreement on scholarly agreement between Nanjing University of the People's Republic of China and the Johns Hopkins University of the United States of America (1981). Unpublished. Nanjing.

Bastid, M. (1987). Servitude or liberation? The introduction of foreign educational practices and systems to China from 1840 to the present. In R. Hayhoe & M. Bastid (Eds.), *China's education and the industrialized world,* (pp. 3–20). New York: M. E. Sharpe.

Biggerstaff, K. (1961). *The earliest modern government schools in China.* (Ithaca, NY: Cornell University Press.

Butt, R. (1979). My days in China. In *Living in China* (pp. 84–97). Beijing: New World Press.

Campbell, S. (1951, January) Reforming the colleges, an interview with Tsao Weifeng, *China Monthly Review* (pp. 8–10). Shanghai.

Chung, L. C. (1934). *A history of democratic education in modern China.* Shanghai: Commercial Press.

Cleverley, J. (1977). Deflowering the cultural revolution: Letter from China. *Change, 9*(5), 15–17.

College Education: Socialist Orientation Reiterated. (1979). *Beijing Review, 22,* 17, 8–9.

Complete text of the agreement between the Hunan government and the Yale mission forming the Siangya Med. Educ. Assoc. (1913). New Haven, CT: Yale University.

Contract. (1979). [Between Xinxiang Teachers' College and Ed Porter). Unpublished. Henan, Xinxiang, China.

Contract. (1987). [Between Henan Teachers' University and John Leggett]. Unpublished. Henan, Xinxiang, China.

Covell, R. (1978). *W. A. P. Martin: Pioneer of progress in China.* Washington, DC: Christian University Press.

Crook, I., & Crook, D. (1979). An Anglo-Canadian couple's 30 years in China. In *Living in China* (pp. 40–62). Beijing: New World Press.

Draft agreement between the Hunan Medical College and the Yale-China Association. (1980). New Haven, CT: Yale University.

Fenn, W. P. (1976). *Christian higher education in changing China, 1880–1950.* Grand Rapids, MI: Erdmans.

Goldstein, S. M. (1984). *The People's Republic of China: A basic handbook* (4th ed.). New York: The Asia Society.

Gu, M. Y. (1984). The development of reform of higher education in China. *Comparative Education, 20,* 141–148.

Hawkins, J. (1981). Chinese education. In E. Ignas (Ed.), *Comparative educational systems* (pp. 91–134). Itaska, IL: F. E. Peacock.

Hayhoe, R. (1984). A comparative analysis of Chinese-Western academic exchange. *Comparative Education, 20,* 39–56.

Holden, R. (1964). *Yale in China, the mainland 1901–1951.* New Haven, CT: The Yale in China Association.

Hookham, H. (1972). *A short history of China.* New York: New American Library.

Hsu, F. (1985). *Americans and Chinese.* Honolulu: University of Hawaii Press.

Hu, C. T. (1984). The historical background: Examinations and control in pre-modern China. *Comparative Education, 20,* 7–25.

Hucker, C. (1975). *China's imperial past.* Stanford, CA: Stanford University Press.

Ignas, E. (1981). The traditional American system. In E. Ignas (Ed.), *Comparative educational systems* (pp. 1–44). Itaska, IL: F. E. Peacock.

Giles, H. A. (1923). *Gems of chinese literature.* Hong Kong: Kelly & Walsh, Ltd.

Klochko, M. A. (1971). Science and scientists in Peking. In S. E. Frazier (Ed.), *Education and communism in China* (pp. 465–494). London: Pall Mall.

Kormondy, E. (1982). The People's Republic of China: Revitalizing an educational system. *Change, 14*(5), 32–37.

Louie, K. (1984). Salvaging Confucian education (1949–1983). *Comparative Education, 20,* 27–38.

Maley, A. (1983). Xanadu—a miracle of rare device. *Language Learning and Communication, 2*(1), 97–104.

Martin, W. (1900a). *A cycle of Cathey; or, China, south and north.* Edinburgh, Scotland: O. Anderson and Ferrier.

Martin, W. (1900b). *The siege in Peking.* New York. Fleming H. Revell.

Memorandum [establishing Yellow River University]. (1984). Henan, Zhengzhou.

Memorandum of agreement between the Johns Hopkins University and Nanjing University. (1984). Unpublished. Nanjing.

Montaperto, R. (1979). Introduction to China's schools in flux. *Chinese Education, 11*(4), 5–21.

Murray, D. (1982). The great walls of China. *Today's Education, 71*(1), 55–58.

Orleans, L. A. (1960). *Professional manpower and education in communist China.* Washington, DC: U.S. Government Printing Office.

Orleans, L. A. (1987). Soviet influence on China's higher education. In R. Hayhoe & M. Bastid (Eds.), *China's education and the industrialized world* (pp. 184–198). New York: M. E. Sharpe.

Peking University Educational Revolution Group. (1972). Insist on the unity of politics and vocational work: Comprehensively grasp conditions for enrollment. *Chinese Education, 13*(1–2), 99–103.

People's Republic of China Suspends the Fulbright Program. (1989). The Board of Foreign Scholarships. Washington, DC: U.S. Information Agency.

Price, R. F. (1987). Convergence or copying: China and the Soviet Union. In R. Hayhoe & M. Bastid (Eds.), *China's education and the industrialized world* (pp. 158–183). New York: M. E. Sharpe.

Qin, F. M. (October, 1986). A familiar yet strange place. *Graduate Student Newsletter (Shandong University),* pp. 3–4.

Regulations on the work and daily life of foreign experts in China. (1986). Beijing: Foreign Experts Bureau.

Scovel, J. (1983). English teaching in China: A historical perspective. *Language Learning and Communication, 2*(1), 105–109.

Scovel, T. (1983). The impact of foreign experts, methodology, and materials on English language study in China. *Language Learning and Communication, 2*(1), 83–91.

Spence, J. (1980). *To change China.* New York: Penguin.

[Report of U.S.-China exchanges]. (1986, January 15). *The Chronicle of Higher Education,* p. 24.

Teng, S. (1961). *China's response to the West.* Cambridge: Harvard University Press.

U.S.-China Education Clearinghouse. (1980). *An Introduction to education in the People's Republic of China and U.S.-China educational exchanges.* Washington, DC: Author.

Wang, K. (1981). English and other foreign language teaching in the People's Republic of China. *College English, 43,* 653–662.

Wu, J. (1983). Quchang Buduan: A Chinese view of foreign participation in teaching English in China. *Language Learning and Communication, 2,* 111–115.

Zachariah, M. (1979). "Massliners" versus "capitalist roaders" in China's education ring: Round four to "capitalist roaders". *Comparative Education Review, 23,* 101–114.

Index

About the Author

EDGAR A. PORTER is a member of the faculty in the School of Hawaiian, Asian, and Pacific Studies at the University of Hawaii. He is the author of several articles including "Foreign Involvement in China's Colleges and Universities: A Historical Perspective," "Everyday Encounters in China," and "Romance in China," and he is currently editing *Journalism from Tiananmen*.